This Room

U·X·L
HISPANIC AMERICAN
ALMANAC 2ND EDITION

U·X·L
HISPANIC AMERICAN
ALMANAC 2ND EDITION

Sonia G. Benson, Nicolás Kanellos, and Bryan Ryan, Editors

U·X·L®

THOMSON
————*————
GALE

Detroit • New York • San Diego • San Francisco • Cleveland • New Haven, Conn. • Waterville, Maine • London • Munich

U•X•L Hispanic American Almanac, 2nd Edition

Sonia G. Benson, Nicolás Kanellos, and Bryan Ryan, Editors

Project Editor
Carol DeKane Nagel

Permissions
Kim Davis

Imaging and Multimedia
Robyn Young

Product Design
Mary Claire Krzewinski, Michael Logusz

Composition
Evi Seoud

Manufacturing
Rita Wimberley

LIBRARY OF CONGRESS CATALOGING-IN-PUBLICATION DATA

UXL Hispanic American almanac / Sonia G. Benson, Nicolás Kanellos, and Bryan Ryan, editors.— 2nd ed.

p. cm.

Rev. ed. of: Hispanic American almanac. 1995.

Summary: Explores the history and culture of Hispanic Americans, people in the United States whose ancestors—or they themselves—came from Spain or the Spanish-speaking countries of South and Central America.

Includes bibliographical references and index.

ISBN 0-7876-6598-3 (hardcover : alk. paper)

1. Hispanic Americans—Juvenile literature. [1. Hispanic Americans.] I. Benson, Sonia. II. Kanellos, Nicolás. III. Ryan, Bryan. IV. Title: UXL Hispanic American almanac. V. Title: Hispanic American almanac.

E184.S75H556 2002   973.468'0468–dc21
                                     2002007376

Printed in the United States of America
10 9 8 7 6 5 4 3 2 1

CONTENTS

READER'S GUIDE

U•X•L Hispanic American Almanac, 2nd Edition, features a comprehensive range of historical and current information on the life and culture of Hispanic America, the community of people in the United States whose ancestors—or they themselves—came from Spain or from the Spanish-speaking countries of South and Central America, Mexico, Puerto Rico, or Cuba. The *Almanac* is organized into fourteen subject chapters including immigration, family and religion, jobs and education, literature, and sports. The volume contains 120 black-and-white photographs and maps, a glossary, and a cumulative subject index.

Related reference sources:

U•X•L Hispanic American Biography, 2nd Edition, profiles one hundred Hispanic Americans, both living and deceased, prominent in fields ranging from civil rights to athletics, politics to literature, entertainment to science, religion to the military. A black-and-white portrait accompanies each entry, and the volume concludes with a subject index.

U•X•L Hispanic American Chronology, 2nd Edition, explores significant social, political, economic, cultural, and educational milestones in Hispanic American history. Arranged by year and then by month and day, the chronology spans from 25,000 B.C. to 2002 and contains more than one hundred black-and-white illustrations, extensive cross references, a glossary, and a subject index.

U•X•L Hispanic American Voices, 2nd Edition, presents twenty-one full or excerpted articles, memoirs, essays, speeches, letters, and other notable works of Hispanic Americans. Each entry is accompanied by an introduction, boxes explaining events discussed in the text, and a glossary of terms used in the document. The volume also contains one hundred black-and-white illustrations and a subject index.

Advisors

Special thanks are due for the invaluable comments and suggestions provided by U•X•L's Hispanic American Reference Library advisors:

Margarita Reichounia
Librarian, Bowen Branch
Detroit Public Library
Detroit, Michigan

Linda Garcia
Librarian, Southern Hills Middle School
Boulder, Colorado

Comments and Suggestions

We welcome your comments on *U•X•L Hispanic American Almanac* as well as your suggestions for topics to be featured in future editions. Please write: Editors, *U•X•L Hispanic American Almanac,* U•X•L, 27500 Drake Rd., Farmington Hills, MI 48331-3535; call toll-free: 1-800-877-4253; fax: 248-414-5043; or send e-mail via www.gale.com.

INTRODUCTION

Who Are the Hispanic Americans?

Hispanic Americans are people who live in the United States whose ancestors—or they themselves—came from Spain or the Spanish-speaking countries of South and Central America, Mexico, Puerto Rico, or Cuba. While the Spanish language is a unifying factor among Hispanics, they are a highly diverse group. Hispanics come from many different countries, and so have different histories, customs, and ways of speaking the Spanish language.

Several factors besides language unify the Hispanic American population as a distinctive community. One such factor is the origins of the group as a whole. The Hispanic American culture began with the European conquest of the New World. At that time, the Spanish intermarried with Native American and African American peoples. Hispanic American traditions, arts, language, and physical characteristics are products of the mixing of these three groups.

Another unifying factor is that many Hispanic Americans share the history—whether recent or long ago—of immigrating to a new country. In the United States Hispanics have often established small communities within the already established ones. In these smaller communities they can continue the traditions of their home countries and speak the Spanish language while working or going to school within the larger community.

A third factor is that the majority of Hispanic Americans are working-class citizens or are professionals who come from working-class backgrounds. Often facing exploitation and discrimination in the American workforce, Hispanic Americans have struggled together for equality on the job and in the schools of the United States.

The Rise of Hispanic Americans

Since the 1970s, Hispanic Americans have received an increasing amount of attention in the United States. This has happened for several reasons. First, the Hispanic population of the United States has been rapidly growing. In fact, the number of Hispanic Americans is increasing at a much faster rate than the total population. With the 2000 Census, Hispanics became—or tied with African Americans to become—the nation's largest minority group.

Hispanic immigration is a second reason for the increased attention given to this group. Although the United States is a nation of immigrants, many Americans worry about the size of the new immigrant population and its effects on society. From time to time throughout history, some Americans have focused these concerns on undocumented immigrants from Mexico. They have also become concerned about the political and social turmoil in Central America and the Caribbean that has forced many people from those countries to immigrate to the United States. The problems are complicated and solutions are difficult to find.

The bilingual-bicultural movement has also focused attention on Hispanic Americans. Programs that provide education and other services in Spanish as well as English put heavy demands on schools, local governments, and other social groups. Some Hispanic Americans have argued that bilingual programs are harmful to Hispanic Americans since they do not prepare Spanish-speaking people to fully participate in an English-speaking country. But many find the programs beneficial because they help Hispanic Americans to appreciate and to preserve time-honored traditions and a rich culture that are a central part of the American heritage.

Finally, the general American populace has become more aware of Hispanic Americans because they have earned more economic and political power. The large number of Hispanics concentrated in some areas of the United States gives them buying power. The dollars they spend influence businesses owned by non-Hispanics. The businesses they own influence local economies. Hispanics are also an important voting bloc. Hispanic votes now elect Hispanic Americans to political positions in states such as Florida, California, Texas, New Mexico, and New York. In other states, Hispanic votes greatly influence the election of non-Hispanics to office.

These issues and others are pushing Hispanic American concerns to the top of the American agenda. As the population of Hispanic Americans grows, so will its impact and influence on American society, business, and politics.

WORDS TO KNOW

A

agriculture: the knowledge and practice of farming, or raising plants and animals for food.

altar: a special table for religious things that serves as a place for prayer.

altarista: a contemporary Chicano artist who expresses him- or herself by making altars.

Anglo: a person of English heritage. Anglo is also used to describe that person's culture.

autobiography: a true story that someone writes about her or his life.

Aztlán: the legendary homeland of the Toltecs and Aztecs. Chicanos identify this land of origin as the region of the American Southwest.

B

babalao: a spiritual healer, witch, or advisor in the santería religion.

ballad: a song that tells a story.

barrio: a Hispanic term meaning "neighborhood."

bejareque: thatched huts used by the native peoples of the Caribbean before the arrival of Christopher Columbus.

bilingual: the ability to speak two languages easily.

bilingual/bicultural education: programs in the United States in which the learning and teaching is conducted in both English and Spanish, and students learn about both Anglo and Hispanic cultures.

birthrate: the average number of children that each woman has.

bohíos: thatched-roof huts used by the Caribbean Indians.

botánica: a shop that sells herbs and folk medicines.

bracero: a day laborer; originally temporary Mexican farm and railroad workers brought to the Southwest to work under a special program.

C

cacique: the village chieftain in Caribbean tribes.

caló: the special language created and used by *pachucos* (young Mexican Americans of the 1940s and 1950s known for their special youth culture and the zoot suits that they wore).

Catholicism: the beliefs and practices of the Christian church led by the Pope in the Vatican in Rome, Italy.

Celts: a people who lived in central and western Europe about 500 B.C. They rode horses and carried iron weapons. Their culture and languages still live in Ireland, Scotland, Wales, and parts of France and Spain.

census: the official counting and description of the population of a country.

charrerías: contests of Mexican cowboys that influenced the modern rodeo. Also called *charro fiestas.*

charro: a Mexican cowboy.

Chicano: a name for Mexican immigrants to the United States; the word comes from *Mechicano,* a Native American name for Mexico.

Chicano movement: a group of twentieth-century Mexican American writers and activists who celebrated their culture and historical background in their works.

chinampa: a man-made island or floating garden, developed by the natives of Mesoamerica to increase agricultural production.

chiripeo: the part-time odd jobs available at low wages to Puerto Ricans on the island.

cimarrones: runaway slaves.

citizenship: the rights and responsibilities of a person from a certain country.

civilization: a group of people, often living together in communities, who have laws, arts, and sciences.

code-switching: changes made by a bilingual person from one language to another in the same conversation or even the same sentence.

colonia: a small colony of Hispanics living in an American city.

colony: a group of people who leave their home country to live in another land controlled by their home country. The new land is also called a colony.

color barrier: The rule that kept African Americans, some Hispanic Americans, and other people of color from playing in American professional baseball. Jackie Robinson, an African American, broke through the color barrier on April 10, 1947.

compadrazgo: godparenthood.

compadres: co-parents or godparents.

concentration: a place where many people or things are brought together.

confianza: trust.

conjunto: a style of Hispanic music first made popular in Texas and northern Mexico, also called *música norteña;* the word conjunto also refers to the band that plays this music. The band is usually made up of a guitar, a base guitar, a drum, and an accordion.

conquest: taking over people or land by winning in war.

corrido: a Mexican ballad, or song that tells a story.

criollo: a person of Spanish or European ancestry born in the New World.

crónica: a local newspaper column that often makes fun of the people and customs of the area.

culture: the collection of customs of a group of people, including their lifestyle, language, food, religion, arts, and recreation.

D

discovery: finding new lands or new knowledge.

discrimination: treating people poorly because of their differences.

diversity: the differences that give variety to people or places.

E

education: learning and teaching.

employment: working at a job.

encomienda: an economic system in which a Spaniard in the New World was given land and a number of native slaves by Spain's king or queen or one of their representatives.

entrepreneur: the person who takes responsibility for a business.

exile: a person who cannot return to her or his homeland for political or other reasons.

expedition: a journey for a special purpose, either exploration or conquest. The people and their transportation are also called an expedition.

exploration: the search for new lands or new knowledge.

extended family: a family that includes children, parents, and other relatives, such as grandparents, aunts, or uncles, usually living together in the same house.

ex-voto: a gift presented to a saint as thanks for answering a prayer.

F

la familia: a Hispanic term that usually means the extended family (children, their parents, grandparents, and other relatives), a very important part of Hispanic society.

feast: a large meal prepared to celebrate a special day.

fluent: able to speak a language easily, without hesitation.

folk ballad: a poem or song that tells a story. Folk ballads are usually based on the everyday lives of people.

folk plays: plays created and presented by common people, based on everyday lives.

folk religion: the beliefs and spiritual practices that grow out of the everyday lives of common people.

formal education: learning and teaching that takes place in a school. Informal education takes place at home or in the community.

frontier: the land farthest from the center of a country, usually where the fewest people live; sometimes used as another word for border.

G

Germanic tribes: groups of people who came from several areas outside the Roman Empire in Europe and Asia. Many of these groups built their culture around war.

godparents: a man and woman who accept responsibility for helping parents raise a child. They usually accept the responsibility in a religious ceremony.

H

hacienda: a large ranch or farm based upon a system of farming introduced to Spain by the Romans.

hermandade: brotherhood.

Hispaniola: the island in the Caribbean Sea where Christopher Columbus established the first European settlement in the New World. Today, Haiti and the Dominican Republic share this island.

horsemanship: the skill of riding and taking care of horses.

hybrid: a combination of two or more things to make something new and different.

I

Iberian Peninsula: the European landmass surrounded by the Atlantic Ocean on the west and northwest and the Mediterranean Sea on the south and east. Spain and Portugal now occupy it.

immigrant: someone who moves to a new country from another country.

immigration: coming to live in a new country from another country.

income: the money that people make at their jobs.

independence: the freedom that a country or person wins from the control of another country or person.

indigenismo: a movement among Hispanics that celebrates the Native American origins of Hispanic culture.

industry: the work done by businesses and factories.

Islam: the religion, also called Muslim, started by Muhammad around the year 620 A.D. Islam is now the main religion in the Middle East and North Africa.

J

jíbaro: originally a Native American word for "highlander"; *jíbaro* is a term Puerto Ricans use for rural mountain people, but it has also become a symbol of the national identity of Puerto Ricans.

K

kinship: the relationship a person has with his or her relatives.

kiva: a secret underground ceremonial chamber, especially as used in Pueblo culture for ceremonies and meetings.

L

labor force: the group of people working in a country or other place.

legacy: something left behind by ancestors for their descendants.

literacy: the ability to read and write.

M

macana: a wooden war club used by the Native Americans of the Caribbean.

marriage: the legal or religious union of a man and a woman as husband and wife.

media: newspapers, magazines, radio, television, films, and other sources for information and entertainment. The mainstream media are those whose audience includes all Americans. Hispanic media are directed at Americans who speak Spanish and who are interested in Hispanic culture.

Mesoamerica: "Meso" means middle, so this term means "middle America." Mesoamerica is used to refer to the land of southern Mexico and Central America.

mestizo: a person of mixed Spanish and Native American ancestry.

migrant worker: a person who moves from one place to another following jobs.

migration: moving from one place to another.

milagrito: a small charm made of tin, silver, or gold used to represent a prayer for healing.

mission: the building used by monks and other religious people in frontier settlements to spread their religion.

mulatto: a person of mixed African and European or Native American ancestry.

mural: a large work of art painted onto a wall.

música norteña: a style of Hispanic music first made popular in Texas and northern Mexico. (Also see **conjunto.**)

música tropical/moderna: the name given to a style of music that includes fast and slow dance songs and is now popular among Hispanic Americans.

N

Native Americans: people from the many different groups who already lived in North and South America when Christopher Columbus first arrived.

native language: the first language that a child learns, usually at home from her or his parents.

network: a group of radio or television stations that produce shows to broadcast to a large audience.

New World: a term used by Europeans for North and South America.

nitaínos: principal advisors among the Arawak Indians, quite often in charge of the labor force.

norteño: northern; the people and culture of northern Mexico.

novel: a long story about fictional characters and events.

nuclear family: a family consisting of children and their parents living together in the same house.

Nuyorican: literally "New York-Rican"; a term used to distinguish Puerto Ricans born or raised in New York from those on the island.

Nuyorican literature: the novels, poetry, and other writings of Puerto Ricans who were born or raised in New York City.

O

oral tradition: storytelling using the spoken word.

orisha: one of the African gods of the santería religion.

orquesta: orchestra; the word refers to a style of Mexican American music organized around a violin and also to the ensemble that plays it.

P

pachuco: a young Mexican American living in the 1940s and 1950s who was a part of the special youth culture of that time. These young people were known for wearing zoot suits and speaking a special language called caló.

Paleolithic: the Old Stone Age, the earliest period of human development, which ended over 10,000 years ago.

patria chica: the home region in the home country.

patriotism: the love that a person has for her or his country.

pelado: a witty, humorous underdog character in Mexican popular theater.

pictographs: a type of writing that uses pictures to represent words or sounds.

pilgrimage: a journey to a religious place.

pillar: a support that is very important to holding up something.

piraguas: a narrow, high-prowed canoe perfected by the Caribbean Indians.

plantation: a large farm for growing certain crops, such as sugarcane and cotton.

playwright: a person who creates a play.

popular theater: the plays, musicals, and shows put on by theaters to attract the general public. Popular theater is concerned more with entertainment than art.

population: the whole group of people who live in a certain country or other place.

posada: a ceremony put on during the Christmas season in which a couple takes the roles of Joseph and Mary and goes door to door in their neighborhood asking for shelter. *Posada* is also a Spanish term for an inn.

poverty: poorness; not having enough money to live on.

pre-Columbian: before the arrival of Christopher Columbus in the New World.

presidio: the Spanish name for their frontier forts.

Protestantism: the beliefs and practices of many Christian churches not led by the Pope, including Baptists, Methodists, Presbyterians, and others.

R

Reconquest: the long war that Spaniards fought to take their land back from the Moors, a group of Muslims originally from North Africa.

refugee: a person who runs away from a dangerous place to find a safe place.

revista: a popular theater entertainment involving music and comedy.

revolutionary: a person who works or fights to change the government or kind of government of a country.

rodeo: a contest for cowboys in which they test their skill riding horses and roping cattle.

role: the part that a person plays in a play or movie, in the family, or in society.

Roman Empire: an important civilization that covered much of Europe during the first five centuries A.D. Its capital was the city of Rome, now in Italy.

S

salsa: a style of music that combines jazz and the rhythms of Cuban dance music, first made popular by Cubans of African heritage.

santería: a religious sect based on a mixture of African religions and Catholicism.

santero: in the Southwest, a sculptor of wooden saints; in the Caribbean, a worshipper of one of the gods of santería.

santo: a sculpture of a Catholic saint.

sculpture: the art of making statues and other figures out of stone, plaster, wood, or metals.

segregation: separating people in schools and other public places because of their race or culture.

settlement: a village, town, or city in a colony.

shrine: a place that is important for religious reasons.

skilled professional: someone who works at a job that requires special training or education.

slavery: a practice in which one person owns another and forces him or her to work without pay.

the Southwest: Arizona, New Mexico, and parts of California and Texas make up the Southwest of the United States.

standard English: the variety of English accepted as correct by most English speakers. It is usually the English heard on television and radio and seen in newspapers.

statehood: becoming or being a state in the United States.

stereotype: a common but simplified and often untrue image of a person or group.

subsistence farming: growing just enough food to live on, with no extra food to trade or sell.

T

theater: the building in which actors present plays. Theater is also used to refer to the plays and the business of putting on plays.

touring troupes: groups of actors that travel from city to city to put on plays.

trade: buying and selling between people or countries.

treaty: an agreement between two or more countries to end a war, keep the peace, or build relations.

U

undocumented immigrant: a person who lives or works in the United States who is not a citizen of the United States and who does not have permission to stay in the country.

unskilled worker: a person who works at a job that does not require special training or education.

V

vaquero: a cowboy.

Y

yerberías: shops selling medicinal plants, herbs, and potions.

yuca: a root used for food.

Z

zemíes: gods of the Arawak Indians. They are also small religious figures made of clay that represented these gods.

zoot suit: the outfit often worn by *pachucos* (young Mexican Americans who lived during the 1940s and 1950s known for their special youth culture). The zoot suit included baggy pants and a wide-brimmed hat with feathers.

U·X·L
HISPANIC AMERICAN
ALMANAC 2ND EDITION

1

A Historical Overview

Three Legacies: Hispanic American Roots in Native American, European, and African American Cultures

---

FACT FOCUS

- Hispanic history and culture combines the history and culture of Native Americans, Europeans, and Africans.
- The ancient people of the Americas discovered how to raise their own food. Farming helped some Native Americans to develop important civilizations before Christopher Columbus discovered the New World.
- Advanced civilizations included the Pueblo people of the American Southwest, the Aztecs of central Mexico, and the Mayans of Mexico's Yucatán Peninsula.
- The Spaniards who came to the New World brought a culture that had been influenced by many European and North African peoples. Romans, barbarians, and Muslims all left their mark on Spain.
- Africans were first brought to the New World as slaves. They often worked on sugarcane plantations in the Caribbean and in mines.
- Some Africans escaped from slavery or led rebellions against slaveholders. In eastern Cuba and in Haiti, these Africans set up their own settlements.
- Slavery ended in Mexico in 1829 and in Cuba in the 1880s.

The history of the Hispanic American people is actually an intertwined history of three peoples: Native Americans, Europeans, and Africans. The Native Americans crossed a prehistoric land bridge between Asia and North America and developed a wide variety of civilizations in the Americas. Europeans, led by the Spanish, came in search of new trade, new treasures, and new lands. Africans were brought as slaves by Europeans to supply the labor needed to build a new world. Each of these three groups left behind its legacy for today's Hispanic Americans.

WORDS TO KNOW

agriculture: the knowledge of farming, raising plants and animals for food.

Celts: a people who lived in central and western Europe in about 500 B.C. They rode horses and carried iron weapons. Their culture and languages still live in Ireland, Scotland, Wales, and parts of France and Spain.

civilization: group of people, often living together in cities, who have laws, arts, and sciences.

culture: the collection of customs of a group of people. It includes lifestyle, language, food, religion, arts, and recreation.

Germanic tribes: people who came from several areas outside the Roman Empire in Europe and Asia. Many of these groups built their culture around war.

Iberia: the peninsula on which Spain and Portugal are found.

immigrant: someone who moves into a new country from another country. The United States is a nation of immigrants.

Islam: the religion, also called Muslim, started by Muhammad around A.D. 620. It is now the main religion in the Middle East and North Africa.

The Native American Legacy

The First Immigrants to the Americas

More than fifty thousand years ago, ice covered much more of the polar regions than it does now. At this time groups of Asians began crossing a land bridge that connected northeastern Asia and Alaska in North America. These first American immigrants moved slowly southward. On their way, they hunted giant mastodons (prehistoric mammals resembling today's elephants) and gathered wild plants for food. Traveling a few miles per generation, they spread out to cover the Americas. Some settled in Canada and some settled in the Mississippi Valley. Others made their homes in the American Southwest, Mexico, Central America, and the Caribbean. Still others continued to South America, to the Andes Mountains and the Amazon jungles. Some journeyed all the way to Cape Horn at the southern tip of South America.

These first Americans traveled in small groups following the trail of animals. Each group chose a leader for his skill in hunting and his bravery in defending his people from other groups. They lived in caves and crude shelters, but these were temporary. They were always ready to move to follow their food supply.

Their religious beliefs were simple. Like other Paleolithic (Old Stone Age) hunters in Europe, Africa, and Asia, they worshiped the animals they ate for food. To express their beliefs, they drew mastodons and tapirs (a mammal related to the horse and the hippopotamus) on the bones that they used as tools.

Hunting and gathering provided a healthy diet. These first Americans ate game, fish, and wild fruits and vegetables. As long as these food sources remained plentiful, Native Americans did not need to find new sources. So, some groups were still hunting and gathering when the Europeans arrived. However, other groups were forced to find new sources for their food. A change in climate about 7200 B.C. changed the environment in many parts of prehistoric America. For example, in Mesoamerica (present-day southern Mexico and Central America) the lush greens that provided food for large animals disappeared. The area became hotter and drier. The hunters became scroungers, eating wild plants and small animals for protein. During this period, which lasted until 2500 B.C., these people became better and better at gathering and storing food. Many Mesoamerican groups also discovered that they could grow some of the plants that they had been gathering.

Discovering how to farm was the first major step toward civilization. The people of Mesoamerica began to plant and irrigate the seeds of wild plants such as maize (corn), squash, beans, and amaranth (a grain). They also tamed some of the wild animals they found around them such as turkeys and small dogs. There were no large animals such as cattle or horses to tame, however. For the most part, these animals had not survived the change in climate. The exception was the buffalo, which roamed the northern part of the continent. Without cattle and horses, the peoples of North America had no beasts of burden. For this reason they carried things themselves.

As new techniques of farming brought larger plots of crops, villages grew. Where the land was not good for farming, the people of Mesoamerica made improvements. They cut hillsides into terraces (large steps) and created chinampas (man-made islands in ponds and lakes). Abundant harvests freed some people to do other activities use-

WORDS TO KNOW

legacy: something left behind by ancestors for their descendants.

Mesoamerica: meso means "middle," so this means "middle America"; the land of southern Mexico and Central America.

Native Americans: people descended from the many different groups of people who already lived in North and South America when Christopher Columbus first arrived.

pictographs: a type of writing that uses pictures to represent words or sounds.

plantation: a large farm for growing certain crops, such as sugarcane and cotton.

The Reconquest: the long war that Spaniards fought to take their land back from the Moors, a group of Muslims originally from North Africa.

Roman Empire: an important civilization that covered much of Europe during the first five centuries A.D. Its capital was the city of Rome, now in Italy.

slavery: the institution in which one person owns another and forces him or her to work without pay.

subsistence farming: growing just enough food to live on, with no extra food to trade or sell.

ful to the village. Potters, toolmakers, and even entertainers (musicians, acrobats, and dancers) became common.

Religious practices also developed. Farmers needed precise weather predictions

3

so that they could plan their planting and harvesting. Shaman priests (priests who use magic for curing the sick) studied the heavens and learned to track the seasons and forecast weather changes. As farmers looked to their priests more and more for guidance, these religious figures gained more power as leaders.

With the seeds of civilization in place, different groups of Native Americans developed their own particular cultures. Some thrived by continuing to hunt and gather. Some raised just enough food in gardens to meet their own needs. This is known as subsistence farming. Others built farms large enough to supply food for their people and to trade. These Native Americans established great civilizations. Among these, the civilizations of the Mexican plateau, Central America, and the Andes Mountains were especially noteworthy. They left behind scientific, artistic, and architectural achievements that still affect our lives.

Native American Cultures in Spanish America

The Native Americans most closely associated with the history of Hispanic Americans are those groups that lived in the Caribbean, Florida, Mexico, and the American Southwest.

The Inhabitants of the Caribbean

Little is known for certain about the people who lived in the Caribbean Islands before the arrival of Spanish explorer Christopher Columbus. Historians and anthropologists estimate that the population of these islands may have numbered anywhere from 60,000 people to as much as 7 million. Native Caribbean peoples probably migrated from Venezuela in South America to the islands more than one thousand years before the arrival of Columbus. When Columbus encountered the New World, there were four major cultures in the Caribbean: the Guanahatabey, the Ciboney, the Arawak, and the Carib.

The Guanahatabey were the oldest culture group. They lived primarily on the Guanahacabibes Peninsula of modern-day western Cuba. The Guanahatabey were extremely primitive. They depended on shellfish for their food. They had no dwellings and left no evidence of social organization.

The Ciboney people had a Stone Age culture. They lived primarily in western Cuba and on the southwestern peninsula of the island of Hispaniola (the island now occupied by Haiti and the Dominican Republic). Smaller groups of Ciboney lived on the Bahama Islands and on Jamaica. The Ciboney were known for their kindness and gentle manners. They developed a crude form of farming to help supply their food, but fishing was more important to them.

While some of the Ciboney lived in caves, the majority lived in *bajareques* (primitive thatched huts). Their leader was the *cacique* (village chieftain). The Ciboney people did not develop art forms, but they did use various herbs and plants for medicines. Because of their lack of military power, some of the Ciboney were forced into slavery by the Arawak.

The Arawak probably came from Venezuela and spread across the Greater Antilles and the Bahamas. There were two

The Caribbean. *Reproduced by permission of The Gale Group.*

major groups: the Lucayo, who occupied the Bahamas, and the Taino, who inhabited central and eastern Cuba, as well as Hispaniola, Jamaica, and Puerto Rico.

Arawakan settlements ranged from a few *bohíos* (thatched-roof huts) to villages of more than 5,000 people. The Arawak soci-

ety was matrilineal. This meant that family possessions and wealth were passed down through mothers. Their leadership, however, was male dominated. Each Arawak village was headed by a cacique. The cacique was not an all-powerful ruler, but he was still the final authority in all village matters. Cacique leadership was hereditary. When the cacique died, his son took his position. If he had no son, the eldest son of his sister became the new cacique. The cacique was helped by his *nitaínos* (principal advisers). The nitaínos were mostly the oldest men in the village, and they were usually put in charge of the labor force. The *behique* (priest) occupied an important position in the society. He interpreted the signs of the *zemíes* (gods) and was also a medicine man. Each village had a zemí house, where ceremonies were performed. Finally, there were the *naboríes* (commoners).

Arawakan villages were located in areas that were good for farming. Although the Arawak harvested corn, yams, beans, and peanuts, their principal food was *yuca,* or manioc (a tropical plant with nutritious edible roots). From the yuca plant they made a type of unleavened bread called *cassava.* The Arawak supplemented their diet with fish, mollusks, turtle eggs, snakes, bats, and iguanas. They also grew tobacco. The behique used it in religious ceremonies in order to attract spirits.

The Arawak had very few metal-working skills, but they were good potters and excellent basket weavers. They made basket fish traps and a special type of basket for carrying water. The Arawak also excelled at wood carving. They constructed canoes without the help of metal tools and used these boats to trade with nearby islands. They carved wooden zemí figures and the *macana* (a wooden club used as a weapon). Since cotton was grown on the islands, the Arawak weaved it into hammocks, nets, and bags.

The Arawak culture dominated the Caribbean region for a long time. But, in the years before Columbus's arrival in the New World, this culture was challenged by the Carib. The Carib were the last of the Native Americans to come to the Caribbean islands. Little is known about them except that they were island raiders. By 1492 they had taken control of most of the Lesser Antilles, and Carib warriors had already terrorized the Arawak population of Cuba, Puerto Rico, and Hispaniola.

Knowledge of the Carib way of life is sketchy at best. They farmed, but unlike the Arawak, they grew crops for food only and not for trade. Their religion did not have the zemíes of the Arawak, as well as the ceremonial rituals. Carib leadership was simpler than that of the Arawak. The Carib cacique was mainly a military leader who planned raids but did not solve village problems. The Carib raided islands for two reasons: to find female slaves and male prisoners. The male Arawak captured by the Carib were cooked and eaten. (The word *carib* means cannibal in the Arawak language.)

The Carib decorated themselves with body paint and jewelry. They applied flower petals and gold dust to their body paint before it dried. They wore chains of stone and coral around their arms, wrists, and legs. They also pierced their noses, lips, and ears to hold ornaments made from fish spines and turtle shells.

As one might expect, the Carib excelled in making weapons. Their arsenal included bows, spears, and macanas. The Carib *piragua* (a narrow, high-prowed canoe) was the fastest canoe in the Caribbean, and it was capable of traveling great distances. Carib expansion in the Caribbean was limited only by the arrival of the Spaniards, and later the British, French, and Dutch.

The year 1492 marked the beginning of the end for the Native Americans of the Caribbean. The Ciboney and Arawak, whom Columbus described as gentle people of great simplicity, were overwhelmed by the coming of Spanish explorers. They died of European diseases such as smallpox and measles and of overwork in Spanish settlements. A little over a century after Columbus's arrival, the Carib were defeated by European military strength.

The Natives of Florida

Spanish explorers landed on the shores of Florida in 1513. At that time, there were an estimated 100,000 Native Americans living there. They were divided among six major groups: the Timucua, the Tocobaga, the Apalachee, the Ais and Jeagas, the Tequesta, and the Calusa.

The Timucua occupied a diagonal region from northeast Florida to the Tampa Bay area. They were mostly hunters, but they also practiced subsistence farming. About 40,000 strong, they were the most numerous of the Florida natives. The Tocobaga, who lived around the Tampa Bay area, numbered about 7,000. They were primarily fishermen, but they also grew corn, beans, and squash. The Apalachee population of Florida lived in the panhandle area and numbered about 25,000. The Apalachee grew corn and vegetables for food, but when these ran out they would turn to hunting and fishing.

The Ais and Jeagas, who numbered only around 3,000, were the most primitive. They never learned farming. Living on the eastern coast of Florida, they could survive as fishermen and gatherers. South of the Ais and Jeagas, there were some 5,000 Tequesta. They also did not farm, but they were excellent fishermen. Finally, there were the 25,000 fierce Calusas living in an area that extended from Cape Sable to the Tampa Bay area. This group lived on shellfish.

Native American Civilizations in the Mexican Plateau

Many Native American cultures lived in North America before the arrival of Spanish explorers, but the civilizations of Mexico and Central America are the most famous for their art, architecture, science, politics, and culture.

The Mayan Civilization. Around 7000 B.C. the Native Americans who lived in the southern part of the Mexican plateau discovered a plant that produced edible grain. They called this plant *teozintle*. These people, known as the Otomí, worked many years to improve teozintle into the plant we now know as corn. With this new source of food, the Otomí people could stop moving from place to place to hunt and gather food. They could begin to build permanent homes. By 5000 B.C. the Otomíes were growing a variety of crops, such as corn, squash, beans, and chili. They were also weaving clothing from vegetable fibers. Eventually, they acquired the skills of making pottery and utensils. Perhaps from the Otomí came the Mayan civilization of Central America and southern Mexico.

Mayan civilization can be divided into three periods: the Preclassic (800 B.C. to A.D. 300), the Classic (A.D. 300 to 1000), and the Postclassic (A.D. 1000 to 1500). During the Classic period, the Mayan civilization was centered in the southern jungles of the Yucatán Peninsula. Today, this area includes the Mexican states of Chiapas and Tabasco and the nations of Guatemala, Belize, and Honduras. Among the great Mayan cities of the Classic period were Tikal in Guatemala, Copán in Honduras, and Palenque in Mexico. The Classic period ended shortly before A.D. 1000. No one is sure what caused the Maya to abandon these cities. Some think that the land no longer produced good harvests. Others believe that it was a civil war.

The Postclassic period began around A.D. 1000. Leaders from the southern Yucatán Peninsula had moved to Mayan settlements in northern Yucatán. There, they began to transform the settlements into independent cities that controlled the land around them. This type of political unit is called a city-state. Among the great city-states of the Postclassic period were Mayapan, Chichén Itzá, and Uxmal.

Thanks to the work of archaeologists and the accuracy of Mayan records, we know more about the Maya than any other Native Americans. Unlike the Aztec, the Maya never built a centralized empire. At the peak of their civilization, they occupied approximately 200,000 square miles. In that vast area were many city-states with a shared language, culture, and religion. The Mayan government was a simple one. A ruler, chosen based on heredity, directed each city-state with the help of priests and nobles.

During both the Classic and Postclassic periods, the Maya made many cultural contributions. This was reflected in their dress, customs, buildings, and arts. Mayan intellectual achievements included written language. They used pictures to represent words, a system called either hieroglyphics or pictographs. They carved this picture writing in wood and stone and painted it with watercolors on fiber paper. They used it to write their own literature. The *Popol-Vuh,* the sacred book of the Maya, traces the creation of man prior to 3151 B.C. The book of *Chilam Balam* is a masterpiece of Mayan literature. The Maya excelled in chronology, the study of time. Their year had twenty months of eighteen days each. They added five extra days at the end of the year. The Maya were also excellent mathematicians, even using zero as a place holder.

Mayan architecture (the design and craftsmanship of their buildings and monuments) was original and outstanding. They used burnt limestone to build their cities and pyramids. Their cities were a collection of temples and monuments decorated with carvings and wall paintings. They consistently used advanced architectural techniques.

When the Spaniards first arrived in Yucatán in 1511, the Mayan civilization was falling apart as a result of civil wars. Soon the Spaniards began to destroy the few Mayan cities that were left standing. The Spanish conquerors built Catholic churches on top of the Mayan temples.

The Aztec. Around A.D. 1200 the city of Atzcapotzalco ruled the Central Valley of Mexico. At this time there arrived a tribe of nomads who called themselves Aztec. They said they came from Aztlán (Place of the Herons). Legend has it that one of the Aztec gods, Huitzilopochtli, had ordered his people to move southward from northern Mexico. They were to settle where they saw an eagle on a cactus with a snake in its mouth. They wandered from one place to another, searching for this sign. Finally, the Aztec

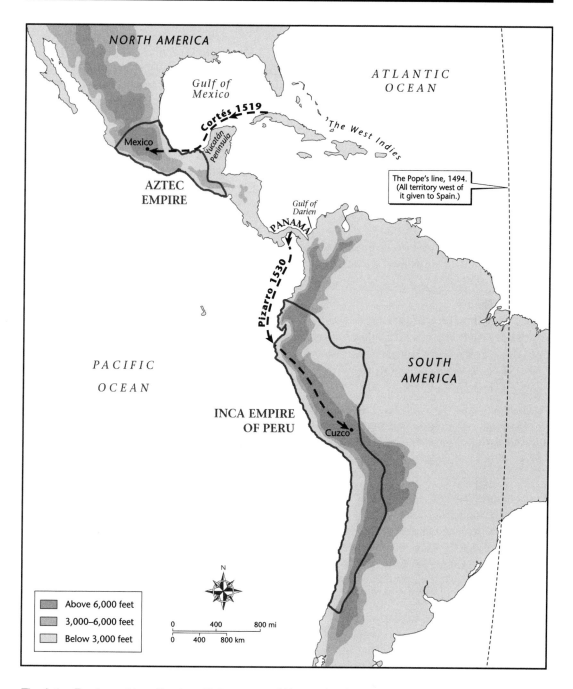

The Aztec Empire and Inca Empire with the routes of Hernan Cortés and Francisco Pizarro. *Reproduced by permission of the Gale Group.*

saw the sign on the shores of Lake Texcoco, east of present-day Mexico City. Atzcapotzalco's rulers allowed the Aztec to settle on the lake's shores in exchange for a tribute, or payment. In 1325 the Aztec began to build their capital, Tenochtitlán, in honor of another god, Tenoch.

The Aztec were an aggressive people. In 1428 they launched a surprise attack on Atzcapotzalco. The Aztec armies soon conquered the Central Valley. By the early sixteenth century, Aztec dominance extended from the Central Valley of Mexico to parts of Guatemala. An estimated 20 million people lived in that empire.

In theory the Aztec government was a democratic one. Each tribe was permitted to choose its own leaders and make its own laws. In addition, each tribe sent a representative to the Supreme Council, which elected the emperor. In practice, however, the Aztec nobility and the priests acquired most of the power. They directed the empire more and more, making it less of a democracy.

The Aztec religion was less spiritual than the Mayan religion, and it was certainly more bloodthirsty. Their ferocious war god, Huitzilopochtli, demanded human sacrifices, so Aztec warriors were educated from childhood to seek prisoners of war to be offered as sacrifices. In 1487, for example, the Aztec celebrated the opening of the temple of Huitzilopochtli by sacrificing more than twenty-five thousand captives. In short, the Aztec waged war to satisfy their war god.

The Aztec capital of Tenochtitlán was a magnificent city. It had an estimated population of 200,000 people. It was built on an island in Lake Texcoco. Canals linked parts of the city and causeways connected the city to the mainland. Tenochtitlán even had its own aqueducts to bring pure drinking water to its citizens. The giant market of Tlatelolco exhibited fresh produce grown on *chinampas* (floating gardens). In the center of the city, there was a magnificent temple, tended by five thousand priests. This capital was a city of beauty and pageantry.

The Aztec had outstanding knowledge of the medicinal properties of plants, and they were able potters and weavers. In some ways, however, the Aztec were not as original as the people who lived before them. Their pyramids were merely copies of Toltec architecture, and their sculptures never quite matched those of the Maya. Their writing never went beyond simple pictographs painted on cloth, skin, and paper they made from a local plant. They did not advance in mathematics or astronomy, and their calendar was a copy of the Toltec calendar. In spite of its lack of originality, the Aztec civilization was a splendid one.

The Aztec Empire was prosperous, but it had a very serious weakness. It created a lot of enemies, especially the tribes it conquered. The people who supplied the victims for the bloodthirsty war god Huitzilopochtli looked forward to the day when a powerful savior would come to destroy the hated Aztecs. In 1519 these tribes were expecting the scheduled visit of the blond Toltec deity Quetzalcoatl. He was going to bring justice and punish the evil ones. Instead of Quetzalcoatl, a blond-haired, blue-eyed Spaniard named Hernán Cortés came. He and his fellow Spaniards landed in Veracruz and quickly moved northward to conquer the Aztec Empire. They leveled Tenochtitlán in 1521 and built Mexico City on the same site. The Spanish saved the weaker tribes from the Aztec. However, these Spanish "liberators" would become the new masters for the next three centuries.

The Pueblo Culture of the American Southwest

There were many Native American cultures in the American Southwest before Columbus came. Some were nomadic, moving from place to place in search of food. Some were sedentary. They settled, built permanent homes, and farmed to produce their food. Perhaps the most important was the Pueblo culture. Descendants of the prehistoric Anasazi people, the Pueblos lived in western New Mexico and the upper Rio Grande area of that state. In addition, there were Pueblo villages in northeastern Arizona. Among the Pueblo peoples at the time of the Spanish arrival were the Zuñi, Hopi, Keres, and Tano.

The Pueblos were a sedentary people whose lives depended primarily on farming. When Spaniards arrived in the 1540s, they found approximately 66 Pueblo villages in the area of New Mexico. The people in these villages grew corn, beans, squash, and cotton. Chili pepper, a trademark of the Southwest, was apparently not known to the Pueblos. Since water was essential to the dry region where the Pueblos lived, they had a system of irrigation that gathered the runoff from infrequent rains. Each Pueblo village also had a cistern to store water. In farming, these people had not developed the plow, but they did make use of the digging stick.

Because the Pueblos were very concerned about raids by other groups in the

HISPANIC FOOD

The food of Hispanics in the New World became a mixture of Spanish, African, and Native American foods.

Spanish explorers and colonists brought wheat, oats, barley, rye, pork, beef, mutton (from sheep) and chickens with them to the New World. From Africa came rice, coffee, sugarcane, spices, and many spicy dishes. Native American cultures passed on many of their unique foods to the Europeans and Africans who came to the New World. Among the most important staples were maize (corn), beans, potatoes, sweet potatoes, and peanuts. Some other important Native American food plants were tomatoes, chili peppers, cacao (for chocolate), and vanilla. Native Americans also introduced Spanish settlers to the turkey. These foods soon spread to Europe, Africa, and the rest of the world. Other Native American foods did not spread to the Old World, but they did influence Hispanic food. Among these are some squashes from Mexico and cactus fruit from the deserts of northern Mexico and the American Southwest.

region, they built their villages on hilltops away from their fertile fields. They made their houses out of stone or adobe strong enough to withstand an enemy attack. The houses had neither doors nor windows. The only entrance was through hatches in the roofs using portable ladders. Essential to the Pueblo village was the *kiva*. This was a secret underground chamber that served both as a ceremonial center and a meeting place. Only males were allowed in the kiva.

Pueblo government organization was simple. Land belonged to the community, and each village was ruled by a council of elders varying from ten to thirty members. Because each village chose its own leaders and made its own rules, the Pueblos never united into nations.

The Pueblos were religious people who worshiped the sun and the elements. It is estimated that they devoted half of their time to religious activities. The most important ceremonies were the communal dances, combining drama, dance, music, and poetry.

As a sedentary people, the Pueblos had time to create works of art. Their artistic impulses found expression in basketry, weaving, and pottery. Pueblo basketry was known for its geometric design. Although they did not learn weaving until A.D. 700, they perfected this art through the use of colored patterns and a technique called tie-dyeing. The Pueblos did not have a potter's wheel, but they crafted pottery by hand and showed gradual refinement in design, color, and symbols.

In spite of more than 450 years of contact with European explorers and settlers, the pre-Columbian Pueblo of the Southwest have survived to the present.

The Spanish Legacy

The Spanish explorers who came to the New World in the late 1400s and early 1500s brought with them more than the language spoken in Spain at that time. They also brought with them a long history and a culture that had itself been created through mixing native cultures with the cultures of invaders and colonizers.

Early Iberians

The earliest known inhabitants of the Iberian Peninsula (present-day Spain and Portugal) were game hunters and cave dwellers. More than fifty thousand years ago, they left behind drawings on their cave walls of the animals they ate. Several thousand years before the birth of Christ, a more advanced culture migrated to the Iberian Peninsula from Africa. These Iberians lived in villages and practiced agriculture, but little else is known about them.

About 1000 B.C. a wave of warriors, hunters, and part-time livestock keepers converged on the peninsula from somewhere in present-day Hungary near the Danube River. These Celtic peoples brought with them their own culture and their own language, Gaelic. When they mixed with the Iberians, they established a new and unique Iberian-Celtic culture. These Gaelic-speaking nomads also settled in other parts of Europe. They are best known for their influence on the cultures of Scotland, Wales, and Ireland. In northwest Spain in a province known as Galicia, Gaelic characteristics have survived to the present time. There, such Gaelic cultural items as the bagpipe and kilt are still used in ceremonies.

Walpi, an ancient Hopi Pueblo village. *Reproduced by permission of Owen Seumptewa.*

Gaelic culture in the rest of Spain, however, was replaced by a series of invasions and colonization efforts. The invaders greatly changed the linguistic, racial, and economic systems of the peninsula. The first to come were the Greeks and Phoenicians (natives of ancient Phoenicia, now Syria and Lebanon). They arrived at about the same time as the Celts to mine tin and establish a series of trading outposts. Their small numbers were not enough to replace the Iberian-Celtic culture, but the Greeks and Phoenicians did influence the native culture with their art and technology. The Iberian-Celts developed sculpture and other art forms that took on the characteristics of Greek classical realism. They also picked up transportation vehicles and mining techniques from the visitors.

Next to come were groups from Carthage, a civilization on the North African coast that had been greatly influenced by Greece. Carthaginians replaced the Greeks and Phoenicians for a short time in the second century B.C. However, in 133 B.C. the Romans defeated the Carthaginian army at Numantia. This was the first of many victories that would ensure the expansion of the Roman Empire into most of Europe, including the Iberian Peninsula.

Roman Colonization

The Roman colonization of Iberia happened on a large scale. Unlike the previous invaders, the Romans brought their families and settled the land. They enslaved the natives and set up a plantation system based on slave labor. The Romans continued to control the peninsula until their empire began to crumble about A.D. 400.

From the Latin-speaking Romans, Iberia acquired some of its most significant linguistic, cultural, political, and economic institutions. These live on in Spain and Latin America.

The Romans were the first to refer to the eastern part of the Iberian Peninsula as Hispania. Their Latin language mixed with the native tongues. Altered by hundreds of years of evolution, it became Castilian, which we now call Spanish. The Romans introduced their political system, their judicial system, and their religion. Politics were organized at the city level, a process the Romans called *civitas*. Unlike the common-law tradition that would later develop in England and its colonies, Roman courts had no juries. Judges made the final decisions on all cases brought before their courts. Similar court systems exist today in many countries. Finally, Christianity, especially in its Catholic denomination, was one of Rome's most enduring contributions to the culture of Iberia.

The Romans also influenced the style of town planning and the system of landholding characteristic of Spanish culture. The town plan revealed the importance of the government and the church. The typical Spanish and Spanish American town was organized around a town square or plaza. The Catholic church was prominently located on the square and the remaining space around the plaza was given to government buildings. A bathhouse, an amphitheater, and a coliseum were also built near the town center. The plantations that the Romans established on the Iberian Peninsula were models for the large farms and ranches later found in Spanish culture.

The Invasion of Germanic Tribes

Other groups following the Romans into Spain contributed to the mix of cultures that would be part of the Hispanic tradition throughout Latin America and the United States. The most aggressive of these groups were Germanic tribes originally from Asia Minor. They had been migrating westward for some time, slowly spreading out to every region controlled by the Roman Empire. As they did, they added Roman customs to their own. When the Roman Empire finally fell, these Germanic tribes began to establish their own areas of control.

Then, the first wave of Germanic tribes were overrun by other Germanic warrior tribes, who pillaged existing communities and took the land for themselves. Vandals, Berbers, and Visigoths were among the groups that moved into the Iberian Peninsula. Even though Roman political influence faded in Iberia, its culture remained to influence the Germanic barbarians. They began to speak one of the variations of Latin evolving on the peninsula. They also embraced Christianity with great fervor. Eventually, Christianity became the unifying force that brought together the mixed cultures of the Iberian Peninsula into one new culture.

Under the Germanic tribes, Spain lived through an era known as the Dark Ages. The once-large Roman Empire was cut into numerous small regions, each controlled by a local rich noble. These nobles replaced the Roman political and economic systems. Feudalism, a system in which nobles controlled the land and people around their castles, became common. The cult of the warrior was also established. Knights and squires protected their lord, his land, and his servants. They also enforced the rules of the nobles, who had the power to collect taxes and force artisans and peasants to supply their needs. The nobles spent the bulk of their time raiding one another in order to increase their territory.

The warrior cult in this society was a central component of the culture. Warriors were educated in the martial arts, and they followed a rigid code of conduct, which included a strong belief in Christianity. The influence of the Germanic warrior cult on Spanish culture would be evident later in the Crusades and the Reconquest (both religious wars against Muslims). The warrior cult also influenced early encounters with the Native Americans of the New World.

Spain under Islam

Perhaps Iberia would have remained under the control of feudalism, like the rest of Europe, if it had not been for the invasion of Arabic-speaking Muslims from North Africa. Known as Moors, these newcomers arrived at the beginning of the eighth century and stayed for eight hundred years. Next to the Romans, the Moors had the greatest influence on the culture of the Iberians. During the life of Muhammad, the founder of the Islam religion, Muslims conquered the Arabian Peninsula. In the thirty years after his death, Islam expanded to Persia (modern-day Iran) and Egypt. The Moors came to Spain during the third wave of Islamic expansion. This wave extended the sphere of Islamic control from Afghanistan in the east to Portugal in the west.

The first Moors crossed from Morocco to Spain via the Strait of Gibraltar in A.D. 713.

They brought with them an advanced culture that sparked life into the feudal Iberian culture of the Dark Ages. The Muslims left few stones unturned in their quest for knowledge. They borrowed and improved upon much of what was known in the world at that time. From the Far East, they learned the art of making steel and the secrets of making medicines. Their philosophy, agriculture, and architecture saved Spain from going backward during the Dark Ages. From their experience in the deserts of North Africa, the Arabs had learned how to preserve and manage water resources. They put this knowledge to good use in the hot, dry Iberian Peninsula. This ability to manage water was passed on to later generations. It proved helpful when the Spanish found themselves in the hot, dry regions of the Americas.

The Moors pushed Christian control into the northern reaches of Iberia. Still, many Christians stayed behind in the Moorish areas of Spain. They were tolerated by the Moors and allowed to develop their Christian and Castilian cultures. With the Moors came thousands of Jews, who were also tolerated. These Jews often served as merchants, teachers, and doctors in such great Muslim cities as Sevilla, Granada, and Cordoba.

The Reconquest

In the eleventh century, the Moors' centralized rule began to break into smaller kingdoms. The Christian Castilians moved to take back little by little the lands that they had lost to Islamic expansion. This Reconquest, as it was called, proceeded slowly because the Christians had little political unity and few economic resources. In 1469

Queen Isabella of Castile married King Ferdinand of Aragon. This union of the leaders of the two largest kingdoms in Spain brought unity to the Christians. In 1492 their unified army defeated King Boabdil, the Moorish ruler of Granada. This victory forced the Moors out of Spain once and for all. Because of their success against the Moors, Isabella and Ferdinand were also able to bring local nobles under their control, uniting all of Spain. In 1493 they received the support of Pope Alexander VI, so they had complete control over the political and religious systems of Spain.

The many years of war against the Moors strengthened the warrior cult the Germanic tribes had brought to the Iberian peninsula. Therefore, by 1492 valor, honor, audacity (daring), and tenacity (strong and persistent) were among the most important values held by Spaniards. They had also inherited other characteristics from the many groups that had invaded, influenced, and inhabited Iberia. When Columbus received the support of Isabella and Ferdinand and sailed west to encounter the New World in 1492, he took with him Spain's multiethnic past. This mixture of cultures became the Hispanic stamp that Spain imprinted on its colonies in the New World.

The African Legacy

When the Spanish began colonizing the Caribbean Islands, they brought a weapon with them greater than any knife, gun, or cannon: disease. Soon after the arrival of the first Spaniards, the native Arawak and Carib people began to die from European diseases to which they had no immunity (the body's natural resistance). As colonization continued the diseases spread. The native populations on the islands of Hispaniola, Cuba, and Puerto Rico were greatly reduced. When the Spanish settlements grew enough to begin taking advantage of the islands' economic resources, workers were needed. Thousands of Africans were forced into slavery and brought across the Atlantic Ocean. First they worked in mines and then they worked on the large sugar plantations that became the focus of the island economies. The Africans who came would greatly influence the racial makeup and culture of the Caribbean people.

Africans Forced into Slavery

In the early 1400s, the Portuguese became the first Europeans to buy and sell Africans for the purpose of slave labor. However, slavery did not become profitable until the plantation system of raising crops was developed in Brazil, the British colonies, and the Caribbean Islands.

The source for slaves in Africa was the western coast between the Senegal River to the north and Angola in the south. Europeans, especially the Portuguese, favored these regions for a number of reasons. First, some of these areas already had a heritage of slavery. One group would enslave members of another, forcing them to work on large farms. Therefore, the European traders could take advantage of existing networks of slave hunters among the Africans. They could also take advantage of experienced workers already familiar with the demands of large farms and plantations.

The expeditions by European slave traders in West Africa brought great anguish

Queen Isabella la Católica. *Reproduced courtesy of the Library of Congress.*

to individual Africans, their families, and whole societies. Families were broken up as the young men (the most valuable) were torn from their roots. That was only the beginning of the suffering, however. In preparation for the voyage across the Atlantic Ocean, captured Africans were first crowded into slave castles called *barranconas*. Thousands died there. On the ocean voyage, thousands more died in the crowded hulls of the slave ships on their way to the Caribbean Islands or Brazil. Once in the New World, these young Africans were sold like cattle at huge auctions.

In the Caribbean Islands, most slaves were sent to work on the hundreds of plantations established by Europeans. Others were sold to artisans to serve as helpers or

Arab slavers with captives to be sold. *Reproduced by permission of Archive Photos, Inc.*

to rich merchants to work as servants in the large households. At first, slave owners preferred male slaves. Eventually, however, hundreds of thousands of African women were sold into slavery. Slave owners found that women worked just as hard as men. They also realized that when they encouraged marriage and families among their slaves, they could ensure future generations of new slaves.

The growth of slavery in the Caribbean New World was closely linked to sugarcane production. Among the early settlers of the islands, there was little need for slaves. Peasants tended their own small farms and Spanish workers served on the larger *haciendas* (ranches or large farms). During this period the production of sugarcane grew slowly and so did the number of slaves. Between 1550 and 1650, the slave population only increased from about 1,000 to 5,000.

Africans in Cuba

In 1763 the British took control of Cuba after thirty years of war among the European powers. Under British direction the Caribbean island soon experienced a period of rapid economic growth. This included the introduction of a large-scale sugar plantation system. As sugarcane production expanded, the need for slave labor increased rapidly. Sixty thousand Africans had been brought to Cuba in the three centuries before 1770. Between 1770 and 1790, another 50,000 arrived.

The slave population continued to grow in the next century. By 1827 African slaves numbered approximately 280,000, or 40 percent, of the Cuban population. At mid-century blacks (African slaves and free Afro-Cubans) outnumbered whites. They made up 56 percent of the population. According to one study, 550,000 slaves were imported into Cuba between 1812 and 1865. This was in spite of the worldwide ban on slave trade that the British imposed during this period. Again, the expansion in Cuban sugar production accounted for the increase. On Cuba the percentage of blacks had been among the smallest in the Caribbean throughout the early colonial period. But, with the increases of the 1800s, the percentage became greater than anywhere else.

The history of Africans in Cuba is not simply a history of slavery. In the years between 1500 and 1800, Cuba had a significant population of free Africans. These freedmen worked in a variety of trades and achieved a level of independence not common among the blacks of the British colonies. Their presence and acceptance by white Cubans would allow them to build African culture into the foundation of Cuban culture.

Africans also fought slavery. Some escaped one by one, and others led rebellions against the colonial slave masters. Whenever they could, *cimarrones* (runaway slaves) escaped to a part of Cuba called the Orient province. There they built numerous fortified towns. In 1727 three hundred slaves from one plantation rebelled, killing

Slaves arrive in America. *Reproduced courtesy of the Library of Congress.*

almost all of the whites. A year later, all of the copper mines were closed in Santiago because of uprisings in that province. In the 1790s, Pierre Dominique Toussaint-Bréda (known as Toussaint L'Ouverture) led a slave revolt against the French colonists in Haiti. His rebels destroyed that colony's sugar industry. After the civil war that eventually made Toussaint L'Ouverture the first African governor in the New World, thirty thousand French colonists fled along with their slaves to Cuba.

During the 1800s, slave rebellions in Cuba became more common. This was due in large part to the high percentage of free-

A 1795 drawing of members of the Free Black Militia stationed in Spanish colonies in Florida and elsewhere. *Reproduced courtesy of the Library of Congress.*

born slaves newly arrived from Africa. They had strong memories of freedom and greatly resented its loss. The rebellious slaves sought freedom and revenge. Whites were often killed. For this reason, the fear of rebellions grew within the white population. In response to slave uprisings and in an attempt to deter them, whites often executed slaves, both rebels and innocent bystanders.

A changing world finally lifted the chains of slavery from the black Cubans. The industrial revolution was spreading throughout the world in the 1800s, requiring new methods and materials to meet the needs of new markets. In the second half of the nineteenth century, some Cuban and Spanish

businessmen realized that Cuba's sugar industry needed to update its production methods. They began to make changes. To succeed, Cuba would need a new labor system suited to the new production methods. In the modernized, competitive, expanded sugar industry of the late 1800s, wage labor was cheaper and more efficient than slavery. In the 1880s economic and social forces came together to end slavery in Cuba.

Africans in Puerto Rico and Mexico

Immediately after the settlement of Puerto Rico by Spaniards, slave traders began transporting African slaves to the island. Even so, the African population of this island was never as large as the African population in Cuba. In fact, it never exceeded 14 percent. In 1775, for example, out of a total Puerto Rican population of 70,250, only 6,467 were slaves. As a result, one hundred years later when slavery was abolished, the transition to wage labor was easier in Puerto Rico than in Cuba.

In the nineteenth century, the slave traffic to Puerto Rico did increase. Yet, slavery was not as important in the rural culture of Puerto Rico as it had been in Cuba. More important was the large class of rural poor whites and persons with mixed European, African, and Indian heritage. These country folk eked out a living as peasants, tenants on subsistence farms, or craftsmen in the towns and villages. This group came to be known as *jíbaros* (a South American word for "highlander" or "rustic"). They remain to this day an identifiable group in both Puerto Rico and on the U.S. mainland.

Just as in Cuba, the importance of slaves to the Puerto Rican economy increased because of an expansion in sugar production. Unlike Cuba, however, the percentage of Africans in the total population changed little because European immigration also increased. Even so, as slaves and later as free men, Africans worked their way into the jíbaro culture of Puerto Rico and added their own unique customs to the mix.

Africans were also transported to Mexico to serve as slaves. They were concentrated mainly in Veracruz on the Gulf of Mexico and in Guerrero on the Pacific around the port of Acapulco. They worked on sugar plantations, but there were not as many Africans in Mexico as in the Caribbean. Slavery in Mexico was abolished in 1829 by the new republican government that emerged after independence.

African Influences on Hispanic Culture

Africans from the Spanish Caribbean Islands and Mexico have greatly influenced Hispanic culture. In music, the tropical sound found in *salsa, merengue, mambo, rhumba,* and *jarocho* has its roots in the percussion-rich rhythms of Africa. To see this all one has to do is observe a *conjunto* (band) playing a variation of this music. Each band needs a player for the congas, bongos, timbales, and maracas. On the Caribbean islands, the religions of Africa mixed with the Catholicism brought over from Spain. This mixing has produced a set of religious practices known popularly as *santerismo.* The food and language of the Caribbean also bear the stamp of Africans.

Many Cubans, Puerto Ricans, and Mexicans carry the coloring, features, and culture of their African ancestors. These things, along with the history of slavery in these areas, have influenced Hispanic culture, giving it an awareness of race. At some times and in some places this awareness has led to racism. Fortunately, in recent years the Caribbean and Mexican people of African descent have made great efforts to overcome this racism.

2

The Meeting of Two Worlds

FACT FOCUS

- When Christopher Columbus discovered the New World in 1492, he set in motion the mixing of cultures that would one day create Hispanic culture.
- On his first voyage, Columbus actually landed at a small island he called San Salvador on October 12, 1492. San Salvador is either present-day Watling Island or Samana Cay in the Bahamas.
- On his second voyage, Columbus founded the first Spanish town in the New World, La Isabela, on the island of Hispaniola.
- In his three voyages, Columbus saw most of the Caribbean islands and the Gulf Coasts of Mexico and Venezuela.
- The arrival of Spaniards in the New World destroyed many Native American cultures. Hundreds of thousands of Native Americans died of diseases introduced by Spanish settlers. Many died of forced labor and warfare.
- In 1513, Spanish explorer Juan Ponce de León was the first European to explore Florida. In 1565 Pedro Menéndez de Avilés founded Saint Augustine, the first permanent European town in the United States.
- Hernán Cortés began to explore Mexico in 1519. In 1521, his armies destroyed Tenochtitlán, the capital city of the Aztecs. He had Mexico City built on the ruins of the Aztec city.
- From 1540 to 1542, the Spanish monk Marcos de Niza and explorer Francisco Vásquez de Coronado each led an expedition to explore the American Southwest. They sought, but did not find, the Seven Cities of Cíbola, which according to legend were filled with gold.
- The Spanish discovered Upper California in 1542 but did not settle there until 1769.
- Hernando de Soto explored Florida and the American South from 1539 to 1542. On March 4, 1541, his expedition discovered the Mississippi River.

WORDS TO KNOW

colony: the new land inhabited by a group of people who leave their home country to live in another land controlled by their home country.

conquest: taking over people or land by winning in war.

expedition: a journey for a special purpose, either exploration or conquest. The people who undertake the journey and their transportation are also called an expedition.

frontier: the land farthest from the center of a country, usually where the fewest people live. It is sometimes used as another word for border.

Hispaniola: the island in the Caribbean Sea where Christopher Columbus put the first European settlement in the New World. Today, Haiti and the Dominican Republic share this island.

New World: the name that Europeans used for the continents of North and South America.

presidio: a Spanish frontier fort.

settlement: a village, town, or city in a colony.

the Southwest: Arizona, New Mexico, and parts of California and Texas.

The history of the Hispanic people in North America begins with the meeting of two worlds. The year 1492 would begin almost four centuries of contact, conflict, and exchange between Spanish and Native American cultures. As a result of these meetings, some cultures would be destroyed. Some would be changed forever. Others would be born. These new Hispanic cultures of North America mixed Spanish, Native American, and African ways. They combined the legacies of those who went before them.

Spanish Exploration and Conquest in North America

Near the end of the 1400s, the countries of Europe began an era of exploration and discovery that would greatly increase the size of the known world. For Spain, this era came at a fortunate time. The kingdoms of Castile and Aragon had just been united through the marriage of Isabella and Ferdinand. The Spanish had just pushed the Moors out of their stronghold in Granada and forced them back to North Africa. Spain was strong and it had a surplus of trained soldiers. United under one king, one religion, and one sword, Spain was ready to make its greatest contribution to the Renaissance. It was ready to explore and colonize a New World. For the next 150 years, Spain would lead the race to build an empire in this New World.

The Voyages of Christopher Columbus

Christopher Columbus was not the first European to set foot on the New World. Research suggests that the Viking explorer Leif Eriksson had reached North America about five hundred years before Columbus. Yet, even if Columbus was not the first European to arrive in the Americas, his expedition was the first to establish a permanent presence in the New World.

Christopher Columbus was probably born in Genoa (now in Italy) in 1451. He became a sailor at an early age. He collected and studied maps to improve his knowledge of the sea. Based upon his studies, Columbus decided that the world was round and that ships could reach the Far East by sailing west. He planned a voyage westward to the rich island of Cipango (Japan) and the mainland of Cathay (China), where the Great Khan—Ghengis Khan, ruler of the Mongols—lived. He hoped to persuade one of the European kings or queens to finance his voyage, but he was turned down on several occasions. Finally, Columbus convinced Queen Isabella of Castile to support his quest. He not only received money for his voyage, but he also persuaded the queen to appoint him admiral in the Spanish navy and governor of any land he should discover.

On August 3, 1492, Columbus sailed from the southwestern Spanish port of Palos de Moguer with three ships: the *Niña,* the *Pinta,* and the *Santa María,* his flagship. The ships sailed southwest along the coast of Morocco to the Canary Islands. They departed from the Canary Islands on September 6 on a westward course. Columbus had predicted that his journey would take a few weeks.

Finally, thirty-three days after leaving the Canary Islands, the Spaniards sighted land. Columbus made landfall on October 12, 1492, on an island he called San Salvador, either present-day Watlings Island or Samana Cay in the eastern Bahamas. On October 27 the three ships landed on northeastern Cuba. Certain that he had reached either Cipango or Cathay, Columbus sent representatives to find the Great Khan and

Christopher Columbus. *Reproduced courtesy of the Library of Congress.*

his gold-domed cities. Instead, he found poor native Arawaks living in *bohíos* (huts).

Columbus then sailed eastward to an island he named La Española—Hispaniola—which today is shared by Haiti and the Dominican Republic. On the treacherous coast of Hispaniola, Columbus lost his flagship. His crew built a makeshift fort they called La Navidad with what remained of the *Santa María.* This would be shelter for the thirty-nine men who stayed behind. Columbus took the *Niña* and the *Pinta* and set sail for Spain. He reached Palos de Moguer on March 15, 1493.

Columbus was certain he had reached the Far East and he was able to convince the queen. In response she granted him seventeen ships and twelve hundred men for a

NORTH
AMERICA

ATLANTIC OCEAN

Gulf of
Mexico

Bahamas

Watling
Island

Rum Cay

Samana Cay

Long Island
Ragged Island

Crooked Cay

Bahia
Bariay

Cuba

Cap
Haïtien

La Navidad

Samana
Bay

Virgin
Islands

Windward
Passage

Hispaniola

Guadeloupe
Marie Galante

Santo
Domingo

Puerto
Rico

Jamaica

Dominica

Martinique

Caribbean Sea

Margarita Island

Ensenada
Yacua

Trinidad

VENEZUELA

Serpent's
Mouth

Gulf of
Paria

Panama

Veragua

Orinoco River

PACIFIC OCEAN

SOUTH AMERICA

Christopher Columbus's discoveries in the New World, 1492. *Reproduced by permission of the Gale Group.*

second voyage. Choosing a more southerly course, Columbus discovered the Virgin Islands and Puerto Rico before he reached Hispaniola in November 1493. There he found La Navidad destroyed and no trace of his men. Apparently, the gentle Arawak of the island had grown tired of the abuses of the Spanish troops and had killed the men.

Columbus sailed farther east on the north coast of Hispaniola. On a promising-looking bay, Columbus founded La Isabela. The fortified compound became the first permanent European settlement in the New World. In March 1494, Columbus explored the interior of the island. A month later he set sail from Hispaniola and discovered Jamaica during the summer. Obsessed with finding the Great Khan, he sailed for Cuba and back to Hispaniola. Finally, in 1496 he returned to Spain.

Although he had very little to show for his efforts, Columbus remained in the good graces of the Spanish queen. When he requested the finances for a third voyage, she agreed. During this expedition in 1498, he sailed south from Hispaniola and on July 31 discovered the island of Trinidad. He then sighted the Venezuelan coast and discovered the mouth of the Orinoco River. He concluded that the Venezuelan coast was Cathay. When Columbus returned to Hispaniola, a settlers' revolt had taken place against his brother Bartholomeo, whom he had left in charge after his second voyage.

When complaints against the Columbus brothers reached Isabella in Spain, she sent Francisco de Bobadilla to investigate. He was the queen's chief justice and royal inspector. In 1500, a year after his arrival in Hispaniola, Bobadilla had Christopher Columbus arrested and sent to Spain in chains. Isabella stripped Columbus of his titles. Even so, she was still willing to give him another chance: a fourth voyage. With four ships and 150 men, Columbus sailed from Spain in May 1502. After discovering the island of Martinique, he made a few brief stops in the Lesser Antilles and Puerto Rico. He then headed for Hispaniola. There he was denied permission to land by the Spanish authorities on the island. He sailed west and cruised the coast of Central America.

After an eight-month search for the Great Khan, Columbus headed for Hispaniola, only to be shipwrecked off Jamaica. Finally, in 1503 rescuers from Hispaniola arrived. In November 1504, Columbus returned to

COLUMBUS'S FIRST VOYAGE TO THE NEW WORLD

August 3, 1492: Columbus sails from the port of Palos de Moguer in southwestern Spain with three ships: the *Niña, Pinta,* and *Santa María.* The ships sail southwest along the coast of Morocco to the Canary Islands.

September 6: The three ships depart from the Canary Islands on a westward course.

September 25: Martín Alonso Pinzon, captain of the *Pinta,* sights land in the middle of the Atlantic Ocean. It turns out to be a false sighting.

October 12: Columbus's ships arrive at a small island—either present-day Watling Island or Samana Cay—southeast of Florida in the Bahamas. Columbus names the island San Salvador.

October 27: The expedition makes landfall on the northeastern coast of Cuba.

March 15, 1493: The *Niña* and *Pinta* arrive back at Palos de Moguer.

Spain. Two years later he died an unhappy man in the Spanish city of Valladolid. He had opened up the New World for Spanish conquest, but he had not reached his own goals.

New Lands in the Caribbean

The Conquest of Hispaniola

Columbus discovered Hispaniola—La Española—on his first voyage to the New

Frontispiece from the original 1493 edition of Christopher Columbus's letter to the Catholic kings describing his discoveries. *Reproduced by permission of Arte Público Press.*

World. It was there that he left behind the thirty-nine sailors of the *Santa María* in the makeshift fort called La Navidad. It was also there that on his second voyage he established the first permanent Spanish settlement in the New World, La Isabela. Many recognized Hispaniola and the other islands of the Caribbean as new lands. However, Columbus continued to believe that he had reached "the Indies." This was Europe's name for India, China, and Southeast Asia. In putting settlements on Hispaniola, he hoped to establish trade with the "Indians" led by the rich and powerful Great Khan. In reality, the Arawak and Carib natives had little surplus to trade. What they had was not the treasure sought by the Spaniards.

Most of the Spanish settlers who came with Columbus had lived in the tradition of the Spanish Reconquest (see chapter 1). They were used to fighting with foreigners, such as the Islamic Moors, in order to seize land for Christianity and their kingdom. In Spain they had been rewarded for defeating these infidels (non-Christians). They had been given the land owned by the Muslims and allowed to set up their own feudal estates, on which they were granted power over peasants and servants. This reward was known as the *encomienda*. Upon settling in Hispaniola, Columbus's men demanded that he reward them by granting them encomiendas over the Arawak and Carib infidels. Columbus opposed this tradition, but he agreed in order to avoid problems with his men.

The Spanish attempt to establish feudal estates on Hispaniola brought tragedy to the native populations. The Arawak and Carib were unaccustomed to trade on the scale expected by Columbus. They were also unprepared to provide the hard labor and tribute (payment) necessary for the encomienda system. They were worked to death in gold mines that yielded little gold. In working to feed the Spaniards, they died of starvation. And finally, they died in large numbers of diseases introduced by the Spanish invaders. They had no natural immunity (resistance) to diseases such as smallpox and measles. Hispaniola's native population and culture was almost completely lost. They lived on primarily in the mixed-race children born to the Spanish conquerors. Their land was also lost to the Spanish.

The Conquest of Cuba

Columbus encountered the island of Cuba on his first voyage to the New World in 1492. However, it was not until 1508, two years after Columbus's death, that the Spanish royalty took an interest in putting a colony on the island. That year Sebastián de Ocampo sailed around Cuba and started to spread tales that there was gold and silver to be found there. Two years later Diego Velázquez was sent to lead a group of three hundred Spanish soldiers in the conquest of Cuba. Velázquez had sailed to Hispaniola on Columbus's second voyage. In over fifteen years on that island, he had become rich and famous among the colonists.

Velázquez's army landed on Cuba at Puerto Escondido, where it encountered Arawak warriors. The Arawak were led by Hatuey, who was already familiar with the Spanish on Hispaniola. He led the warriors on Cuba in several deadly raids against the Spanish. But, in the end, the Spanish defeated the Arawak because of their better weapons. Hatuey was captured by Velázquez and burned at the stake. Today, Hatuey is remembered in Cuba as its first hero, a symbol of the island's resistance against foreigners.

First, Velázquez worked to take control of the Arawak population in that area. Then, in 1512 he directed the building of the town of Nuestra Señora de la Asunción de Baracoa. Thus, Baracoa became Cuba's first permanent settlement. By 1515 Velázquez had founded the cities of Santiago and Havana. By 1517 he had conquered the entire island. Velázquez became the governor of Cuba and remained in that position until the 1520s.

The early Cuban economy soon turned to the *encomienda* system. Under this system on Cuba, each Spaniard was given a certain number of Native American slaves and a certain amount of land. These resources were put to use raising livestock and gold mining. The pork, cattle hides, and gold from Cuba were soon in high demand in the other Spanish colonies, so the first Cuban settlers became rich. Velázquez repeated his previous exploits and made a second fortune on Cuba.

While the Spaniards prospered, the Arawak suffered. As had been the case on Hispaniola, Native Americans on Cuba soon died in large numbers because of the Spanish invasion. One cause was European diseases. Another cause was overwork in the mines. There turned out to be very little gold in Cuba. Faced with decreasing sources for gold, the Spaniards worked the Native Americans harder to get the same yield. Finally, starvation killed some of the natives of Cuba. Spanish livestock trampled the fragile crops that the Arawak used for food. The reduced harvests weakened the people and left them open to disease.

Cuba's first economic boom came to an end when silver was discovered in Mexico and Peru. The fickle colonists on Cuba left to find riches elsewhere. Eventually the economy rebounded, however. Because of its location, the island provided a perfect point of exchange for products from Mexico and Peru in the west to Europe in the east. In Cuban harbors New World silver was loaded onto ships bound for Spain and Old World goods arrived for distribution in the colonies.

By the mid-1500s, Havana's fine harbor had helped it become Cuba's leading city. It became Cuba's capital in 1607. Attracted by its riches, the British and the French both tried to take Havana from the Spanish. They each attacked the city numerous times. The Spanish responded by building stronger fortifications to protect the city. They also sent a strong navy to Cuban waters to protect ships. Fleets of ships loaded with gold and silver were gathered together in Havana Harbor. They were then escorted back to Spain to protect them from pirates. By the 1700s Havana was the New World's greatest port.

The Conquest of Puerto Rico

Unlike Hispaniola and Cuba, Columbus did not discover Puerto Rico until his second voyage in 1493. The Taino tribe of Arawak Indians living on the island called it Borinquén. Columbus charted the island and named it San Juan Bautista, but he made no attempt to settle it. At the time he was focusing on Hispaniola. It would be sixteen years before the Spanish would arrive to settle Puerto Rico. They would be led by another member of Columbus's second expedition, Juan Ponce de León.

After his voyage with Columbus, Ponce de León returned to Spain. In 1502, however, he was recalled to Hispaniola by the governor. He was needed to put down a revolt in Higuey (now Haiti) on the eastern part of the island. While performing his military duties in the village of Salvaleón, he heard that there was gold on the nearby island of Borinquén. He got a license from the governor of Hispaniola to explore the island and search for gold.

In 1508 Ponce de León and fifty Spaniards arrived to conquer an island inhabited by 30,000 Taino Indians. The Spaniards defeated the large population of natives by using terror tactics as they approached each village. These tactics were effective primarily because the Taino society was not organized to defend itself. It also lacked good means of communication. Against the better weapons and military organization of the Spanish, the Taino were no match. Their island of Borinquén became the Spanish colony of Puerto Rico, or "rich port."

After some disputes among his superiors in Hispaniola and Spain, Ponce de León was named governor of the island. As governor he became famous for using his fierce greyhound dog to frighten the Taino into obeying. But, his reign lasted only a couple years. In 1511 disputes among his superiors resulted in his dismissal.

The settlers who followed Ponce de León to Puerto Rico quickly set out to raise livestock and other foodstuffs for the expanding colonial market. The encomienda system also arrived. The land and Taino slaves were used to grow sugarcane. As on the other Caribbean Islands, the Native Americans provided labor only for a short time. They lacked experience with large-scale farming, so they were not very effective. Harsh treatment and disease killed a majority of the Taino by the 1580s. On Puerto Rico, Cuba, and Hispaniola, the Spanish would eventually replace the forced labor of Native Americans with the forced labor of Africans.

Spanish Expeditions to Florida and the American South

There is some evidence that explorers from England and Spain may have sailed along the Atlantic coast of Florida before 1513. Even so, Juan Ponce de León is credited with discovering the peninsula in that year. His expedition was approved by the Spanish crown and his discoveries were well recorded. Legend tells us that while Ponce de León was in Puerto Rico, he heard of an island called Bimini. This island was famous among the native people of the Caribbean because it had a "fountain of youth." This spring could make those who drank its waters young again. Ponce de León may have been in search of this fountain, but he had other reasons for his voyage.

The Discovery of La Florida

Juan Ponce de León had a great deal of influence among the Spanish nobility. The Ponce family was one of the most important in Spain, and it had married into another strong family, the Leóns ("lions" in Spanish). Ponce de León used this influence to obtain a permit from King Ferdinand to discover and settle Bimini. This was in February 1512. According to the permit, the explorer would

Juan Ponce de León receiving water taken from the fountain of youth. *Reproduced by permission of the Corbis Corporation (Bellevue).*

have to pay for the ships and equipment himself. He would agree to give one-tenth of the treasure he found to the king. He would also agree to provide the king with a report of his discoveries. In return Ponce de León would become the king's representative on the island. He and his men would have the right to divide the native population among themselves for use as slaves.

Ponce de León's initial plans to make the voyage in 1512 were delayed. He was needed to command a fort in Puerto Rico. The following spring he resumed his quest. He obtained the ships and supplies that he would need and on March 3, 1513, he set sail from San Germán, Puerto Rico. The expedition sailed on three caravels, the small, sturdy, wooden ships well suited to the winds of exploration. The three ships were called the *Santiago,* the *Santa María de la Consolación,* and the *San Cristóbal.*

The expedition sailed north northwest. On March 14 it reached San Salvador, Columbus's first stop in the New World. After making repairs and gathering supplies, Ponce de León directed the three ships to the northwest. On March 27, Easter Sunday 1513, he sighted the Florida mainland. He sailed along the coast until April 2, looking for a place to land. Sometime during the following week, he went ashore to take possession of the newly discovered land. There is no clear record of the landing place. Some historians believe that it was between the Saint Johns River and present-day Saint Augustine. Others believe that it was at Cape Sable. Ponce de León named the new land La Florida. He may have been referring to the beauty of the land's plant life. Or, he may have chosen the name because Easter Sunday is known as *Pascua Florida* in Spanish.

In April the expedition sailed along the coast of Florida. During the month of May, the three ships rounded the southern tip of the peninsula and sailed north along its Gulf coast. Throughout his voyage Ponce de León believed that Florida was an island, not Bimini, but a large new island. From time to time along their voyage, the Spaniards tried to make contact with the natives of Florida. Each time the attempts ended in battle. Having found no fountain of youth, no gold, and no place to easily settle, Ponce de León decided to return to Puerto Rico.

On June 15 the Spaniards set sail through the Florida Keys. One week later they came upon some small islands. Because his group was able to capture 170 turtles there, Ponce de León named the islands the Tortugas ("turtles" in Spanish). Two days later he sent the navigator Antonio de Alaminos and one of the caravels to continue the search for Bimini. Ponce de León returned to Puerto Rico on October 10, 1513, to report the large new island that he had discovered and named La Florida. Alaminos returned four months later. He had discovered the small island of Bimini, but he had not found the fountain of youth.

A Lion Returns to Florida

After his discovery of Florida in 1513, Ponce de León sailed to Spain to ask the king for a permit to colonize Florida and Bimini. The permit was granted on September 27, 1514. Ponce de León would have the responsibility of colonizing the islands and converting the native people to the Catholic faith. They were not to be enslaved if they accepted the religion. The king ordered Diego Columbus (Columbus's nephew), who was living on Hispaniola, to help supply the expedition. In return Ponce de León agreed to share the riches of Florida with the king.

As had been the case on his first trip to Florida, Ponce de León was delayed by other duties. So, it was not until 1521 that he finally left for Florida. He supplied two ships with two hundred men, fifty horses, and many farm animals. He also took several Catholic priests to serve the colonists and to spread the Catholic religion among the native people. In February of that year, the expedition sailed out of San Germán, Puerto Rico.

The landing point of Ponce de León's second voyage is not known for sure. Historians believe it was near Charlotte Harbor on the Gulf coast of Florida. On his first trip, Ponce de León had heard that there was gold there and he probably wanted to see if the stories were true. As soon as they landed, the explorer and his men were attacked by the native Calusa Indians. An arrow pierced Ponce de León, but the "old lion," as he was called, continued to bravely lead his men. When the Calusa attacked again, he ordered retreat and set sail for Cuba. The expedition made it to Cuba, but Ponce de León died there a few days later. He was buried later on Puerto Rico. Juan Ponce de León died without having established a colony in Florida, still believing that it was an island.

Pedro Menéndez de Avilés. *Reproduced courtesy of the Library of Congress.*

The Conquest of Florida

Over the next forty years, Spain discovered that Florida was not an island. But, it failed several times to place a colony in Florida. In 1564, however, a group of French Protestants succeeded in founding Fort Caroline at the mouth of the Saint John's River, near where Jacksonville is today. This angered the Spanish king, and he ordered Pedro Menéndez de Avilés to drive the French out of Florida.

Menéndez, one of the best commanders in the Spanish army, laid out his strategy carefully. On June 29, 1565, he set sail from Cádiz, Spain, for Puerto Rico. On August 15 he left San Juan, Puerto Rico, with eight hundred soldiers and colonists. The expedition arrived in Florida on August 28, the feast day of Saint Augustine. For this reason Menén-dez named the area Saint Augustine. After sailing north for a brief skirmish with the French, Menéndez returned to settle the area.

On September 6, 1565, Menéndez sent some of his men ashore to build a crude fort. Two days later Menéndez landed and claimed the area for the king of Spain, Philip II. Thus, Saint Augustine became the first permanent European settlement in what would become the United States.

Over the next three months, the Spaniards from Saint Augustine and the French from Fort Caroline fought four battles. In battle, Menéndez was ruthless. His army killed 130 French at Fort Caroline. In another two battles along the Florida coast, he and his men killed 330 French, even after the French had surrendered. By November 16, 1565, Menéndez's army had captured another 170 French soldiers. Florida now belonged to Spain. King Philip II commended Menéndez for his work.

Menéndez dreamed of creating a Spanish colony from Florida all the way north to Canada. The dream, however, would never become a reality. On February 20, 1574, Philip II recalled Menéndez to Spain to give him command of the Spanish Armada, a large fleet of battleships. The king planned to use the armada to invade England. But before Menéndez could lead the invasion, he fell ill and died on September 17, 1574. The invasion was delayed until 1588. Sir Francis Drake and other English captains, along with several storms in the waters around Great Britain, destroyed the Spanish Armada. The disaster signaled an end to Spanish domination of the seas.

Spain was weakened in Europe, but it held onto its lands in the New World for some time. Florida remained a Spanish colony until 1763. Then, Spain handed it over to the British in order to regain Cuba, which the British had captured. In 1783 the British returned Florida to Spain in exchange for the Bahama Islands. The sun finally set on Spanish Florida in July 1821. At that time, the United States purchased the peninsula for $5 million.

The Expedition of Pánfilo de Narváez

Stories of gold in the northwestern parts of Florida began to spread in Cuba after Ponce de León's voyage along the Gulf coast. Two expeditions that set out to find this gold ended up exploring much of the present-day states of the American South. Pánfilo de Narváez led the first expedition near the end of the 1520s. Hernando de Soto led the second ten years later. Neither group found gold, but they did find adventure.

In the mid-1520s, the king of Spain appointed Pánfilo de Narváez governor of Florida. He also gave Narváez the right to discover, conquer, and settle the land from the Rio Grande to Florida. Narváez and his six hundred men left the Spanish port of Sanlúcar de Barrameda on June 27, 1527. The expedition began to have bad luck as soon as it reached the New World. After arriving in Hispaniola, 140 men deserted. Between Hispaniola and Cuba, a hurricane wrecked two ships. The expedition spent the winter of 1527 in Cuba. It sailed again on February 20, 1528, with only 400 men.

In the waters off Cuba, Narváez's ships hit several sandbars. They continued on with great difficulty. On April 12, 1528, the ships anchored near Tampa Bay. A few days later, Narváez landed and took possession of the land in the name of the king. He then sought out the local Native Americans to ask about gold. They told the Spaniards through sign language that the gold was to the north. They would find the gold in Apalachee, present-day Tallahassee. It is likely that the natives invented the story so the Spaniards would leave them alone.

Lured by the tales of gold, Narváez decided to march inland with three hundred men. They set out on May 1, 1528, with very little food and supplies. On June 25, after a fifty-six-day march, the tired Spaniards arrived in Apalachee. Instead of gold, the Spaniards found fierce Apalachee people. Tired and hungry, the men marched toward the sea. They had been told by a prisoner that they could find food at the village of Aute, present-day Saint Marks or Apalachicola. But, the Apalachee there had set fire to the fields. They also attacked the tired, hungry Europeans.

The Spaniards decided to build barges and sail to Mexico. They believed it was nearby. They sawed down trees with their swords and pikes and made them into planks. They turned their horseshoes into nails. They ripped their shirts and put them together to make sails. They also killed their horses and used the hides for water skins. Finally, on September 22, 1528, five barges set sail carrying 242 men.

The makeshift fleet sailed close to the Gulf coast of present-day Florida, Alabama, Mississippi, and Louisiana for more than a month. Narváez's barge left the others and was never seen again. The four remaining barges were caught in a hurricane near the coast of Texas. Eighty men managed to survive by reaching present-

Alvar Núñez Cabeza de Vaca. *Reproduced by permission of the Granger Collection, New York.*

day Galveston Island. Because of their experience, they named the island Isla de Malhado (Badluck Island).

The Adventures of Cabeza de Vaca

Soon after the Spaniards had landed, the Native Americans on Isla de Malhado took them captive. Cold, hunger, and disease followed during a bitter winter. The Spaniards even resorted to cannibalism in order to survive. Of the eighty men who reached Malhado, only fifteen survived the winter. Their captors forced some of the survivors to act as medicine men. One Spaniard, Alvar Núñez Cabeza de Vaca, became famous among the Native Americans as a medicine man by using Catholic rituals. He simply made the sign of the cross and recited a Hail Mary and the Lord's Prayer.

In April 1529 the Native Americans took the fifteen survivors to the Texas mainland. There, twelve of the Spaniards managed to escape. Cabeza de Vaca and two others stayed behind because they were too sick to travel. One of these three died, but Cabeza de Vaca and Lope de Oviedo survived and were taken back to Malhado. After twenty-two months of captivity and movement, the two Spaniards began their journey to freedom. They first crossed a number of inlets and arrived at a large bay, present-day Matagorda Bay. There, they met several

Native Americans on the shore. These people told them that their tribe had three other Spaniards at a village farther inland. These three were the only survivors among the twelve escapees. The other nine had died from cold and hunger.

Lope de Oviedo had grown tired of the way he was treated by the Native Americans. So, he left Cabeza de Vaca behind and returned toward Malhado. He was never seen again. Two days after his departure, the rest of the local tribe arrived near Matagorda Bay with their three prisoners. Cabeza de Vaca, Andrés Dorantes, Alonso del Castillo, and the black man Estevanico were reunited for the first time in more than three years. The four Spaniards spent the winter of 1532–33 together with the natives. In August 1533 they moved with their captors to an area near present-day San Antonio. There, the Native Americans separated the four. But before this, the Spaniards agreed on an escape plan.

Cabeza de Vaca lived with one tribal group until September 13, 1534. A day later, Castillo, Dorantes, and Estevanico arrived. On September 15 they began the most daring, difficult, and remarkable escape in the history of the New World.

After making their break, the four Spaniards wandered from tribe to tribe, posing as medicine men. Their journey took them over 1,000 miles through present-day Texas, New Mexico, and Arizona. They walked barefooted and naked over the harsh land of the Southwest. They learned to conquer the freezing winds of winter and the blistering sun of summer. They ate spiders, salamanders, lizards, worms, and prickly pears.

Finally, in February 1536, eight years and thousands of miles after leaving Cuba, their

Title page of Alvar Núñez Cabeza de Vaca's *La relacion,* 1542. Reproduced by permission of Arte Público Press.

ordeal ended. They came upon a company of Spanish soldiers in northern Mexico. A few days later, they arrived in San Miguel. They had survived because they had worked together and kept their faith. On May 15, 1536, the four left San Miguel. They arrived in Mexico City on June 24, 1536.

More adventures would lay ahead for each of these four survivors. But, for the time being, their stories of eight years of bad luck would stir the imagination of their fellow Spaniards. Cabeza de Vaca returned to Spain and spent three years writing his story. Published in 1542 as *La relación,* the

Hernando de Soto. *Reproduced courtesy of the Library of Congress.*

account of his trip provided the first descriptions of the plants, animals, and people of the American South and Southwest. It would spark several future expeditions.

The Expedition of Hernando de Soto

Born in 1500 in Spain, Hernando de Soto left for Central America when he was in his teens. Later, he joined Francisco Pizarro in his conquest of Peru. After living in Peru for a few years, de Soto returned to Spain in 1536. There, he sought out Alvar Núñez Cabeza de Vaca, who had just returned from his eight-year journey. Despite Cabeza de Vaca's report, de Soto remained convinced that Florida was covered with gold.

On April 20, 1537, Charles V named de Soto governor of Cuba and captain-general of Florida. A year later de Soto sailed for Cuba. Once there, he made provisions for governing the island. Then on May 18, 1539, he left Cuba for Florida. His expedition included 650 men and a large herd of pigs and other livestock.

On May 30, 1539, the Spaniards arrived at Tampa Bay. Soon after landing they discovered Juan Ortiz, a member of the Narváez expedition. He had been saved by the daughter of the cacique Hirrihigua. However, they did not discover gold. So, de Soto and 550 men marched north along the coast to Apalachee. They spent the winter there. During the winter of 1539, the Spaniards celebrated a feast of thanksgiving. The following spring de Soto led his men northeast to avoid attack by the Apalachee and to seek gold. They soon reached present-day Georgia.

According to recent research, de Soto's route was as follows. In April 1540 his group crossed the Savannah River and entered South Carolina. After failing to find gold, the Spaniards headed north and arrived at Xuala, present-day Marion, North Carolina. They then crossed the Great Smokey Mountains into Tennessee. From the mountains they headed southwest through Georgia and Alabama. On October 18, 1540, de Soto and his men reached the village of Mauvilla, near Mobile Bay. At this village the Choctaw chief Tascaluza and his men attacked de Soto's group. Although the Spaniards managed to kill about 3,000 Choctaws, they lost 22 men and 148 were wounded.

The Discovery of the Mississippi River

Because of his failures, de Soto decided not to keep a rendezvous he had planned in

HISPANIC AMERICAN TALES

Early American history has many tales of exploration, adventure, romance, and triumph over hardship. Anglo-American culture includes stories about the Jamestown colony in Virginia and the Plymouth colony in Massachusetts. In his book *General Historie of Virginia* (1624), Captain John Smith tells of his capture by the native Powhatans. He was going to be killed, but he was saved by Pocahontas, the chief's daughter. Pocahontas later married John Rolfe, another English colonist. The Thanksgiving story tells of the Pilgrim settlers in Massachusetts. Happy to have survived the hard winter of 1620, they gathered with the native Wampanoags to have a feast of thanksgiving.

Hispanic American culture has similar stories. Alvar Núñez Cabeza de Vaca tells the story of his adventurous journey in his 1542 book *La relación.* Early Hispanic history has its tale of a young Native American woman saving a European explorer. A member of the Cabeza de Vaca's expedition, Juan Ortiz, was lost near Tampa Bay, Florida, in 1528. He was saved by the daughter of the chief Hirrihigua. Ortiz was found eleven years later when Hernando de Soto's expedition arrived at Tampa Bay. Hispanic history also has its Thanksgiving. De Soto and his 550 men spent their first winter in Florida near Apalachee. During that winter of 1539, these Spaniards held a feast of thanksgiving.

Pensacola, Florida. He had instructed Diego de Maldonado to go to Cuba and return with supplies. De Soto never showed up to get his supplies. Instead, he led his men northwest into present-day Mississippi. The Spaniards spent the winter of 1540–41 in the land of the Chicasaw people of northern Mississippi.

On March 4, 1541, de Soto ordered his men to break camp and leave the area. Before the Spaniards could leave, they were attacked by the Chicasaw. During the battle the attackers set fire to the camp. Twelve men, fifty-nine horses, and three hundred pigs were killed. To escape, the Spaniards

retreated to the northwest. On their way they came upon a great river, the mighty Mississippi. De Soto and his men spent more than a month building barges to cross the river.

The Spaniards crossed the great river on June 19, 1541, and then marched to a place near Horseshoe Lake, Arkansas. Again, de Soto heard tales of gold and silver from the local Native Americans. So, he pushed on into the territory of the Plains Indians. Instead of gold and silver, the Spaniards found buffalo skins. They continued west, seeing the Arkansas River on September 13. As winter approached, de Soto decided to

Hernán Cortés.

turn back to the southeast. The expedition spent the winter of 1541–42 at Autiamque, present-day Redfield, Arkansas. It was a harsh winter. The total number of men lost on the trip climbed to 250. Looking for relief from their misery, the Spaniards headed south. But, the Arkansas countryside offered no relief. Depressed by the situation, de Soto fell ill. He died on May 21, 1542, in Guachoya, now McArthur, Arkansas.

Luis de Moscoso quickly took command of the expedition. He first ordered that de Soto be buried outside of Guachoya. But, de Soto's death and burial presented the Spaniards with a problem. De Soto had already convinced the local Natchez people that he was immortal. Moscoso began to fear that if the Natchez found out that de Soto had died, they might attack. So, he ordered that de Soto's body be dug up. The Spaniards then wrapped the body and

weighted it with sand. Under the cover of night, they took a canoe out onto the Mississippi. There they sent the explorer to the depths of the great river he had discovered. Moscoso told the Natchez that de Soto had gone to heaven. He would return soon.

Moscoso decided to head toward Mexico. He felt that traveling southwest over land would be the best course. However, along their route the Europeans found the food scarce and the Native Americans hostile. Returning toward the Mississippi and its supply of food, they spent the winter of 1542–43 along the river. Early in 1543 they began to build seven boats. They also killed their horses and pigs and dried the meat. On July 2, 1543, they launched the boats down the river. Two weeks later they reached the mouth of the Mississippi.

Leaving the great river behind, they sailed along the coast of Louisiana and Texas. Finally, on September 10, 1543, they arrived at Tampico on the Gulf coast northeast of Mexico City. Of the original 650 men, 311 survived the journey. They had walked and sailed more than 3,500 miles. Again, the Spanish explorers failed to find gold or silver. But again they returned with information about the plants, animals, and people of the American South.

The Conquest of Mexico

In 1518 Hernán Cortés set out from Cuba to explore the mainland of Mexico. He had been chosen by Diego Velázquez, the governor of Cuba, to confirm reports from previous explorers. Columbus's fourth voyage had taken the Spanish along the coast of Central America in 1502. Later voyages by Francisco Hernández de Córdova and Juan

Hernán Cortés meeting the Aztec emperor Moctezuma in Tenochtitlán. *Reproduced courtesy of the Library of Congress.*

de Grijalva had taken the Spanish along the Yucatán and Mexican coasts. From these trips, reports had come back to Cuba that there were large native civilizations in the interior. Cortés hoped to find them.

Cortés and his army of four hundred men left from Santiago de Cuba. They made stops at the island of Cozumel off the northeast coast of the Yucatán Peninsula and in the Tabasco region west of the peninsula. In Tabasco Cortés received several young women as gifts from the Native Americans. One of these women, Malinche, became his mistress and interpreter.

The Meeting of Two Great Civilizations

The Spaniards landed on the Gulf coast in April 1519 at a bay Cortés named Veracruz. When they met the local inhabitants of the coast, they heard the stories themselves. There was an advanced civilization and a magnificent city farther inland. The people were the Aztec and the city Tenochtitlán. Cortés ordered some of the Spanish ships destroyed so that his men would not be able to return to Cuba. Then, he set out for the interior and the source of the stories. Cortés was a conquistador (conqueror). He had been raised in the warrior cult of southern Spain during the Reconquest over the Moors. His goal in the New World was not to study new cultures or to trade with them. He wanted to establish himself as the ruler of a new land.

Along the way to the interior, the Spaniards were confronted by the natives of Cholula. With the assistance of information given to him by Malinche, Cortés was able to defeat the Cholulans. He continued toward Tenochtitlán. In Tlaxcala, Cortés found people willing to join him against the Aztec. The Tlaxcalans had long been victims of Aztec aggression. They believed Cortés would give them an opportunity for revenge.

Moctezuma was the Aztec emperor who ruled the great city of Tenochtitlán. His spies informed him when the Spaniards landed on the coast and as they approached. Moctezuma believed that Cortés was the god Quetzalcoatl, who was expected to return one day. He also believed that the other Spaniards were immortal. By the time Cortés and his men arrived at Tenochtitlán, Moctezuma had no idea what to do. Cortés took advantage of the situation and imprisoned the king in his own palace. Then, the Spaniards and their Tlaxcalan allies set up camp inside the walls of the Aztec city.

At one point Cortés was called away to the coast to deal with another Spanish expedition sent to replace him. Instead, he persuaded the new group to join him. Upon returning to Tenochtitlán, Cortés found the city in rebellion. The Aztecs had finally turned against the invaders after a year of abuse. Led by Cuitlahuac, Moctezuma's brother, they forced the Spaniards out on July 1, 1520. The Spaniards called this *La noche triste* (The Sad Night). During this same rebellion, the Aztec people stoned Moctezuma to death.

The Fall of Tenochtitlán and Rise of Mexico

Cortés was not a man to give up easily. So, he retreated to the town of Coyoacán to set up his headquarters and plan his return. He decided to use his four hundred soldiers, the Spaniards from the second expedition, and the thousands of Tlaxcalans to lay siege to the city. They did not allow anyone or anything in or out of Tenochtitlán. In time, Cortés's force attacked the starving Aztecs. It also attacked the neighboring Tlatelolcans. Both groups were devastated by the Spanish firepower and by the European diseases introduced earlier. Cuitlahuac, the hero of the Aztec rebellion, died not in battle, but rather in a sickbed. After Cuitlahuac's death, Cuauhtemoc, a Tlatelolcan, took command. Despite his efforts, he and the defenders of Tenochtitlán were forced to surrender. He was later executed by the Spanish. To many Mexicans today, Cuauhtemoc is a hero and Cortés is a villain.

Victorious, Cortés ordered the destruction of Tenochtitlán. In its place, he directed the building of Mexico City. Afterward, he and his conquistadors spread out to explore and conquer the rest of the valley of Mexico. Cortés took for himself a huge area of land southeast of Mexico City. It covered practically all of the state of Oaxaca. In 1529 he was given the right to use the title El Marqués del Valle de Oaxaca (Marquis of the Valley of Oaxaca).

Eventually, due to political intrigue and the jealousy of some of his peers, Cortés was stripped of his power and land and sent back to Spain. He was replaced by professional viceroys, representatives of the king. The Spaniards then ruled Mexico for three hundred years until 1821. They stamped their Hispanic mark on Mexican society, but they could not erase the influence of the native peoples of Mexico.

Spanish Exploration of the American Southwest

The story of Alvar Núñez Cabeza de Vaca's journey in the lands north of Mexico spread quickly among the fortune seekers in Mexico City. As it did, it was mixed with a legend that had started during the Muslim invasion of the Iberian Peninsula centuries before. According to the legend, seven Portuguese bishops had fled the invasion by crossing the Ocean Sea (Atlantic Ocean). In the land that they found, they built the Seven Cities of Antilla, rich in gold and silver. Cabeza de Vaca's report suggested to some that the Seven Cities were in the land north of Mexico.

Fray Marcos de Niza and the Seven Cities of Cíbola

One man who was convinced that Cabeza de Vaca had·seen the Seven Cities was Antonio de Mendoza, the viceroy of Mexico. He chose the friar (monk) Marcos de Niza to explore the mysterious land to the north. Fray Marcos was an experienced traveler. He had been part of the conquests of Guatemala and Peru.

On March 7, 1539, Fray Marcos left the northern Mexican village of Culiacán. Included in his expedition was Estevanico, the black man who had been with Cabeza de Vaca on his journey. On March 21 they crossed the Río Mayo. Fray Marcos decided

to send Estevanico and a few of his Native American guides ahead as scouts. Estevanico was to leave behind a cross to mark each settlement that he found. The larger the settlement, the larger the cross.

For two months the friar and his men followed a route marked with crosses. The crosses kept getting larger. The friar thought he was approaching the Seven Cities. Messengers sent by Estevanico told Fray Marcos that he had seen the Seven Cities. The local Zuñi people called them Cíbola. Certain that he would soon come to the Seven Cities, Fray Marcos pushed northward up the Sonora Valley into southeastern Arizona.

In late May Fray Marcos received news that Estevanico was dead. He had been killed by the Zuñi as he had been approaching the first city, present-day Hawikuh, New Mexico. Still, Fray Marcos pressed on toward the first city of Cíbola. He later reported a city larger than Mexico City. However, he feared for his life, so he did not enter the city. Instead, he raised a cross and claimed possession of the city in the name of the king of Spain. Then Fray Marcos and his men began their return to Mexico. They arrived in Mexico City in September 1539. In Mexico City Fray Marcos reported to Viceroy Mendoza that there was much gold in Cíbola. The people of these cities covered themselves in it, he claimed.

The Expedition of Francisco Vásquez de Coronado

Fray Marcos's report seemed promising, so Viceroy Mendoza decided to send a second expedition. He chose the governor of Nueva Galicia, a northern Mexican province, as leader. Francisco Vásquez de Coronado gathered three hundred Spaniards,

Francisco Vásquez de Coronado. *Reproduced by permission of the Corbis Corporation (Bellevue).*

including Fray Marcos, and eight hundred local Native Americans for his expedition. They left Compostela, Nueva Galicia, on February 23, 1540. By April 1 the large group had only covered 350 miles. Coronado decided he could move faster if he pushed ahead with a smaller group of one hundred men. He left Tristán de Arellano in charge of the main force.

With Fray Marcos as his guide, Coronado and his men marched through the Sonora Valley into southwestern Arizona. Then, they veered eastward. On July 7, after a 1,000-mile

journey, they arrived at the first of the Seven Cities, Hawikuh. The Zuñi town did not have the gold Fray Marcos had described in his report. Instead, hostile warriors awaited the Spaniards. Coronado's scouts proved that Fray Marcos had either lied in his earlier reports or he had believed the false reports of others. The Seven Cities filled with gold were actually seven villages with adobe houses. Coronado sent Fray Marcos back to Mexico City to report the truth to Viceroy Mendoza.

While waiting for Arellano and the main force to catch up, Coronado continued to

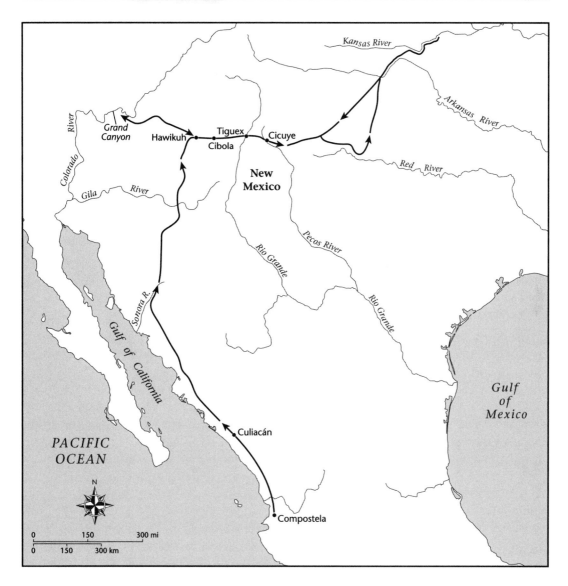

Francisco Vásquez de Coronado's expeditions to the American Southwest, 1540–42. *Reproduced by permission of the Gale Group.*

send out scouting parties to search for gold. One of these scouting parties went into the Hopi villages of northeastern Arizona. They found no gold, however. Another group was led by Captain López de Cárdenas. It dis-

covered no precious metals, but it did find the Grand Canyon. A third group was led by Hernando de Alvarado. It set off to explore a province the local Native Americans called Tiguex, now Albuquerque, New Mexico.

Then they traveled to Cicuye on the upper Rio Grande and eastward along the Pecos River. They took on a Pawnee guide whom they called El Turco (the Turk). He told the Spaniards of a rich land called Quivira. But, Alvarado decided to return to Tiguex to wait for Coronado.

Coronado and the main force joined Alvarado, and the whole group camped at Tiguex during the winter of 1540–41. They demanded that the local Pueblo people supply their food. Eventually, these demands angered the Pueblos. They revolted and Coronado was forced to battle them throughout the winter. On one occasion Coronado directed the burning at the stake of two hundred Pueblo prisoners.

On April 23, 1541, Coronado and his men set out to reach Quivira. El Turco led the way. First, they reached the border of present-day Oklahoma. The Native Americans there informed the Spaniards that Quivira was far to the north. Coronado left his army behind on June 1, taking thirty men. After marching five weeks, he and his party reached Quivira on July 6. There was no great city. There was only a settlement of seminomads. Coronado and his men explored the area for more than a month. The soil was fertile, but there was no gold. While in the area of present-day Wichita, Kansas, the Spaniards became suspicious of El Turco. First, they found out that he was telling the local Native Americans not to help them. After torturing him they found out he had been lying. There were no riches in Quivira. The Spaniards killed him.

The disgruntled Spaniards left Quivira in late August. They spent the winter of 1541–42 in Tiguex. In the spring of 1542,

Coronado decided to return to Mexico City. Several friars in the group decided to stay behind to preach the Christian faith to the Native Americans. As soon as the soldiers left, however, the Native Americans killed the friars.

In July 1542 Coronado returned to Mexico City. He had fewer than one hundred of the three hundred Spaniards who had left Compostela. He was brokenhearted and impoverished by his quest for Cíbola and Quivira. He died in Mexico City in 1544.

Spanish Exploration of California

The Mythical Island of California

The first expeditions to Baja (Lower) California were made in 1532 by Hernán Cortés, the founder of Mexico City. He was looking for the fabled Northwest Passage, a water route leading from the Atlantic to the Pacific Ocean. Instead he found land off the west coast of Mexico. Because the Spaniards thought it was an island, they gave it the name of a mythical island from Spanish literature. California was the name of an island in the novel of knights called *Las sergas de Esplandián* (The Deeds of Esplandian). Seven years later, Francisco de Ulloa proved that California was not an island but a large peninsula.

The Mexican viceroy Antonio de Mendoza was always looking for new treasures. He believed California might offer such treasures. In 1542 he chose a Portuguese sailor, Juan Rodríguez Cabrillo, to lead another search for gold. Cabrillo was to sail north from La Navidad, a town on the west coast of Mexico. On September 28, 1542,

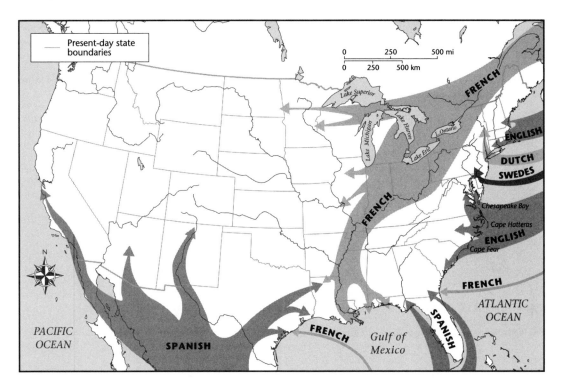

Major paths of early European penetration in the United States. *Reproduced by permission of the Gale Group.*

Cabrillo came upon an excellent port, San Diego. He then continued northward. Searching the coast, he found no sign of treasures. Cabrillo died on January 3, 1543. Bartholomé Ferrelo took command of the expedition. He continued to sail north all the way to the Oregon coast. But, disease broke out among the crew and Ferrelo decided to return to Mexico. The expedition arrived at La Navidad on April 14, 1543.

The Spanish "Rediscover" California

The Spanish lost interest in exploring California after the Cabrillo-Ferrelo expedition. However, in the late 1500s, Mexico began to trade with Spain's colony in the Philippines. At this time the Spaniards real-

ized that Alta (Upper) California could offer ports where Spanish ships could repair and resupply. They also recognized the threat from British pirates in the area. English admiral Sir Francis Drake had claimed the California coast for Britain in 1579.

In 1584 the Spanish sent Francisco de Gali to scout the coast of Alta California. Eleven years later, the Portuguese sailor Sebastião Rodrigues Cermenho explored the California coast on his return from the Philippines. Rodrigues Cermenho followed Gali's general course, but he went closer to the coast. In December 1595 he came accross a bay. It was named after the Mexican viceroy at that time, Monterey. He arrived at the Mexican port of La Navidad one month later.

Royal Presidio Chapel, Monterey. *Reproduced by permission of Archive Photos, Inc.*

Monterey sent the experienced sailor Sebastián Vizcaíno to scout the coast of Alta California in May 1602. Vizcaíno spent eleven months exploring the coast. He made detailed records of the coast, including the area around the entrance to Monterey Bay. But his crew paid a high price. One-quarter of the original crew died of hunger. The exploration of Alta California was proving to be costly.

The Last Frontier

Spain finally pushed to colonize Alta California, but not because it offered treasures. Russians had begun to trade on the Pacific Coast, and the Spaniards were afraid that Russia would seize the area. The governor of Baja California, Don Gaspar de Por-

tolá, was chosen to lead a new expedition. Father Junípero de Serra, the head of the Franciscan monks in Baja California (a peninsula in northwest Mexico), was also part of the group.

In January and February 1769, two ships left for San Diego carrying supplies. Two parties also left for San Diego by land. One party, with Portolá at its head and Serra as its chaplain, left Loreto in Baja California on May 15. The other, commanded by Fernando Rivera Moncade, left the Baja California town of Velicatá on March 22.

The two groups traveled hundreds of miles through difficult terrain. On July 1, 1769, they joined the ships at San Diego. Two days later Father Serra planted a cross on a San Diego hill. The Spaniards then began to build a mission, a center for the Catholic church in the area. San Diego was the first of twenty-one missions that the Franciscan order of monks built in Alta California.

Portolá left San Diego and headed north to find Monterey Bay. He arrived there in October 1769, but he did not believe that it was Monterey. So, he pushed northward. Days later he arrived at a large bay. He knew it was too large to be Monterey, so he named it San Francisco. He wanted to continue his search, but since his men were tired, he decided to return to San Diego. The group arrived on January 24, 1770.

Portolá was still obsessed with finding Monterey. On May 31, 1770, he and Father Serra boarded the ship *San Antonio* to search for the bay. A few days later, they finally reached Monterey. Father Serra stayed to build the second mission in Alta California. Portolá returned to Mexico. Spain now had two forts, or presidios, to guard its empire in

A 1786 illustration of a soldier at the Monterey Presidio. *Reproduced courtesy of the Bancroft Library, University of California.*

A 1786 illustration of a soldier's wife in Monterey. *Reproduced courtesy of the Bancroft Library, University of California.*

Alta California. Monterey was to the north and San Diego was to the south.

Don Antonio María Bucareli, the new Spanish viceroy in Mexico, wanted to start another settlement in California. In 1773 he called on Captain Juan Bautista de Anza, the head of a fort in northern Mexico. De Anza was to set up a route between Monterey and Sonora in northwestern Mexico.

In January 1774 de Anza set out on a scouting mission. He stopped first at the point where the Gila and Colorado rivers meet. There, he established good relations with the Yuma people and their cacique Palma. He crossed the river and pushed on through the desert. On March 22, 1774, he reached San Gabriel, one of the Spanish missions near present-day Los Angeles. He went on to Monterey. Then, de Anza and his men returned to Mexico City to report to the viceroy. Together, they decided to build the new fort in San Francisco.

De Anza gathered an expedition of 240 settlers and enough supplies to start a settlement. The group left northern Mexico in October 1775. As the expedition reached Yuma country, they were welcomed by Chief Palma. On January 2, 1776, they reached San Gabriel. In March they arrived in Monterey. The presidio of San Francisco was founded on September 17, 1776. It stood at Spain's northernmost frontier. His mission accomplished, de Anza returned to Mexico City. He later became governor of New Mexico.

The Alta California provinces made little progress. The Yuma lost patience with the Spaniards, and in 1781 they revolted. The Spaniards put down the revolt, but the Spanish settlements did not grow. They were remote and isolated, with few people or resources. In 1821 California joined the independent Republic of Mexico.

3

The First Hispanic Americans

Hispanic People in Texas, the Southwest, and California Become U.S. Citizens

---

FACT FOCUS

- Mexicans living in Texas became the first Hispanic Americans when that state joined the United States in 1845.
- After the Mexican War ended in 1848, Mexicans in New Mexico, Arizona, California, Nevada, Utah, and Colorado became American citizens.
- New Mexico and Arizona kept a strong Hispanic culture until the 1880s, when railroads connected them to the East and Midwest.
- After the Mexican War, prejudice and unfair laws forced many Hispanics born in California to move to Mexico.
- Hispanic Americans born in the United States are influenced by mainstream American culture. Schools, jobs, television, radio, and newspapers are changing their views.

Many of the first Hispanic Americans did not choose to come to the United States. It came to them. During the early 1800s, Anglo settlers from the United States began to move westward. They were looking for new land and new opportunities. Some were looking to push the borders of the United States from the Atlantic Ocean to the Pacific Ocean. At the same time, Hispanic settlers from Mexico were moving northward into Texas, the Southwest, and California. Where these two groups made contact, there was sometimes cooperation but often conflict. When borders moved because of war or treaty, some Hispanics found their homes in the United States. These residents of Texas, New Mexico, Arizona, and California became the first Hispanic Americans.

Texas

Texas under Spain and Mexico

Alonso Alvárez de Pineda first claimed Texas for Spain in 1519 after sailing along

WORDS TO KNOW

Anglo: a person of English heritage. It is also that person's culture.

citizenship: being a member of a community or a country. The way a person behaves in regard to his or her rights and responsibilities as a citizen are part of citizenship.

discrimination: treating people poorly because of their differences.

independence: the freedom that a country or person wins from the control of another country or person.

mission: a building used by monks and other religious people for purposes of spreading the Catholic religion in frontier settlements.

statehood: becoming or being a state in the United States.

trade: buying and selling between people or countries.

treaty: an agreement between two or more countries to end a war, keep the peace, build relations, or exchange land for other benefits.

In 1716 the Spanish returned to build several missions. These Catholic centers were to convert the Native Americans to Christianity and keep the French out of Texas. There were some small battles with the French. In the battle that started the war for Texas, seven Frenchmen attacked a Spanish town guarded by one soldier and a monk. Spain won control of Texas in 1722.

Spain found it very hard to settle Texas. The local Comanche tribes attacked settlers, destroyed forts, and raided ranches for livestock. Most of the Hispanic settlers gathered in villages along the lower Rio Grande Valley. By 1749 there were 8,993 Hispanics and 3,413 friendly Native Americans living in this area called Nuevo Santander. Laredo was on the north bank of the river and Mier, Camargo, and Reynosa were on the south bank. By 1776 Reynosa was larger than Philadelphia at that time. After these towns were established, settlers began to push another 100 miles north to the Nueces River Valley. There, they provided a buffer zone between the Comanche and French intruders and Spanish towns to the south. By 1835 their ranches had become home to 5,000 people and 3 million head of livestock (cattle and sheep).

When the United States acquired the vast Louisiana Territory in 1803, Spain began to fear that the new country would next want Texas. Anglo settlers had already made their way to Texas. Would they accept Spanish rule or lean toward the United States? The problem got worse in the 1820s when Mexico started its war for independence from Spain. Spain could not fight this war and protect its northeastern border. It did not have enough resources.

its Gulf coast. Spain did little to settle Texas until the 1680s. At that time the Spaniards feared that the French would take control of Texas if nothing were done. In May 1690 Antonio de León founded the first Spanish settlement in Texas. It was San Francisco de los Tejas, near the Neches River. A year later Spain made Texas a separate province. In 1693 the Spanish governor left because of Native American attacks.

To solve its problem, Spain decided to settle Catholic Anglos between the United States and its Spanish colonists. It thought that these people would be loyal to Spain because of their religious beliefs. Moses Austin and three hundred families settled in eastern Texas. But, in 1821 Spain lost the war with Mexico and its claim to Texas. The new leaders of Mexico would now have to worry about their northeastern border.

Mexico's first independent government was led by Augustine Iturbide. He was a former Spanish officer who wanted to be king of Mexico. But, he was defeated in 1823. A more democratic government was started in 1824. The new Mexican constitution called for a president, a congress, nineteen states, and four territories.

Anglo Settlers in Mexico's Texas

Texas was far from Mexico City and it still had few people. To solve this problem, the Mexican congress decided to bring more Anglo settlers to Texas. Between 1824 and 1830, thousands of Anglo families entered east Texas. Land was much cheaper than in the United States. So, these families bought hundreds of thousands of acres. By 1830 Texas had 18,000 Anglo settlers. It also had 2,000 African slaves.

From the beginning, Anglo Americans found it difficult to live under Mexican rule. They did not use the Spanish language. They disliked Mexican laws and its legal system. Mexico, like Spain, did not have juries for trials. Judges decided each case. The Anglo Texans did not like being far from the seat of government, Saltillo in Coahuila, which was 500 miles from some of the Anglo settlements. The Anglo Texans

Antonio López de Santa Anna. *Reproduced by permission of the Corbis Corporation (Bellevue).*

felt the distant government did not protect them from Comanche attacks. Finally, many of the Anglo Texans used slaves for labor and they feared the Mexican government would soon abolish slavery. In fact, in 1829 Vicente Guerrero, the second Mexican president, did abolish slavery.

During the 1830s conditions between Anglo Texans and the Mexican government got worse. The Mexican congress passed laws against Anglo immigration. A couple of coups d'état (violent overthrow of an existing government) put a conservative military man at the head of the government. As president, General Antonio López de Santa Anna put the army in charge of the

The Alamo, San Antonio, Texas. *Reproduced courtesy of the U.S. Department of the Interior and the National Park Service.*

states and territories. When the military blocked trade between Texas and the United States, the Anglo Texans fought back. Both sides prepared for a showdown.

Texan Independence and Statehood

Santa Anna first sent General Martín Perfecto de Cos to San Antonio to enforce Mexico's new laws. Then, Santa Anna joined the army. The Anglo Texans, led by Colonel William B. Travis, gathered in the mission of El Alamo to resist the Mexicans. Two American frontier heroes, Davy Crockett and Jim Bowie, were among the Anglo Texans. The Mexican army did not attack immediately. First, it laid siege to the mis-

sion, but this was not successful. The Anglo Texans had Kentucky rifles that could shoot farther than the Mexican muskets and cannons. So, they were able to pick off many Mexicans. Finally, Santa Anna ordered the attack. There were many more Mexican soldiers and they stormed the Alamo. They killed the Anglo defenders, even after they had surrendered.

The defeat at the Alamo became a rallying cry for the Anglo Texans. They pulled together and became stronger. Eventually, the tide turned. Santa Anna's army was defeated at San Jacinto, and the general was captured. In victory the Anglo Texans declared their independence and forced

Santa Anna to accept their demands. The Republic of Texas was born in 1836.

The new country welcomed settlers from the United States, and they began to come in large numbers. Between 1836 and 1845 almost 90,000 new Anglos arrived. Many brought their slaves. The growing number of Anglo Texans called for Texas to become one of the United States. Statehood was delayed, however, because of the issue of slavery. Several northern states did not want to add another slave state to the Union. On December 29, 1845, however, Texas was admitted to the Union as the twenty-eighth state.

Hispanic Americans in Texas

The 1836 constitution for the Republic of Texas made citizens of all people living inside its borders. Hispanic Texans and Anglo Texans were to have the same rights. The state constitution of 1845 followed the same guidelines. In a decade the Hispanics living in Texas had gone from being Mexicans to being Texans and then Americans.

Anglo Texans did not always welcome their Hispanic neighbors. They held these first Hispanic Americans responsible for the abuses of the Mexican government. Hispanics were mistreated or forced to leave their land. Hispanic merchants and teamsters (wagon drivers) were forced out of business. In many cases the Hispanic residents of Texas were not allowed to enjoy the rights promised to them by the state constitution.

Hispanics in Texas also had very little political power. Only one Hispanic Texan helped to write the state constitution. Some at the constitutional convention wanted to deny Hispanics the right to vote. They were given the right to vote, but it was hard for

THE HISPANIC MELTING POT

New Spain (Mexico and the Caribbean) was a melting pot for races and cultures from the beginning. But just as in the United States, this melting pot did not create a single race or social group. At the top of this New World society were Spaniards born in Spain. Spaniards born in the New World were next. These people were called *criollos.* In Mexico, especially, people of mixed Native American and Spanish blood became the core of the society. These people were called *mestizos.* In the Caribbean, there was more mixing of Africans with the other groups. People of mixed African blood were called *mulattos.* Finally, there were Native Americans and Africans. Early on, these people had very little power in society. Today, Hispanic Americans reflect all of these groups in their race and culture.

them. The primary elections were for white voters only and Hispanics were not considered white. For the main election, there was a poll tax. Each voter had to pay money to vote. Therefore, poor Texans, including many Hispanics, could not afford to vote. Finally, Anglo Texans often harassed Hispanic Texans who tried to vote. A few rich

Hispanics did gain some political power. Juan Seguín became the mayor of San Antonio. But later, Anglo residents forced him out of office. In 1850 the state legislature had no Hispanic members. All 64 of its members had been born outside Texas and Mexico.

The Southwest and California

The Mexican War

The Texas rebellion caused hard feelings between Mexico and the United States. Mexico suspected that the United States had supported the rebels. Also, although government officials in Mexico City never accepted Texan independence, Washington immediately welcomed it. Then in February 1845, the U.S. Congress voted to accept Texas as a state. Mexico broke off diplomatic relations in response. Finally, a dispute over the border between the two countries started a war. Texans claimed the Rio Grande as their southern border. Mexico disagreed. It said that the Nueces River, a few hundred miles to the north, was the actual border. The United States accepted the Texas claim.

James K. Polk, the new president, had promised the American people that he would add more land to the United States. He first tried to buy land from Mexico, but he was turned down. When the Texas border dispute arose, he sent General Zachary Taylor across the Nueces River to block trade on the Rio Grande. On April 25, 1846, Mexican soldiers responded by attacking the Americans at Port Isabel at the river's mouth. The U.S. Congress declared war against Mexico on May 13. Two years of war followed. Taylor won victories in north-

eastern Mexico. General Stephen Watts Kearny took control of Santa Fe (now in New Mexico) and marched on to California. General Winfield Scott landed at Veracruz and then occupied Mexico City.

The war ended in February 1848 when the two countries signed the Treaty of Guadalupe Hidalgo. The treaty officially set the border of Texas at the Rio Grande. It also allowed the United States to buy New Mexico, Arizona, California, and parts of Nevada, Utah, and Colorado for $15 million.

Hispanic Americans in the Southwest and California

The Treaty of Guadalupe Hidalgo protected the rights and property of Mexicans who now found themselves in the United States. They could return to Mexico if they chose. Or, they would become citizens of the United States with all the rights of citizenship if they stayed. The U.S. government would protect their property and respect their religion and culture. Similar rights were extended to the Mexicans who became Americans after the Gadsden Purchase in 1853. At this time the United States paid Mexico $10 million for the southern parts of New Mexico and Arizona.

The new Hispanic Americans in New Mexico, Arizona, and California did not really enjoy the rights of American citizens, however. Anglo settlers often discriminated against their Hispanic neighbors.

New Mexico and Arizona

When the Treaty of Guadalupe Hidalgo ended the Mexican War, New Mexico and Arizona found themselves part of the United States. At first things did not change much

The Battle of Buena Vista during the Mexican War, at which Zachary Taylor defeated the forces of Antonio López de Santa Anna to end the northern campaign. *Reproduced courtesy of the Library of Congress.*

for Hispanic New Mexicans. Unlike in Texas, Hispanic New Mexicans remained in the majority until the early 1900s. Hispanics were especially numerous in the northern parts of the territory near Santa Fe and Albuquerque. Many Anglo settlers did arrive, but most of them lived in southeastern New Mexico. Because they were in the majority, Hispanics in this territory continued to have a lot of political and economic power. From 1850 to 1911, Hispanics held the key political positions. They also controlled the territory's legislature until the 1890s.

Arizona was part of the territory of New Mexico until 1863. After it was separated from New Mexico, Arizona continued to be

a good place for Hispanics for several years. Hispanic Arizonans kept political power in Tucson, the capital of the territory. There was also cooperation between Hispanics and Anglos during the 1860s and 1870s. Politicians and businesspeople worked together to keep up the valuable trade with the Mexican state of Sonora.

However, in the 1880s things began to change. Railroads were built to connect Arizona with the eastern United States. A large group of Anglo settlers arrived, and they preferred to trade with the United States. The capital was moved to Prescott where Anglos were in the majority. Eventually, political and economic power in the Arizona territory shifted to the Anglo population. Hispanics did keep political power in southern Arizona, however. Until the 1950s all of the Hispanics in Arizona's territorial and state legislatures had come from the area near the Mexican border.

California

Before the Mexican War, Hispanic and Anglo Californians had usually cooperated with one another. But after the Treaty of Guadalupe Hidalgo gave Alta (Upper) California to the United States, a new group of Anglo settlers arrived. Many of these newcomers were from the U.S. South. The people from that region of the country had a history of slavery. They also had a history of prejudice against people with different racial and cultural backgrounds. This new group of Anglos began to reduce the political and economic power of the Hispanic Americans in California.

Eight Hispanic Californians worked on the state constitution with forty Anglos when California joined the Union in 1849. But, that was the last major political success for Hispanic Californians. The gold rush of 1849 attracted thousands more Anglos. This gave Anglos a greater majority in the state. In 1850 Hispanics were 15 percent of the population. Twenty years later they were only 4 percent. Political and economic power for Hispanic Californians decreased first in northern California. There, many Anglos had come in search of gold. Eventually, the Anglo majority used its power to force out the Hispanics in southern California.

The state legislature passed laws that taxed the six southern counties five times more than other counties. In 1855 it passed laws against the customs of Hispanic Californians. These laws prohibited bearbaiting, bullfights, and cockfights. Local officials used laws against vagrants and foreigners more often on Hispanics than others. The 1850 Foreign Miners Tax tried to make mining more expensive for Hispanics than for Anglos. There was clearly discrimination against the Hispanic residents of California. Many returned to Mexico because of these laws.

Hispanics Lose Land in the Southwest and California

The 1848 Treaty of Guadalupe Hidalgo was supposed to protect the property of Hispanics in New Mexico, Arizona, and California. However, it failed to do so. As more and more Anglos came to the Southwest and California, more disputes over land arose. Hispanics in these areas found out that the records of ownership they had from Mexico did not always work in the United States. The U.S. Congress passed the California Land Act of 1851 to better protect Hispanic land holdings. Instead, Hispanic ranchers lost land because of complex legal procedures. The Congress then passed the Homestead Act in 1862. This allowed people to settle and claim empty lands. In California thousands settled on land already claimed by Hispanics. The Hispanic owners often lost the legal battles over the land.

In New Mexico a special office started in 1854 settled land disputes. But, this office was very slow. It took over fifty years to settle just a few claims. During these long disputes, Anglo con men often cheated Hispanic New Mexicans out of their land. In the 1890s the United States built the Santa Fe Railroad from Kansas through northern

New Mexico. Land speculators known as the Santa Fe Ring invented false schemes to cheat hundreds of Hispanics out of their farms and ranches. In response, many Hispanics organized Las Gorras Blancas (The White Caps). These bands of hooded night riders tore down fences and tried to derail trains. Their hope was to scare Anglo landowners and railroad companies out of New Mexico. In the end they failed. In the early twentieth century, Hispanic New Mexicans lost more land. At this time New Mexico set up state parks. Hispanics had owned much of the land turned into parks.

After the Mexican War, Hispanic political, economic, and land rights decreased in the Southwest and California. These first Hispanic Americans saw their frontier towns changed by Anglo settlers. As they changed, the majority Hispanic-Mexican culture became a minority Hispanic-American culture. The opportunity offered by the New World was often replaced by discrimination. Some of the first Hispanic Americans decided to return to Mexico, the nation of their birth, to escape these problems. Some stayed in the United States. And, by the 1890s other Mexicans would come to the United States to make a new home. They would join the Hispanic communities already in the Southwest and California. They would again influence the culture of the United States.

4

Mexican Immigration to the United States

FACT FOCUS

- Immigration from Mexico to the United States has been influenced by many factors. These include family ties, trade, gold, wars, and work.
- Almost all of the first Mexican immigrants to the United States were *norteños,* northern Mexicans.
- Experienced miners from Sonora, Mexico, introduced many of the mining techniques used in California mines during the 1849 California gold rush. These experienced miners arrived before the large group of Anglo forty-niners (prospectors who went to California during the gold rush) came west.
- The majority of Mexican-origin people today live in the five southwestern states of Texas, New Mexico, Colorado, Arizona, and California.
- Mexican Americans numbered 20.6 million in the 2000 Census and made up about 58.5 percent of the Hispanic population of the United States.

Mexicans have come to the United States for three main reasons. First, the American Southwest was once a part of Mexico, so many northern Mexicans already had family and work ties there. When the region became part of the United States, these northern Mexicans continued to travel and settle there. Second, some Mexicans came to the United States to escape political problems and war in their homeland. This was especially the reason for immigration during and after the Mexican Revolution of the early 1910s (which will be discussed later). However, by far the most common reason that Mexicans have moved north of the border is work. During many periods over the last 150 years, the United States has had a need for workers. Mexicans have often seen more opportunities for work in the United States. Many have left behind their homes to make the difficult journey to a strange new home. No matter what their reason for coming, Mexican immigrants have helped shape the history and culture of the United States.

Early Mexican Immigration to the United States

Before the Mexican War, Mexicans had moved freely back and forth between Chihuahua, Sonora, and Baja California in the south and New Mexico, Arizona, and California in the north. They traveled from one region to another to do business or to visit family. They established a large economic and social network that covered these areas. This network ignored the borders between the regions. When the Treaty of Guadalupe Hidalgo gave the northern regions to the United States, the people still ignored the borders. They still traveled back and forth to do business and visit relatives. Some moved their homes from one region to another. The network of Hispanic towns on both sides of the new border made moving easier. When the people who lived south of the border moved north to find work or to follow family, they became the first Mexican immigrants to the United States. Almost all of these first immigrants were *norteños,* northern Mexicans.

There were several events that helped increase early Mexican immigration to the United States. First, as more settlers came to Texas, New Mexico, Arizona, and California, the demand for food and supplies grew. Northern Mexico was nearby, and it was a good source for these things. Mexico traded cattle hides, tallow (animal fat used for soap, margarine, and candles), and wool with Texas. In New Mexico and Arizona, the U.S. Army needed provisions for its battles with the Native Americans.

From 1848 to 1860, general trade attracted Mexicans to the Southwest to work as wagon drivers and as agents for the merchants. That trade increased during the U.S. Civil War from 1861 to 1865. The Union navy blocked Confederate ports on the Atlantic Ocean and Gulf of Mexico. So, the Confederate states shipped cotton and other products to Europe through eastern Mexican ports such as Tampico. Later, California used the western Mexican ports of Guaymas and Mazatlán to ship products to the eastern United States. In each of these cases, more Mexicans moved north to help with the trade.

The second event that helped increase early Mexican immigration was the discovery of gold in California in 1849. This attracted many Mexican miners from Sonora. These experienced miners arrived before the large group of Anglo forty-niners (prospectors who went to California during the gold rush) came west. The Mexicans introduced many of the mining techniques used in California mines. Mexican miners also took their skills to gold and silver mining centers in New Mexico and Arizona.

The third event was the coming of the railroad to the Southwest after 1880. The railroad made travel and trade easier, so the economy of the Southwest grew. New railroads in northern Mexico also helped that economy grow. By 1900 a railroad network connected Texas, New Mexico, Arizona, and California to most of northern Mexico and parts of central and southern Mexico. The people and economies of the United States and Mexico were now more strongly linked. Economic growth in the U.S. Southwest prompted Mexicans to come north. From 1880 to 1900, 127,000 Mexicans came to the

United States. The railroads made it easier for central and southern Mexicans to travel to the north. For this reason, many of the Mexicans who came to the United States during this time were not norteños.

Some of the new Mexican immigrants came north to work in gold or silver mines. Some came to work as farmers, merchants, and clerks. *Colonias* (Mexican colonies) were set up along the railway lines. In Texas these colonias produced cotton. In Colorado and California they were built in areas where sugar beets were grown. In New Mexico and Arizona, Mexicans built colonias near mines. Many other Mexicans came to work on the railroad itself. They helped build the railroads and maintain the tracks. During the last two decades of the 1800s, many more Mexicans left behind farms in central and southern Mexico to go to northern Mexico and the U.S. Southwest. There they worked as migrant workers. They moved from job to job as the season changed. Soon, these former subsistence farmers became used to working for money to meet their needs.

Central and southern Mexicans were usually very mobile. They were far from their original homes and did not feel attached to the new land. As the railroad and other industries grew farther north, these immigrants followed. By early in the twentieth century, Mexicans had traveled as far north as Kansas City and Chicago.

Adaptation to a New Home

Mexican immigrants were at home in the U.S. Southwest. Even by 1900 this region was still very Mexican in character. However, they did experience many problems.

WORDS TO KNOW

barrio: a Hispanic name for a neighborhood.

Chicano: a name for Mexican immigrants to the United States; it comes from the word *Mechicano,* a Native American name for Mexico.

immigration: coming to live in a new country from another country.

literacy: the ability to read and write.

migrant worker: a person who moves from one place to another following the jobs.

migration: moving from one place to another to live for a short or long time.

patriotism: the love that a person has for her or his country.

revolutionary: a person who wants to change the government or kind of government of a country.

Many did not speak or understand English, the dominant language. They were forced to follow confusing immigration laws. Many were poor before they came and continued to struggle in the United States. Mexicans also faced racism and discrimination. How well the Mexicans adapted to their new life depended on several factors. Mexican Americans born in the United States and longtime residents knew the language and customs of the Southwest well. They were the most likely to succeed. Those who had family in the region had an easier time than those who did not. Immigrants who came from northern Mexico had three advantages. They could easily bring their families with them. They remained close to family and contacts in Mexico. And, they were already familiar with the Anglo culture of the Southwest.

Immigrants from central and southern Mexico had the most difficult time. It was hard for them to bring their families along. They were far from families and social networks in Mexico. They were also not very familiar with the Anglo-Hispanic culture of the Southwest. For these reasons, these immigrants tended to gather around existing Mexican towns. They brought their own customs and soon influenced the existing Mexican-American culture. Their language, food, clothes, and music mixed with the local customs and changed them. The Hispanic-American culture in the U.S. Southwest continued to evolve.

The Mexican Revolution and World War I

Revolutionaries and Refugees

The next major event to cause Mexican immigration to the United States was the Mexican Revolution of the 1910s. After thirty-five years under the dictator Porfirio Díaz, many Mexicans felt that too much wealth was held by too few people. Revolutionaries such as Emiliano Zapata, Francisco "Pancho" Villa, and Francisco I. Madero began to fight for change. The Mexican people were caught in the middle. Many left for the United States. They wanted to escape political persecution, military service, and economic problems. They also wanted to escape the violence of war. The poor, middle class, and rich all had a reason to go to the United States.

During the first years of the revolution, there was little Mexican immigration to the United States. The working classes that had been moving north stayed to fight for the revolutionary cause. The towns of northern Mexico supplied laborers, miners, and middle-class professionals to fight. The rural areas sent cowboys, small landowners, *hacendados* (hacienda owners), and peons (members of the landless laboring class) to fight. Emiliano Zapata led southern Mexicans to regain land taken by rich speculators and hacendados. Eventually, all of Mexico was affected. Many joined the revolution because they thought it would bring good change. Others did not want the revolution because they thought it would hurt them. All in all, Mexicans suffered twenty years of war.

Soon the enthusiasm for a new Mexico turned to disappointment with the revolution. Mexico was being torn apart and many decided to leave. As in the past, the first to leave were norteños. For one thing, the revolution had started there. For another, it was a fast and easy trip. Most of the refugees from the north were from the lower and middle classes. However, some rich families also made the trip. They deposited their money in American banks along the border and lived comfortably. Eventually, the revolution pushed south. As it did, more people were uprooted.

World War I

As Mexico struggled with revolution, the rest of the world was also moving toward war. From 1914 to 1917, the United States managed to stay out of World War I. But, it did supply many of the European countries at war. For this reason, the U.S. economy grew at a fast pace. Soon, there were not

Francisco "Pancho" Villa and Emiliano Zapata at the head of their army during the Mexican Revolution, 1910. *Reproduced by permission of Archive Photos, Inc.*

enough workers for the factories. Then, the United States joined the war. Many American workers became soldiers and went to Europe to fight. The labor shortage increased. Because the war was a barrier to European immigration, the United States turned to Mexico for workers.

Industries in the United States needed Mexican labor. However, American laws of that time made it difficult for Mexican workers to enter the United States legally. Congress passed the Immigration Act of 1917 in February of that year. It required that all immigrants be able to read and write. Each immigrant also had to pay an $8 tax. The law had been designed to keep out eastern Europeans, but it also stopped many Mexicans. Many Mexicans had little educa-

tion. In some Mexican states, almost 85 percent were illiterate. In addition, the $8 tax was more than many could afford to pay.

In June 1917 Congress made some changes in the law to encourage Mexican immigration. The changes would allow farm workers to come even if they did not meet the literacy and tax requirements. Even so, immigration was complicated for Mexicans. For this reason, in 1917 legal immigration from Mexico decreased. Instead, American employers found illegal ways for Mexican workers to enter the country. In the end, the Immigration Act of 1917 and a later 1924 law did not help control Mexican immigration. It encouraged U.S. businesses and farms and Mexican workers to choose an illegal path.

Another 1917 law hurt Mexican immigration. In May of that year, the U.S. Congress passed the Selective Service Act. Only American citizens were included in the military draft. But, any man living in the United States had to register with the local draft board. Mexican citizens living in the United States were afraid of this requirement. Some feared they would be drafted to fight in the American army. Some were in fact drafted. Others feared the United States would discover that they were illegal immigrants and send them back to Mexico.

Even with the legal obstacles, many Mexican workers found a way to come north. The economic growth caused by World War I attracted Mexicans to new areas in the United States. Mexican workers set up new colonias in Los Angeles, Phoenix, Houston, Kansas City, and Chicago. Mexicans worked in oil fields, weapons factories, meat-packing plants, and steel mills.

These World War I era immigrants often found themselves in cities and industries where there were few Hispanics. Adjusting was more difficult for them than for previous immigrants. Another problem for new immigrants at this time was the growing anti-Mexican feeling among Americans. The Mexican Revolution had affected some Americans, who spread the idea that all Mexicans were wild and violent.

The México Lindo Generation

During the Roaring Twenties, the United States saw continued economic growth. Agriculture and mining both grew. More importantly, manufacturing was growing. More and more, Mexican labor was needed in American cities. A flood of workers began coming from the central Mexican states of Jalisco, Guanajuato, Michoacán, and San Luis Potosí.

Like many other newcomers to the United States in the early twentieth century, these Mexicans came from peasant or farming backgrounds. They had little attachment to their home countries, but they had a strong attachment to their *patria chica* (home region). They responded to the difficulties they faced in their new homes by gathering together with people from their own region. Communities with names such as El Michoacanito (Little Michoacán) and Chihuahita (Little Chihuahua) were started. The people in these communities shared similar jobs, food, music, theater, and physical features.

A majority of these groups came to the United States in search of temporary work. Most intended to return to Mexico. Many did. Even those who stayed in the United States kept alive a dream of someday returning to Mexico. They maintained a strong loyalty to their home regions. This patriotism was coupled with a strong commitment to Mexican patriotic holidays. The middle- and upper-class Mexicans who came during this time brought another form of patriotism. They introduced *indigenismo,* or pride in the Native American heritage of Mexico, to the immigrant community. Over a time, these loyalties became a part of the Mexican-American identity. It was even given the name "México Lindo" (Pretty Mexico).

Not Wanted by Society, But Wanted by Business

In the early part of the twentieth century, Mexican Americans faced segregation, abuse in the workplace, police brutality, and rejection by American society. Many Americans believed that Mexican immigrants were a threat to the racial and cultural integrity of the United States. In 1924 Congress passed the National Origins Quota Act to decrease immigration. But employers defended their source of cheap labor. Lobbyists from agriculture and mining persuaded Congress not to include the Western Hemisphere in the 1924 law. Those who wanted to stop Mexican immigration failed.

Mexican Americans also joined together to defend themselves from abuse. El Congreso Mexicanista (The Mexican Congress) was held in Texas. Its goal was to establish a plan to stop legal abuses and violence against Mexicans. The group had little political power, but it showed that Mexican Americans were willing to defend themselves. It was also a model for other organizations. The Asamblea Mexicana (The Mexican Assembly) formed in Houston in 1925 to work for better justice for Mexican Americans in U.S. courts. Local organizations, usually called La Liga Protectora Mexicana (The Mexican Protective League), were started to protect legal rights. These groups especially tried to stop the numerous executions of Mexican American prisoners.

These México Lindo organizations brought leadership and unity to immigrants who came during the early part of the century. They helped a generation of "temporary" immigrants to cope with their new home. But, when the American-born children of the México Lindo generation grew up, they distanced themselves from these groups as they adopted American ways. These second-generation Mexican Ameri-

cans identified with the United States as their permanent home.

The Great Depression and World War II

The Great Depression

The Great Depression changed the lives of every American. It also changed the evolution of Mexican communities in the United States. Mexican workers had been in high demand during the 1920s. With the unemployment of the 1930s, however, they were seen as unwanted competition for jobs. All across the United States, community leaders pushed Mexicans to leave. Many did. Those with growing children and those born in the United States stayed. They had put down roots in their American communities.

During this period a cultural shift took place in the Mexican American community. Loyalty to Mexico was replaced by a Mexican American identity. The people in these communities began to take on American values. They also turned away from aspects of Mexican culture. By the mid-1930s a new mixed culture was evolving. Anglo culture clearly influenced Mexican American cultural expression. At the same time, the decrease in Mexican immigration meant that there was less Mexican influence. Older immigrants barely kept alive pure Mexican traditions, and they continued to lose their influence over younger Mexican Americans born in the United States.

By the end of the decade, many young Mexican Americans had been exposed to the general American culture. They had attended American schools and many had graduated from high school. For young people in poor

A League of United Latin American Citizens (LULAC) convention in Houston, Texas, 1937. *Reproduced by permission of Arte Público Press.*

areas, there were the Civilian Conservation Corps and the National Youth Administration. These were both a part of Franklin Roosevelt's New Deal programs to help Americans earn a living during the difficult years of the Depression. These groups selected young people from a variety of backgrounds to work together. This kept the young people out of trouble and it gave them some income. It also helped them build a shared experience.

World War II

The United States entered World War II in 1941. When it did many Mexican Americans joined the war effort with enthusiasm. Even though they felt discrimination at home, they wanted to show their patriotism. They had become a part of the United States. Unlike their parents, they felt few ties to Mexico. Thousands joined the white

and black Americans in the armed forces. Most Mexican American women stayed behind, but many worked to support the war effort. Many women moved to California and other industrial areas. There they worked in places where Mexicans had never been allowed. Mexican Americans banded together. The League of United Latin American Citizens (LULAC) spread throughout the United States during the war period. This and other similar organizations worked on home front efforts such as bond drives.

With many workers overseas fighting, there was again a labor shortage. Again, the United States turned to Mexico for workers. To organize this effort, the government implemented the Bracero Program. In this program U.S. labor agents went to Mexico and recruited workers. The *braceros* (manual laborers) inspired many others to immi-

A woman recruited for the Bracero Program working in a field. *Reproduced courtesy of the Library of Congress.*

grate on their own. Many of these temporary laborers worked on farms and on the railroad. When the program ended, some stayed in the United States. Others were taken back to Mexico but later returned north of the border. These new immigrants still had close links to Mexico. They reminded the Mexican American community in the United States of their roots.

The Postwar Period

After the war the United States enjoyed a period of prosperity. The economy was strong and the time was good for social changes.

Individual Mexican Americans took advantage of this prosperity. Thousands of Mexican American veterans came back to their barrios (neighborhoods) in cities and small towns. Many decided to get married and have children. Many moved to the growing suburbs. There, the American culture surrounded them and their children. They attended schools that taught mainly Anglo American culture. Their newspaper, radio, and television media focused on Anglo American culture. These Mexican Americans adopted much of the mainstream culture. As they became a part of their communities, they advanced on the job and in their towns.

An Alianza Hispaño Americana parade in Tucson, Arizona. *Reproduced courtesy of the Arizona Historical Society Library.*

As a group, Mexican Americans built on their successes during the war. They tried to gain political power and to make social change. When Mexican American war veterans returned to find still more discrimination, they used their war record to call for changes. One event led to the founding of the American G.I. Forum, a leading advocate for Mexican American civil rights. A funeral home in Three Rivers, Texas, refused to bury a soldier killed in the Pacific because he was Mexican American. The American G.I. Forum fought to give this veteran and other Mexican Americans the respect they deserved. Returning Mexican American veterans also founded many American Legion posts across the country. LULAC and the Alianza Hispaño Americana (Hispanic American Alliance) fought to end segregation in Texas and Arizona. These organizations united Mexican Americans to seek changes.

Finding a New Identity

The late 1960s and early 1970s was a time of great social change in the United States. Young and old debated the Vietnam War and civil rights for minorities. Many fought in the streets over these issues. Young Mexican Americans were no different. Like their parents, they spoke out and fought for civil rights for their people. They also sought a new identity. Their struggle became known as the Chicano movement. In the 1920s the

César Chávez at a United Farm Workers Union rally, 1975. *Reproduced by permission of AP/Wide World Photos.*

word "Chicano" had been used negatively to name lower-class Mexican immigrants. In the 1940s and 1950s, it was used as a slang word to mean Mexicano (person from Mexico). In the 1960s and 1970s, Mexican Americans used it with pride. For these young Chicanos, the label captured their unique situation. It celebrated their Native American and Spanish heritage. It recognized their racial, ethnic, and cultural background. It rejected the feelings of inferiority felt by many older Mexican Americans.

The Chicano movement used some of the symbols of its immigrant ancestors. It also added new elements. Leaders of the movement used history and myth to help define the Chicano character. They identified the U.S. Southwest with Aztlán, the mythical original home of the Aztec people. Members of the Chicano movement rejected Americanization. Instead, the movement combined many cultural elements. Chicanos drew from the subculture formed by urban youths in the 1940s and 1950s. They had their own language (*caló*) and their own style of clothing (the zoot suit, a suit typically consisting of a thigh-length jacket with wide padded shoulders and narrow-leg trousers). Chicanos also drew from the *pinto* (ex-convict) subculture. They revived the art and stories of the Native Americans

A *Cinco de Mayo* parade in Detroit, Michigan, 2001. *Reproduced by permission of AP/Wide World Photos.*

before Columbus. Finally, Chicanos warned that the general American society had a plan to discriminate against them.

The Chicano movement also inspired other organizations in the 1960s and 1970s. Chicano student organizations sprang up throughout the nation. Chicanos formed the Brown Berets, a group that worked in the barrios. César Chávez led the United Farm Workers Organizing Committee to protect the rights of Mexican American migrant workers. In Texas, La Raza Unida political party formed in 1968 to try to win control of community governments where Chicanos were in the majority.

In the 1980s the term "Hispanic" replaced Chicano in common usage. Hispanic refers to any person living in the United States who is of Spanish ancestry (although many groups prefer the term "Latino" and many Mexican Americans proudly use the term "Chicano" in the early 2000s). Leaders of the Mexican American community embraced the term "Hispanic." They believed that it represented an identity that was less nationalistic and radical than the Chicano identity. At present, many Mexican American Hispanics do cultivate a historical and cultural link to Mexico. They do see themselves as racially different from white Americans. But, they also seek a His-

Two men watch for approaching Border Patrol officers from above the steel wall that marks the U.S.-Mexico border in Naco, Mexico, 2001. No one knows how many illegal immigrants are living in the United States. *Reproduced by permission of AP/Wide World Photos.*

panic version of the current American dream of success, education, and prosperity.

Mexican Americans continue to celebrate the *fiestas patrias* (holidays from the homeland) brought to this country by the México Lindo generation. However, today's celebrations focus more on culture than on historical events. For example, during the *Cinco de Mayo* (May 5, the Mexican Independence Day) celebration, very little is said about the historical origin, the 1862 Battle of Puebla. Instead, the day seems to be a celebration of the Hispanic presence in the United States.

Today, immigration from Mexico continues, with both documented and undocumented workers. During the 1990s, with a healthy economy and a large demand for labor, the United States experienced record levels of undocumented immigration. Approximately 3.9 million Mexicans entered the United States in this way between 1990 and 2000.

In September 2001 Mexican President Vicente Fox and U.S. President George W. Bush met to discuss the possibility of an immigration deal that would make it legal for some of the three or four million Mexicans living and working illegally in the United States to work here legally. Something of this nature happened in 1986 with the Immigration Reform and Control Act, which created a process by which illegal aliens who had been in the country for four or more years could become legal immigrants. Fox and Bush agreed that both countries gain economically from the exchange of labor that occurs between the borders. While Bush ruled out the idea of a blanket amnesty for illegal immigrants (that everyone would be allowed legal residence), he said he would consider a program in which some "guest workers" could obtain green cards (allowing them to work legally) and thereby gain legal residency in the United States.

When terrorists attacked the World Trade Center in New York City and the Pentagon in Washington, D.C., on September 11, 2001, U.S. defense and law enforcement officials eyed all illegal immigrants with suspicion. The position of unauthorized immigrants in this country became uncomfortable. Many Mexicans were laid off from their jobs and thousands went back to Mexico, at least temporarily. However, because the Hispanic American vote has been so strongly courted by U.S. politicians, it is likely that the Mexican president will eventually win some rights for Mexicans who are living and working in the United States illegally.

In the meantime, immigration from Mexico continues to ebb and flow with the availability of work in the United States. This new immigration will continue to affect the Mexican American and the general American cultures. Memories of the Mexican land, people, and culture will continue to mix with acceptance of the American land, people, and culture. Longtime residents of the United States will continue to find themselves grouped with newcomers. The Mexican American identity will continue to evolve.

5

Puerto Rican Immigration

FACT FOCUS

- In the mid-1800s, many Puerto Ricans went to New York to plot against Spain to win independence for their island.
- On April 28, 1898, the United States declared war on Spain. The U.S. Navy bombarded the Spanish forts in San Juan, Puerto Rico, and the U.S. Army troops invaded the island to force out the Spaniards. Spain soon surrendered and in the treaty that followed, Spain transferred Puerto Rico, Cuba, and the Philippines to the United States.
- Puerto Ricans have been U.S. citizens since 1917. This has made it easier for them to come to the United States.
- Most Puerto Ricans have come to New York City.
- In the year 2000, there were approximately 3.4 million Puerto Ricans living on the mainland United States and 3.8 million living on the island of Puerto Rico.

Puerto Ricans have been coming to the United States since the early 1800s. At first they came because there was a great deal of trade between the two lands. Merchants came to New York to sell sugar and molasses and to buy American goods. Later, many who were exiled for political reasons came to find better conditions or to work for independence from Spain. More recently, closer economic and political ties between the United States and Puerto Rico have led to increased immigration. Since 1898 the United States has had possession of Puerto Rico and since 1917 Puerto Ricans have been U.S. citizens. Two million Puerto Ricans have come to the U.S. mainland in this century. Most have come since the beginning of World War II. And, because they are citizens, Puerto Ricans have had an easier time moving to the United States than other Hispanic groups.

An aerial view of El Morro fortress and castle, built in the sixteenth century, in San Juan, Puerto Rico. *Reproduced by permission of the Corbis Corporation (Bellevue).*

Early Puerto Rican Immigration to the United States

Immigration from Spanish Puerto Rico

The American colonies had established economic ties with Puerto Rico long before their independence from Britain. This had been difficult because Spain wanted to control all of the trade from its Caribbean colony. For this reason, early commerce between the United States and Puerto Rico was secret. Ships smuggled sugar, molasses, and other plantation products to the United States. On their return trip, they took American manufactured goods. These were much cheaper than similar Spanish goods. By the early 1800s, many Puerto Rican traders had come to New York to direct business. They joined Cubans in the city to found an organization to serve merchants and their families from both islands.

In the mid-1800s many Puerto Ricans went to New York to plot against Spain to win independence for their island. Ramón Emeterio Betances was one of these exiles. Together with other Puerto Rican and Cuban exiles, he helped start the rebellion known as El Grito de Lares on September 23, 1868. *Criollos* (Spaniards born in the New World) from the middle class and free

Afro-Cubans from the coffee-growing region of Lares in western Puerto Rico supported the effort. However, it failed. Spain easily put down the poorly planned rebellion. Even so, Puerto Rican exiles in the United States continued to work for independence. Many settled in to their new homes. They brought their families and found jobs to support themselves. At first, most of the exiles were from the criollo middle class. Soon, however, skilled artisans and laborers came. All were dissatisfied with Spain's rule of their island.

The merchants and exiles in New York represented only a small group of immigrants. Large-scale immigration did not occur until the late 1800s. At this time the Puerto Rican economy and society underwent many changes. In the 1870s the rulers of Puerto Rico decided to free all slaves. Around the same time, coffee began to compete with sugar for the position of most important crop. These two events caused radical changes in the island's labor needs. On farms, day labor became most important. With no consistent work, many workers moved to cities such as San Juan. During this same period, the Puerto Rican population grew dramatically. It increased from 583,000 in 1860 to 1,000,000 in 1900. The need for workers did not grow at the same rate. So, a large number of Puerto Ricans were unemployed. Many of the unemployed left the island to find farm work on other islands in the Caribbean. Eventually, many went to the United States in search of jobs.

U.S. Control of Puerto Rico

In the late 1800s, the United States began to show more and more support for the

Puerto Rican independence movement. In April 1898, an event occurred that brought the United States into an open war with Spain. The USS *Maine,* an American battleship, blew up in Havana Harbor. In response, U.S. President William McKinley persuaded the Congress to declare war against Spain on April 28. In May the U.S. Navy bombarded the Spanish forts in San Juan, Puerto Rico. At the same time, U.S. Army troops invaded the island to force out the Spaniards. The Puerto Ricans cheered the Americans as liberators. Five months after the war had begun, Spain surrendered. In the Treaty of Paris, signed December 10, 1898, Spain transferred Puerto Rico, Cuba, and the Philippines to the United States. Puerto Rico had a new master.

Under the Foraker Act passed by Congress in 1900, the U.S. military government of Puerto Rico was replaced by a political system closely linked to the United States. The island would be called a protectorate in this scheme. The Foraker Act created a

Luis Muñoz-Rivera. *Reproduced by permission of Arte Público Press.*

house of thirty-five representatives. However, the most powerful officials had to be appointed by the U.S. president. A commissioner would represent the protectorate in the U.S. Congress. Luis Muñoz-Rivera, a hero of the independence movement, was the first to serve in this position. He soon found that it carried little political power. In 1917 the U.S. Congress passed the Jones Act. It replaced the old system with a legislature of two houses, each elected by the people. It also gave U.S. citizenship to all Puerto Ricans.

The Jones Act was a political victory for Puerto Ricans. However, employment opportunities suffered because of the closer economic relationship with the United States. New larger sugar plantations used more machinery and fewer workers. The plantations gobbled up land, forcing out subsistence farms and coffee plantations. In the towns and cities, independent shoemakers, carpenters, and other craftsmen were overwhelmed by manufactured goods made in the United States. In addition, the many jobs for women in tobacco factories and maid services declined. As the years passed, job opportunities for island workers continued to decrease. Most of the available jobs were part-time odd jobs. In Puerto Rico these jobs are called *chiripeo*. Unemployment and underemployment caused many Puerto Ricans to leave for the mainland.

U.S. Businesses Seek Puerto Rican Workers

In the early part of the twentieth century, Hawaii's sugar industry needed experienced workers. Plantation owners there recruited a few thousand Puerto Ricans. First, these workers traveled to New Orleans by ship. Then, they went by train to San Francisco. From there, they took a ship to Hawaii. Along the way some of the workers decided not to continue. Small colonias were started in both New Orleans and San Francisco. Most who stayed moved to the East Coast. According to the 1910 census, two-thirds of the Puerto Ricans living on the mainland were in New York.

U.S. immigration policies made Puerto Rican workers attractive to American businesses. Laws passed in 1921 and 1924 raised barriers to immigration from Europe and Asia. So, when labor shortages occurred, employers looked to the Americas for workers. Mexico and Puerto Rico became sources for labor. As American citizens, Puerto Ricans could enter the United

States more easily than Mexicans. By 1930 there were over 53,000 Puerto Ricans living on the mainland with most in New York. There they concentrated in Brooklyn, the Bronx, and East Harlem. As more Puerto Ricans came in later years, these barrios remained at the core of the Puerto Rican community in the United States.

Forging a New Community

More and more Puerto Ricans came to the mainland in the early part of the twentieth century. Soon after settling in northeastern cities, they began to feel the effects of discrimination. In July 1926, non-Hispanics attacked Puerto Ricans living in New York. The Harlem Riots, as the conflicts were called, forced the Puerto Ricans to come together to stand up for their rights. They pulled together by drawing upon the common culture they had brought with them from their homeland. In celebrating this culture, they forged a new community in their new land.

To assert their culture, Puerto Rican immigrants looked back. They looked back to their island roots in a time before the Spanish. The Native Americans had called their island Borinquén. Now in the United States, Puerto Ricans showed their nationalism and ethnic pride by reviving the idea of *Borinquén querido* (beloved Borinquén). Composers such as Rafael Hernández wrote many songs to capture this spirit. His most famous piece was "Lamento Boricano" (Borinquén Lament). The song offered Puerto Ricans in this country a romantic reminder of the beauty and rural simplicity of their homeland.

The Catholic religion also helped unify the Puerto Rican community. Puerto Ricans had brought their own unique form of Catholicism with them to the United States. Soon after they arrived, Catholic churches especially for Puerto Ricans began to spring up. Many churches in New York City focused on the religious rituals and cultural themes familiar to Puerto Ricans. By bringing Puerto Ricans together to worship, the churches also brought together the community.

Community organizations and clubs did much to unite Puerto Rican immigrants in cities like New York. These groups also helped raise awareness of Puerto Ricans in the non-Hispanic population. The most common associations were the *hermandades* (brotherhoods). These societies helped Puerto Ricans in need and promoted ethnic pride. Other organizations included collections of businesspeople and merchants. These groups helped Puerto Ricans feel at home by selling Caribbean food, religious relics, and Latin records. Finally, labor unions helped Puerto Rican workers defend themselves from abuse by American industries.

Already citizens with the right to vote, Puerto Rican immigrants could come together in political groups more easily than Mexican immigrants. By 1918 they were forming political groups and asserting some political power. In the 1920s La Liga Puertorriquena (The Puerto Rican League) brought together several community associations for political action. Like many of the ethnic political groups in eastern cities, this group usually supported the Democratic Party. The Democrats usually made policies that helped ethnic minorities.

The growing Puerto Rican community of the 1920s was greatly challenged in the next decade. The Great Depression of the 1930s brought economic hardship to everyone, including Puerto Ricans. The hard times also led to more discrimination against immigrants. In response to economic and social pressures, many Puerto Ricans returned to their island home. Between 1930 and 1934, about 20 percent of the Puerto Ricans living in the United States went back.

Those who stayed behind hung on to their jobs in New York and other eastern cities. They became more a part of the general American culture of the cities in which they lived. Their children were influenced by their American environment. As it emerged from the Depression, this one time immigrant community began to reflect a Puerto Rican American character.

The Great Migration

The largest migration of Puerto Ricans, almost two million, occurred after World War II. They came for two reasons. Economic policies in Puerto Rico had decreased the number of jobs in agriculture and light industry. At the same time, the postwar economic boom on the mainland offered more jobs and higher wages than were available back home. So, they came in large numbers.

The Post-World War II Era

An interesting thing about the new immigration was that it was airborne. After the war many World War II cargo planes became available for peacetime use. There were so many Puerto Ricans who wanted to come to the United States that entrepreneurs saw an opportunity to use these planes to carry passengers. New airlines were started. By 1947 over 20 airlines provided service between San Juan (Puerto Rico's capital) and Miami or between San Juan and New York. The large numbers of passengers and the competition among airlines pushed the prices down. In the 1950s Puerto Ricans could fly to New Jersey for $40.

These new arrivals crowded into large barrios (neighborhoods) in New York and other eastern cities. As the numbers grew, Puerto Ricans began to settle in Italian American and Irish American neighborhoods. Here there was often hostility between the ethnic groups. Much of this hostility was fought out in the streets by gangs of young men who went by colorful names. These gangs inspired composer/conductor Leonard Bernstein's 1961 musical *West Side Story*. In reality, however, the gang fights were not as romantic as those portrayed by the gang members from the Sharks and the Jets in the musical.

Like earlier groups of Puerto Rican immigrants, these postwar arrivals faced serious social and economic challenges. Most of the work available to them was low paying. Discrimination forced them into low-rent overcrowded housing. Police brutality and a less than sympathetic court system made conditions worse. Even Puerto Rican veterans of World War II and the Korean War found themselves in this battle for acceptance.

To better deal with these challenges, the new Puerto Rican Americans turned to new self-help and civil rights organizations. These organizations did not look back on their beloved island home. They looked around at the urban scene, poverty, and lack of opportunity that faced Puerto Ricans in the United States. The Puerto Rican Forum was founded in New York in the mid-1950s. It proposed actions to ease the effects of poverty. Aspira (Aspire) was founded in 1961 to promote educational programs. It raised money from the public and private sectors to help young people gain a better life. Aspira eventually spread to serve large Puerto Rican communities across the country.

Because of their numbers and the pressures of crowding in large eastern cities, postwar Puerto Rican immigrants did spread out across the country. They moved to textile mill towns in Rhode Island and Connecticut. They moved to steel mill towns in Pennsylvania, Ohio, and Indiana. And, they moved to Illinois to work in the factories of Chicago. Chicago soon had the second largest population of Puerto Ricans, behind New York. Today, Puerto Ricans tend to live in New York, New Jersey, Florida, and Pennsylvania. The Puerto Rican populations within the big cities has actually dropped in the 2000s, with more Puerto Ricans now living in the suburbs.

For a time, Chicago was a center of Puerto Rican population and had its own Puerto Rican organizations. One of the most important was the Caballeros de San Juan (Knights of Saint John). Its main goal was to give leadership to the community and preserve religious values. Other groups known as *hermandades* (brotherhoods) were founded in the 1950s and 1960s. These were similar to organizations that had been founded in New York in the early 1900s.

Religion also served to unite the Chicago Puerto Rican community. Puerto Ricans in this large midwestern city kept alive the folk traditions of their homeland through their worship. Religion also brought Puerto Ricans together with Mexican Americans living in Chicago. Both groups shared many churches in South Chicago and East Chicago.

Community organizations and the church were no match for the unrest of the 1960s. In Puerto Rican barrios, frustration and despair grew into violence. In response to an incident of police brutality, hundreds of young Chicago Puerto Ricans went on a rampage in 1966. They broke windows and set fire to many of the businesses in their neighborhoods. The brutality incident sparked the riot, but tension had been building due to the conditions in the city. Poverty, unemployment, and overcrowding were a part of life in Chicago.

During this decade militant organizations were formed in Puerto Rican barrios. They rejected the ideals of earlier community organizations. Like the Chicano and Black Pride movements, these Puerto Rican groups were led by young people seeking change with new tactics. Foremost among these new militants were the Young Lords. This grassroots group was similar to the Chicano Brown Berets and the Black Panthers (other militant groups seeking change in the 1960s). The Young Lords promoted Borinquén pride and offered a plan to change poverty-stricken neighborhoods. In New York and Chicago, they staged sit-ins at public places and churches to bring about local improvements.

In the early twenty-first century, Puerto Ricans are the second-largest Hispanic group, increasing from 1990 to 2000 by

Luis Muñoz-Marín. *Reproduced courtesy of the Library of Congress.*

about 25 percent to about 3.4 million on the mainland United States. That number does not include the 3.8 million living on the island of Puerto Rico. Puerto Ricans continue to move back and forth between the island and the mainland, keeping the Puerto Rican American culture alive.

The future of this movement between the island and the mainland will be determined by the resolution of the statehood issue. In 1953 the island's governor, Luis Muñoz-Marín, led the push to change Puerto Rico from a protectorate to a commonwealth, a separate political unit with ties to the United States. More recently, the island has debated becoming an independent country, becoming the fifty-first state, or keeping its current status. A vote was taken in Puerto Rico in 1999 to see what Puerto Ricans' opinions were on the issue of Puerto Rico's political status. Less than 3 percent voted for independence. Fifty percent supported maintaining Puerto Rico's position as a commonwealth (a political unit that is voluntarily united to the United States but has more self-governing than a state), while 46 percent voted for U.S. statehood. Independence is a very unlikely option for the future. It would make immigration more difficult and it would also make contact more difficult between family members on the island and those on the mainland. Whatever the future brings to Puerto Rico—independence, commonwealth, or statehood—the millions of Puerto Ricans who have come over the last two centuries have already left their mark on the United States.

6

Cuban and Other
Hispanic Immigration

FACT FOCUS

- Most Cubans have come to the United States to flee from the political situation in their country. In the 1800s, Spanish laws oppressed Cubans. Since 1959, Cubans have wanted to be free from Fidel Castro's Cuba.
- The majority of Cubans have settled in Florida.
- Recently, the United States has received more and more immigrants from Central America. Many people from the Dominican Republic, Nicaragua, El Salvador, Honduras, Guatemala, and Costa Rica now live in Miami, New York, Houston, Los Angeles, New Orleans, San Francisco, and Chicago.
- In the United States, all of these groups have set up communities and organizations to help themselves and others who have come to this country.

Large-scale Cuban immigration to the United States has only occurred within the last fifty years. In fact, more than a million Cubans have entered the country since the Cuban Revolution of 1959. Even so, Cubans have been coming to the United States since the 1800s. From the beginning, Florida has been the destination of a vast majority of immigrants from Cuba. Florida has attracted Cubans because it is only 90 miles north of the island. Florida's historical connection with Cuba has also made it attractive. Each wave of arrivals has shared similar characteristics. Unlike Mexican and Puerto Rican immigration, Cuban immigration has featured equal numbers from the middle class and the working class.

Early Cuban Immigration to the United States

Immigration from Spanish Cuba

Cuban cigar manufacturers began operating in Key West, Florida, in the 1830s, and

WORDS TO KNOW

Central America: the southern portion of North America that extends from the southern boundary of Mexico to the northwestern border of Colombia. The countries of Central America include Belize, Costa Rica, El Salvador, Guatemala, Honduras, Nicaragua, and Panama.

communism: an economic theory that does not include the concept of private property. Instead, the public (usually represented by the government) owns the goods and the means to produce them in common.

refugee: a person who runs away from a dangerous place to find a safe place.

revolutionary: a person who wants to change the government or kind of government of a country.

South America: the fourth largest continent in the world, it makes up most of Latin America. Countries in South America include Argentina, Aruba, Bolivia, Brazil, Chile, Colombia, Ecuador, Falkland Islands, French Guiana, Guyana, Netherlands Antilles, Paraguay, Peru, Suriname, Trinidad and Tobago, Uruguay, and Venezuela.

they welcomed Cuban workers to their factories. Some cigar makers, such as the Spaniard Vicente Martínez Ybor, even closed their Cuban factories and opened new ones in Florida. Key West was close to the tobacco plantations of Cuba, and it was free of the trade laws imposed by Spain. It became so popular among Cuban factory owners and workers that by the late 1860s, Key West was practically a Cuban colony.

Up to this time, the number of Cubans leaving their homeland had been small. However, in 1868 large groups of Cubans began leaving the island for Europe and the United States. This coincided with the beginning of the first struggle for independence. In October of that year, Carlos Manuel de Céspedes, a black general, led a group of Cuban rebels to declare independence for the eastern part of the island. He set up a provincial government in the city of Yara in the Orient province. A bloody war known as the Ten Years' War followed. Spain's attempts to remove the rebels failed, but the rebels were not able to win a clear victory. The war came to an end in 1878 when both groups signed the Pact of El Zajón. It promised amnesty for the rebels and freedom for slaves who fought with the rebels. It also promised home rule.

Cubans began fleeing the war as soon as it had started. At least 100,000 had left by 1869. More left over the next ten years. They fled the political, social, and economic unrest on Cuba. The wealthy went to Europe to live in relative luxury. The middle-class merchants and professionals went to cities on the East Coast of the United States, such as New York. However, the majority of those to leave were workers who crossed to nearby Florida.

The Cuban community in Key West pulled together immediately. They shared the problems of living in a new place. They also shared a feeling of support for the independence fighters back home. Cuban exiles formed revolutionary clubs to raise money for the cause and to help Céspedes. The close connection between Key West and the independence movement would continue through the years.

Once they had built a community base, Cubans got involved in local American politics. By 1875 there were more than 1,000 Cubans registered to vote in Monroe County, where Key West is located. The city's first mayor was Carlos Manuel de Céspedes II, son of the hero of the Ten Years' War.

In 1885 the cigar factories in Key West experienced labor problems. In response the manufacturer Martínez Ybor moved his operations to an area east of Tampa, Florida. The new development was named Ybor City, and soon other cigar manufacturers located their factories in the complex. Numerous cigar workers followed, and Tampa became the center of the cigar industry in Florida. As in Key West, the Cubans pulled together to support each other and the independence movement. Class differences between the wealthy factory owners and the workers were blurred by the desire of both groups for independence.

There were other Cuban communities in Florida, smaller than those in Key West and Tampa. They also supported the independence movement. Soon, a network grew between the different Cuban communities. This network of Cuban communities in Florida had much to be proud of. Cubans led the first labor movements. They owned and operated many important businesses. They had helped initiate bilingual education. Moreover, in cities like Key West and Tampa, Cubans were responsible for many improvements to city services and civic culture.

José Martí. *Reproduced courtesy of the Library of Congress.*

The only real divisions that occurred in the exile community were not between rich and poor Cubans, but between white and black Cubans. Segregation laws in Florida, also known as Jim Crow laws, separated the races and forced blacks to form their own institutions.

Cuban Independence

Cubans in the United States had gained economic and political influence during the late 1800s. With this power they were able to offer a great deal of support to the architects of Cuban independence. The poet and patriot José Martí founded his Cuban Revolutionary Party (PRC) in Tampa. He planned the revolution while living in New York. In 1895 he launched it with the backing of

Cubans in the United States. Martí would not live to see his dream realized, however. Four months after he helped start the war, he was killed. Eight months later Spain sent General Valeriano Weyler, a hardened veteran, to lead the brutal "war with war" campaign to wipe out the rebel movement.

With things going poorly for the rebels, Cuban exiles worked to shape U.S. opinion and policy toward their homeland. Cuban propagandists in the United States worked with the English-language press to stir up sympathy for the Cuban rebels. Public opinion turned against Spain. Even many U.S. politicians and industrialists came to support the Cuban independence movement. But in the end, many of these same political and business leaders wanted the United States to control an independent Cuba.

Soon after the mysterious sinking of the USS *Maine* in Havana Harbor in 1898, the United States was at war with Spain. When the Spanish-American War ended five months later, the United States had won control of Cuba, Puerto Rico, and the Philippines. The United States allowed Cuba, unlike Puerto Rico, to become independent and draft its own constitution. However, a 1901 treaty that the two countries negotiated included a provision (the Platt Amendment) that allowed the United States to intervene militarily in Cuban affairs. It also allowed the building of the U.S. naval base at Guantánamo Bay in southeast Cuba in 1903. Cuba was independent, but it had exchanged Spanish domination for U.S. domination.

With independence, many exiles in the United States went back. However, many had put down roots in the United States. Their children had been born on the mainland and

returning to Cuba did not seem the best choice. Meanwhile, the economic, social, and political changes taking place in independent Cuba were causing new immigration to the United States. These twentieth century immigrants found comfortable surroundings in the Cuban communities already established in Florida in the previous century.

From 1900 to 1950, Cubans continued to flee political turmoil on the island. In the 1920s a small number of young intellectuals moved to Miami to escape the harsh policies of the dictator Gerardo Machado. In Miami these new exiles plotted to overthrow Machado's government. When the U.S. Depression dragged the Cuban economy into collapse, a movement led by workers and students overthrew the dictator. Out of a job and unpopular in Cuba, Machado and his supporters moved to Florida. The governments that followed Machado could not bring peace and prosperity to Cuba. Therefore, Cubans continued to leave for Miami and other Florida communities.

Immigration from Fidel Castro's Cuba

The most dramatic exodus out of Cuba began after 1959. Since that year over one million Cubans have entered the United States. Again, Cubans left their homeland for political reasons. In 1959 Fidel Castro came to power. Castro and his revolutionaries made their triumphant entry into Havana after they had overthrown the brutal regime of the dictator Fulgencio Batista. At first Castro earned a wide and popular following in Cuba. But, over the years many of his compatriots have left because of his policies.

Castro's First Years

In 1935 Batista had led a coup to overthrow the government that had succeeded Machado. He was elected president five years later. He served for four years. In 1952 he seized power as a dictator. His government repressed civil rights and spread corruption. For much of this time, Batista had the support of the United States. In U.S. politics and business, the policy was to invest in Cuba and to protect those investments. Batista was someone the Americans could count on to protect their interests.

In the opinion of many Cubans, the United States controlled Cuba as an economic and political colony. And, Batista was their man in Havana. However, by the end of the 1950s Batista's abuses were so bad that even the Americans began to look forward to a new leader. When a young lawyer turned revolutionary, Fidel Castro, came to power in February 1959, he did not meet much negative response from Washington. Cubans also welcomed the new leader, hoping for better times ahead.

The American response to Castro would change as he began to work toward his goals. Soon after taking power, Castro began a program of land reform and restructuring of the economy. When landowners and the upper classes objected to these policies, Castro used force to repress their protests. More and more he chose socialist ideas and turned to the Cuban Communist Party for support. Eventually, Castro welcomed the support of the Soviet Union. The cold war between the United States and the Soviet Union had now moved to an island 90 miles off the Florida coast.

Fidel Castro. *Reproduced by permission of AP/Wide World Photos.*

In response the U.S. government announced that it would welcome all refugees from Castro's Cuba. The move was an attempt to strike back at Castro and the Soviets. By encouraging middle-class professional Cubans to leave Cuba, U.S. leaders felt they could damage the Cuban economy and hurt the image of communism worldwide. President Eisenhower also believed that Cuban exiles in the United States could plan a new revolution to overthrow Castro. Castro's new policies and the American invitation convinced many Cubans to leave the island for the United States. Landowners and the wealthy came. Middle-class professionals also came.

Thousands of children also came. Wild rumors circulated that Cuban children were being taken from their homes by Castro's men. These children were then being sent to the Soviet Union to receive a Communist education. The Catholic Church and other groups in the United States responded by bringing 14,048 middle- and upper-class children to the United States to escape the rumored program. Here, they were raised and well educated. As a consequence, there are numerous middle-aged Cuban professionals now in the United States who have not seen their parents or other family members since their childhood.

The Bay of Pigs and Cuban Missile Crisis Era

After John F. Kennedy became president in 1961, relations between the United States and Cuba did not improve. President Eisenhower had encouraged Cuban exiles to prepare an invasion of Cuba to overthrow Castro. Kennedy decided to follow the same policy. On April 17, 1961, Cuban exiles trained and armed by the United States attempted an invasion on the shores of the Bahía de Cochinos (Bay of Pigs). They received no direct support from the U.S. military and were easily defeated by the Cuban army. The United States was embarrassed and criticized by the international community. Castro became stronger. Cuban exiles grew more and more angry.

Eighteen months later Kennedy and the United States recovered from the Bay of Pigs failure with success in the Cuban Missile Crisis. The United States had discovered that the Soviets were building missile launching sites in Cuba. Soviet missiles in nearby Cuba would threaten all of the United States. Kennedy's tough response and the U.S. naval blockade of Cuba convinced the Soviets to withdraw their weapons.

After the Cuban Missile Crisis, the U.S. government resumed its policy of welcoming refugees as a way to hurt Castro's Cuba. This policy continued to attract the merchants, technicians, and professionals who were the backbone of Cuba's struggling economy. In the ten years after the Bay of Pigs invasion, almost 500,000 Cubans left the island. Because of the large numbers, U.S. officials started a special program to settle some of the refugees outside of Florida. Thousands went to California, New York, Chicago, and other areas with large Hispanic populations. To help the newcomers, the government provided emergency housing, English-language training, financial aid for the education of Cuban children, and medical care.

President Lyndon B. Johnson continued the policy of welcoming Cuban refugees. Then, in 1965 Fidel Castro encouraged many of his people to leave. He announced that Cubans who had relatives in the United States could leave. However, the exiles in Florida would have to come pick up their relatives at Camarioca Bay. Boats of all types left Miami for Cuba, returning with thousands of new exiles eager to join their families on the mainland. The boats arriving in Miami created a dramatic spectacle. However, because many of the boats were in poor condition, the trip was dangerous. Some boats capsized. To make for safer transport, an airlift was organized. The flights continued until 1973, carrying thousands more Cubans to the United States.

The Mariel Boat Lift

In the late 1970s and early 1980s, several events occurred that would eventually lead to the most dramatic influx of Cubans in this

A boat carrying Cuban refugees approaches a naval pier in Key West, Florida, during the Mariel Boat Lift, 1980. *Reproduced by permission of AP/Wide World Photos.*

century, the Mariel Boat Lift. During President Jimmy Carter's term, the United States tried to improve relations with Castro's Cuba. Some Cuban Americans followed the government's lead and tried to reconcile with Cuba. The dialogue between the two countries prompted Castro to make a generous offer. He would allow many more Cubans to leave, including prisoners of war.

Before anything could happen, however, an incident in Havana complicated the issue and sparked a flurry of activity in both countries. In April 1980 a bus carrying a load of discontented Cubans crashed through the gates of the Peruvian embassy in Havana. Peru granted the passengers political asylum. The event attracted worldwide attention. It was clear that many Cubans wanted out of Castro's Cuba. Faced with this negative press, Castro tried to turn it around.

Castro revised his policy of allowing Cubans to leave gradually. He announced that whoever wanted to leave Cuba should go to the Peruvian embassy. Immediately,

A legally immigrating Cuban woman is reunited with her granddaughter in Miami, 1980. *Reproduced by permission of AP/Wide World Photos.*

10,000 people crowded in. The Cuban government then processed and gave exit visas to these people. Several Cuban Americans gathered together a group of forty-two boats to carry these new exiles off the island. With Castro's approval, these boats began a round-the-clock evacuation of the "Havana Ten Thousand." Because the flotilla of boats picked up the new exiles at Mariel Harbor, the operation became known as the Mariel Boat Lift. The refugees became known as Marielitos. By the time the boat lift ended in late 1980, over 125,000 Marielitos had left Cuba for the United States.

President Carter, like those before him, welcomed the new influx of Cubans. For the United States, it was another sign that the

American way of life was better than Cuban socialism. Castro offered a different view. He claimed that so many Cubans were leaving his country because they had been tempted by the glitter of America's consumerism. The Cuban Americans that he had allowed to travel on the island had convinced his people that life in a capitalist society was easier than life in Cuba. Cubans had not seen the bad parts of American society. Even so, Cuban supporters of Castro had to admit that socialism had not lived up to the promises made twenty years before.

The Marielitos differed from the earlier waves of Cuban exiles. The new refugees showed more variety in class and race than Cubans already in the United States. They were more a reflection of the general Cuban population. Many blacks and mulattoes (those with black and white ancestry) came. Many from the lower class came. Also, Castro cast out many criminals in order to solve some of his problems and cause some for the Americans. These criminals drew a lot of attention, but the majority of the Marielitos were average, hardworking Cubans.

After their arrival this large group of refugees faced more difficulties. Thousands of new arrivals crowded into processing centers. They lived in tent cities and even a football stadium in Miami. They had to stay in the camps for a long period of time, and many became frustrated. Some refugees stayed in these "temporary camps" for months, some for years. Castro accused the United States of discriminating against these Cubans because they were not rich, educated, and white like the Cubans in previous groups.

Castro's charges were valid, but the whole truth was more complex. To leave the camps, refugees needed a sponsor in the United States. And, unlike previous exiles, most of the Marielitos did not have families in this country. At first many unrelated Cuban Americans and other Americans volunteered to act as sponsors. However, as the boat lift faded from the news, sponsors became harder to find. The knowledge that criminals were in this group also made it hard for the rest of the Marielitos. Those who came to work and raise their families were treated as guilty by association with the hard-core criminals.

The Cuban community has now put down such deep roots in the United States that the term "exile" no longer applies to many. The children of Cubans who came to the United States in the early part of the twentieth century have mixed together with refugees from Castro's Cuba. They have formed the Cuban American ethnic group that is such an important part of the culture of Miami and other American cities. They have also joined the Mexican Americans, Puerto Rican Americans, and others in the Hispanic American community.

The Cuban community shares many similarities with the other two major Hispanic groups. Like Mexicans and Puerto Ricans, the early Cubans who came wanted to escape economic, social, and political problems at home. They wanted to make a new life for themselves. To survive in their new home, they built community organizations. They looked to their homeland and drew from their culture to find an identity and build strong ethnic solidarity.

The Cuban community is also different from other Hispanic communities. Overall, Cuban exiles in the United States came from more privileged backgrounds. They brought more money, power, and education to the United States when they came. The upper- and middle-class Cuban immigrants have also been better accepted by the white majority culture in the United States. For these reasons, even though Cubans have been in the United States for a shorter time, they have succeeded at a faster pace than Mexicans and Puerto Ricans.

Cubans have also benefitted from U.S. policies against Castro's Cuba. U.S. administrations from Eisenhower to Reagan have provided a great deal of aid to Cubans to help them settle and adapt. Cubans on the whole have more money, education, and political power than other Hispanic groups. In southern Florida the Cuban community developed a strong lobbying power (campaigning to influence politicians) in order to keep U.S. pressure on Fidel Castro. Over the years, the population has grown and the Cuban American vote in Florida has become very important in presidential elections. Cuban Americans numbered 1.2 million in the 2000 census; they are the third largest Hispanic group in the United States, making up 3.5 percent of the Hispanic population. They are a very influential force in U.S. culture.

Other Hispanic Groups

For many years three groups have been considered the main U.S. Hispanic groups: Mexican Americans, Puerto Ricans, and Cuban Americans. In 2000 it was clear that other Hispanic groups were catching up to the "big three" at a rapid pace. The Dominicans were the fourth largest group and the Salvadorans were next. There were 1.7 million Central Americans in the United States, including Guatemalans, Hondurans, Nicaraguans, Panamanians, and Costa Ricans. There were about 1.4 million South Americans, including Colombians, Ecuadorians, Peruvians, Argentinians, Venezuelans, Chilians, Bolivians, Uruguayans, and Paraguayans.

Dominican Immigration

Immigrants from the Dominican Republic (the country on the eastern half of the Caribbean island of Hispaniola) began arriving in the United States at the turn of the twentieth century. At that time the United States began to play a major role in the country's economy. Sugar became an important crop that attracted investors to the island. North Americans, Europeans, Cubans, and other investors brought their money to buy land. They set up sugar, coffee, and cacao (seed used in making cocoa, chocolate, and cocoa butter) plantations, as well as cattle ranches. Dominican farmers were forced off their land and into the sugar labor force.

Because of American investment, the U.S. government took an interest in the Dominican economy and politics. The early part of the century was marked by economic distress and political turmoil. In response the United States sent U.S. Marines to occupy the Dominican Republic for eight years, from 1916 to 1924. The U.S. government controlled the Dominican economy until 1941. Under U.S. control, schools and hospitals were built. New roads and bridges connected remote areas. Government was

centralized and local political leaders lost power. The U.S. occupation changed the average Dominican's way of life. Many Dominicans gave up subsistence farming and came to rely on wage labor. When jobs became scarce in the Dominican Republic, many people moved to the United States.

By the end of the U.S. occupation in 1924, sugar companies controlled almost a quarter of all farmland. Eighty percent of these companies were American. In the following years, the Dominican National Guard was created. It would have a lasting effect on the nation. The guard was trained by the United States, and it produced a government favorable to the United States. Molina Trujillo, who would reign as dictator from 1930 to 1960, worked his way up through the guard to become the president.

To achieve his nationalistic goals, Trujillo wanted a large and stable work force. He stopped almost all migration to the United States. He also promoted population growth. From 1930 to 1961, the population of the Dominican Republic doubled from 1.5 million to 3 million people. When Trujillo was assassinated in 1961, he left behind a large population that depended on wage labor. In the early 1960s, problems in agriculture pushed many Dominicans to leave the country and move to the city. In 1970 over one-half of the population of the capital city, Santo Domingo, had migrated from the countryside. This migration soon became international. Household heads left the republic for Puerto Rico and the United States.

In the final decade of Trujillo's dictatorship, 9,800 Dominicans immigrated to the United States. In the next two years, from 1960 to 1962, almost 60,000 moved to the

United States. Between 1966 and 1980, the number of legal immigrants admitted to the United States averaged about 14,000 per year. Immigration to the United States, both legal and undocumented, became a partial solution to the growing unemployment problem in the Dominican Republic.

Today, Dominicans are the fourth-largest Hispanic group in the United States. In New York City and the northeastern United States, they are the second-largest group. The U.S. Census in 2000 estimated that Dominicans number 765,000. Like Puerto Ricans, they are a mobile group. The closeness of the Dominican Republic to Puerto Rico and the mainland makes travel back and forth to the island relatively easy. Most immigrants travel directly to the United States. Others go first to Puerto Rico. Recently, however, undocumented Dominicans have begun to enter the United States through Mexico. They cross into the United States by the long U.S.-Mexican border.

Central American Immigration

Central American countries have contributed to the U.S. Hispanic population, some with small groups, some with large. Each group of Central American immigrants has had its own reasons for coming. Costa Rican immigration to the United States has been the least noticeable (there were an estimated 69,000 Costa Rican Americans in 2000). This may reflect the prosperity and political stability of that country. The population of immigrants from Honduras was relatively small in the early 1990s, but grew to 218,000 in 2000 after the devastating Hurri-

Molina Trujillo. *Reproduced by permission of Archive Photos, Inc.*

cane Mitch caused massive destruction throughout Honduras and Nicaragua in 1998. The United States allowed thousands of Hondurans and Nicaraguans to stay and work in the country in order to help ease the situation in Central America. Hondurans are scattered throughout Miami, Houston, New York, and Los Angeles, but there is a long-standing Honduran community in New Orleans. In the early years of banana trade between the United States and northern Honduras, many companies set up their offices in New Orleans. The trade attracted Hondurans to that city.

For a long time, there have been Guatemalans from the middle and professional classes in the United States. The number

Triumphant Sandinistas are greeted on the streets of Managua, the capital of Nicaragua, 1979. *Reproduced by permission of the Gamma Liaison Network.*

had been small, however. More recently, a large group of political refugees fled the civil war tearing apart that country and in 2000 there were approximately 372,000 Guatemalans living in the United States. Many of these refugees are Mayan-speaking Native Americans who speak little or no Spanish. Guatemalan communities are concentrated in Los Angeles, Miami, Houston, and New York. Small rural groups are found, for example, in southern Florida.

The Nicaraguan population in the United States numbered about 178,000 in 2000. The waves of Nicaraguan immigration have been caused mainly by the political uncertainty in that country. Before the Sandinista

socialist revolution of 1979, there were already groups of Nicaraguans living in Miami and Los Angeles. However, the large exodus from Nicaragua to the United States began after the revolution. In the 1980s tens of thousands of Nicaraguans came to settle in Los Angeles, San Francisco, and Miami. Since the 1990s the political situation in Nicaragua has become more stable. The country has an extensive rebuilding program to clean up after Hurricane Mitch, and the new Nicaraguan government has called for exiles to return to their homeland.

In Miami, Nicaraguans live in several well-defined neighborhoods. There, they have put in place the social, cultural, and economic traditions from their homeland. Nicaraguan restaurants, stores, travel agencies, beauty shops, and medical clinics have created a "little Nicaragua" atmosphere. Several newspapers are published within this community. Local radio stations air special programs produced by and for local Nicaraguans. Nicaraguan holidays are celebrated in Miami with the same strong feeling as they would be in Nicaragua. Nearly any product or food found in their homeland can now be found in these immigrant communities.

Like with the Cubans fleeing Castro, the first Nicaraguans to flee the Sandinista Revolution were professionals and government officials. Later exiles included citizens from all classes. English-speaking Nicaraguans from the Caribbean coast as well as Miskito Indians came. Small communities of seafaring coastal Nicaraguans now live in Florida and along the coast of Texas. In Miami, these *costeños* (coastal people) live and work in different neighborhoods from the *ladinos* (Spanish speakers), Nicaraguans from the highlands.

The largest group of immigrants from Central America are those from El Salvador, who numbered 655,000 in 2000. Salvadorans are concentrated in Los Angeles, Houston, Chicago, and Miami. The long civil war in El Salvador caused many professional and middle-class Salvadorans to move to the United States. However, there has not been a mass exodus such as in Cuba and Nicaragua. Most of the Salvadorans living in the United States come from the poorest social groups. They have come from rural areas of El Salvador and from squatter communities in San Salvador and other cities.

7

The Hispanic People

FACT FOCUS

- In the U.S. Census in 2000, Hispanic Americans made up 12.6 percent of the U.S. population, becoming either the largest ethnic minority group in the United States or tying with African Americans for that position.
- Hispanic Americans are a very diverse people. Their different histories have influenced who they are as well as how and where they live.
- The Hispanic population is growing at a faster rate than the non-Hispanic population.
- Cuban Americans tend to be more conservative than other Hispanic groups. They have more education, better jobs, and make more money than other Hispanic groups.
- Mexican Americans tend to be younger and have less education than other Hispanic groups.
- Hispanics as a group are younger and have more children than non-Hispanics in the United States. They have less education and a lower income than other Americans.

In the U.S. Census in 2000, Hispanics numbered approximately 35.3 million people, composing 12.6 percent of the total U.S. population of 281 million. With these figures, Hispanic Americans had reached a long-anticipated milestone, becoming either the largest identifiable ethnic minority group in the United States or tying with African Americans for that position. The numbers from the 2000 Census mean that, with more Hispanic voters, there will almost certainly be more Hispanics elected to the government. They should also ensure a government more attentive to Hispanic concerns. Hispanic Americans in 2000 are still not attaining equal levels of education and income with the rest of the U.S. population, but the 2000 population figures provide hope for a new era of political and social power for U.S. Hispanics.

WORDS TO KNOW

birthrate: the average number of children that each woman has in a certain area.

census: the official counting and description of the population of a country.

concentration: a place where many people or things are brought together.

demographics: statistics about various traits of a nation or other group of people, such as birthrate, education, and income.

diversity: the differences that give variety to people or places.

employment: working at a job.

immigration: coming to live in a new country from another country.

income: the money that people make at their jobs.

median age: the age that falls exactly in the middle of all the ages of a group of people combined.

population: the whole group of people who live in a certain country or other place.

The rapid growth of the Hispanic population of the United States reflects growth in the many different Hispanic groups from different national backgrounds. Hispanic Americans share many cultural elements, but they are a diverse people from many different countries of origin. The major Hispanic groups in the United States are Mexican Americans, Puerto Ricans, and Cuban Americans; these have been the "big three" U.S. Hispanic groups for many years.

Dominican Americans and Salvadoran Americans have also become large groups, and there are many other growing groups from the Caribbean, Central and South America, and other countries with a Spanish heritage. Among all of these groups, there are major historical and demographic (statistics about various traits, such as birthrate, education, and income) differences. Each group has also kept alive its own unique cultural elements.

Hispanic Diversity

History

The history of Mexican, Puerto Rican, and Cuban immigrants to the United States is very different. The Spaniards conquered the Native American people of Mexico, but they did not completely destroy them. Instead, the Spaniards coupled with the Native Americans to produce a new mixed race of Mexicans. This mixed race is known as *mestizo*. Thus, Mexicans have a strong Native American as well as Spanish heritage.

The people of Cuba and Puerto Rico were also conquered by the Spaniards. The Spaniards also coupled with the native Arawak and Carib people to produce mixed-race children. However, many of the native people of the islands were forced into slavery in the mines and fields of Puerto Rico and the sugarcane fields of Cuba. A very large percentage died of overwork or from diseases. So, the Spaniards began importing slaves from Africa to the Caribbean Islands. Eventually, African slaves outnumbered the Native Americans. Both of these groups began to intermarry. Today, Cubans and Puerto Ricans have not

An early rally for Puerto Rican independence in East Lower Harlem, New York. *Reproduced by permission of the Jesús Colón Papers, Centro de Estudios Puertorriqueños. Hunter College, City University of New York (CUNY); Benigno Giboyeaux for the Estate of Jesús Colón and the Communist Party of the United States of America.*

only a Spanish and Native American heritage but a strong African ancestry as well.

Immigration

Immigration patterns to the United States have been different for each of the major Hispanic groups as well. The number of people who migrated to the United States from Mexico was relatively small before 1900. After 1900 Mexican immigration began to increase. The factors that caused this immigration were the Mexican Revolution, poor economic conditions, and rapid population growth in Mexico. Today, the primary cause of Mexican immigration is the demand in the United States for cheap labor and the desire to earn better wages among the Mexican workers. The constant arrival of Mexicans means that within the Mexican American community there is always a large number of newcomers.

Prior to 1959 the number of Cubans who migrated to the United States was very small. In 1959 Cuban revolutionary Fidel Castro (1926–) overthrew the Fulgencio Batista (1902–1975) dictatorship. He soon declared Cuba a socialist state. He outlawed private property and the accumulation of large amounts of wealth. Many Cubans fled Cuba and immigrated to Florida. This first large wave of Cuban immigrants consisted of many educated professionals and skilled technicians. A second large wave of Cubans migrated to the United States in 1980. Unlike the previous group, most of these immigrants were from the poorer classes. They were not as welcome or as well treated as previous Cuban immigrants.

As a result of these two waves of immigrants, the number of Cubans in the United States increased rapidly. In 1959 there were only 30,000 Cubans in the United States. In 2000 there were 1.2 million. Cubans have become a major economic, political, and cultural force in Florida. They are especially influential in Miami. That city has the largest concentration of Cubans in the United States.

The pattern of migration from Puerto Rico to the United States is different from the patterns for Mexico and Cuba. Puerto Rico became a possession of the United States in 1899. Puerto Ricans were granted U.S. citizenship in 1917. Thus, Puerto Ricans who migrate to the United States are not considered immigrants in the same sense as Mexicans and Cubans. Before 1940 Puerto Ricans did not come to the United States in large numbers. After World War II the economy of Puerto Rico began to slump. Migration to the United States increased at that time and has been fairly constant since. In 2000 there were 3.4 million Puerto Ricans living in the United States and 3.8 million living on the island of Puerto Rico.

Geographical Concentration

The ten states with the largest number of Hispanics are California, Texas, New York, Florida, Illinois, Arizona, New Jersey, New Mexico, Colorado, and Washington, in that order. In 2000, fully half of the nation's Hispanic population lived in two states: California, home to 11 million Hispanic people, and Texas, home to 6.7 million. Three-quarters of the U.S. Hispanic population lived in the states of California, Texas, New York, Florida, Illinois, Arizona, and New Jersey combined. New Mexico has the highest percentage Hispanic population at 42.1 percent of its population; California is 32.4 percent Hispanic, and Texas is 32 percent Hispanic. The states with the highest percentage of increase in Hispanic population were mainly in the Southeast, where there had not been a significant Hispanic population in the past. They were, in order: North Carolina, Arkansas, Georgia, Tennessee, Nevada, South Carolina, Alabama, Kentucky, Minnesota, and Nebraska.

Mexican Americans, Puerto Ricans, and Cubans tend to reside in different parts of the United States. The majority of Mexican-origin people live in the five southwestern states of Texas, New Mexico, Colorado, Arizona, and California. Puerto Ricans tend to live in New York, New Jersey, and Pennsylvania, while the majority of Cubans reside in Florida. South and Central Americans tended to live in New York City and Los

Angeles. Most people from the Caribbean live in either New York or Miami.

Hispanics have a higher tendency than the general U.S. population to live in cities. During the decade 1990–2000 the largest cities in the United States went through some dramatic population changes. In 1990, 52 percent of the total population of the one hundred largest U.S. cities was non-Hispanic white. In 2000, whites were no longer the majority in the cities, at 44 percent of the total population.

Most American cities saw a great influx of Hispanics during the 1990–2000 decade, but some more than others. In Los Angeles, the Hispanic population grew from 40 percent to 47 percent (to a total of 1,719,073), while the non-Hispanic white population dropped to 30 percent. In Anaheim, California, the Hispanic population grew from 30 percent to 47 percent of the city's population. In New York, while whites decreased in number by about 11 percent, the Hispanic population gained by 21 percent. Puerto Ricans comprised 37 percent of the city's Hispanic population, the largest share of any Hispanic group. The Bronx and Brooklyn both contained more people of Puerto Rican origin than any other county in the nation. New York also has a significant Dominican and Central and South American Hispanic population.

Large numbers of Hispanic Americans have been moving within the country into areas of the Southeast and the Midwest where there has not been a large Hispanic presence in the past. Charlotte, North Carolina, for example, saw an increase in Hispanic population of 614 percent during 1990–2000. Other cities with large influxes included Indianapolis, Indiana; Memphis,

A Poster for National Migration Week issued by the U.S. Catholic Conference. *Reproduced by permission of Impact Visuals/Mev Puleo.*

Tennessee; Minneapolis, Minnesota; and Little Rock, Arkansas.

Increased numbers in American cities will mean more political power for Hispanics. However, some old battles for equality in those cities are a long way from being won. The Civil Rights Project, a Harvard University research program, analyzed city neighborhoods in light of the 2000 Census and found that half of the U.S. Hispanic population lives in city ghettos, segregated (set apart) from the rest of the community. If Hispanic communities continue to grow but remain segregated, the researchers predicted that living conditions could actually get worse for Hispanics.

Hispanic Traits and Comparisons in the United States

Growth and Birthrate

The Hispanic population has been growing at a faster rate than the non-Hispanic population for decades. Between 1980 and 1990, it increased by 53 percent, in comparison with only 6.8 percent for non-Hispanics. Between 1990 and 2000 it increased by nearly 58 percent. This dramatic rate of growth is attributed to increased birthrates (the average number of children that each woman has) and a rise in the level of immigration since 1990. In 1998, there were 84 births per 1,000 Hispanic women from the ages of 15 to 44 years old, making Hispanic women the group with the highest birthrate among all racial and national origin groups. The birthrate for non-Hispanic white women was 57.2 births per 1,000 women. Mexican Americans have the highest birthrate of the three largest U.S. Hispanic groups, followed by Puerto Ricans and then Cubans.

The immigration rate for Hispanics was also higher than that of other groups. Between 1990 and 1996 there was an estimated average of 15.1 immigrants for every 1,000 Hispanic persons per year, compared to 3.1 immigrants for all persons.

Age

Hispanics are younger than the non-Hispanic population. While Hispanics under the age of 18 make up more than 35 percent of the Hispanic population, in the general U.S. population the under-18 population makes up only 25.7 percent. Hispanics under the age of 18, in fact, make up 17.1 percent of the total population of individuals under 18 years old in the nation, making Hispanic teenagers the nation's largest group of minority teens by far.

The median age (in the middle of all ages combined) for the United States is 35.3, but the median age within the Hispanic community is 25.8. Cubans are the oldest among the Hispanic population, and Mexican Americans are the youngest. The median age for Cubans is 40.7 years, in comparison with 24.2 years for Mexicans. Puerto Ricans are also a young population, with a median age of 27.3; Central Americans are slightly older at 29.2, and South Americans at 33.1 years for the median age.

Education

The level of education reached by Hispanics as compared to non-Hispanics is very different. In the 2000 Census, 57 percent of Hispanic Americans aged 25 and older had graduated from high school, while 88.4 percent of non-Hispanic whites had graduated from high school. While 10.6 percent of Hispanics hold bachelor's degrees from college, 28.1 percent of non-Hispanic whites have them. The number of Hispanics who had less than a ninth grade education was 27.3 percent, while for non-Hispanic whites that figure was only 4.2 percent.

The high educational level of Cubans is seen in the number of Cuban high school and college graduates: 73 percent have a high school education and approximately 23 percent have a college education. Among Puerto Ricans, 64.3 percent have a high school education. Among Mexican Americans, 51 percent have completed high school and only 6.9 percent are college

Population With at Least a High School Education by Detailed Hispanic Origin: 2000

(In percent)[1]

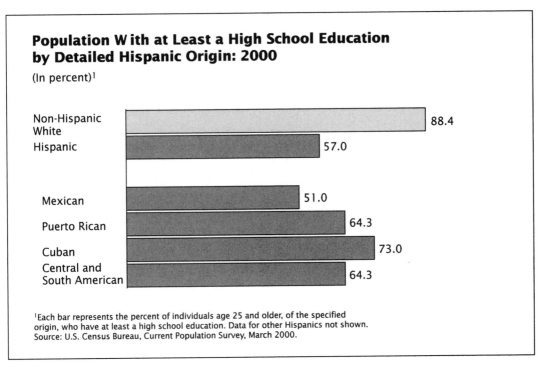

Non-Hispanic White	88.4
Hispanic	57.0
Mexican	51.0
Puerto Rican	64.3
Cuban	73.0
Central and South American	64.3

[1]Each bar represents the percent of individuals age 25 and older, of the specified origin, who have at least a high school education. Data for other Hispanics not shown.
Source: U.S. Census Bureau, Current Population Survey, March 2000.

Population by Hispanic Origin and Educational Attainment: 2000

(As a percent of each population 25 years and older)

■ Hispanic
□ Non-Hispanic White

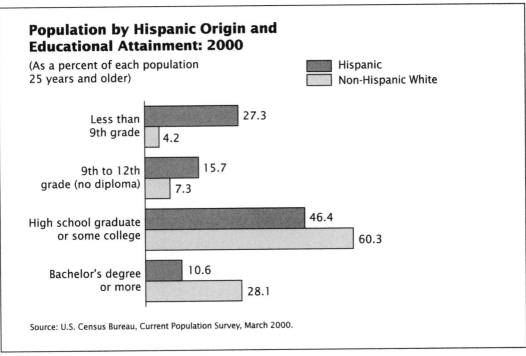

	Hispanic	Non-Hispanic White
Less than 9th grade	27.3	4.2
9th to 12th grade (no diploma)	15.7	7.3
High school graduate or some college	46.4	60.3
Bachelor's degree or more	10.6	28.1

Source: U.S. Census Bureau, Current Population Survey, March 2000.

graduates. One explanation for the high level of education among Cuban Americans is that the majority of Cuban immigrants in the early 1960s were middle class. However, later generations of Cubans are continuing to achieve high levels of education. Among Cuban Americans ages 25 to 34, almost 78 percent are high school graduates and 20.4 percent have a college education.

Work

The occupational status of Hispanics is not as high as that of non-Hispanics, although it is improving. In 2000, over twice as many non-Hispanic males (33.2 percent) held managerial and professional jobs as did Hispanic males (14 percent, up from 11.4 percent in 1990). At the lower end of the occupational hierarchy, there were more Hispanics (22 percent) than non-Hispanics (11.6 percent) working as operators, fabricators, and laborers. The proportion of Hispanics employed in service occupations was 19 percent.

The same was true for the difference between the occupations of Hispanic and non-Hispanic women. While 33 percent of non-Hispanic females held professional and managerial occupations, only about 17.2 percent of Hispanic females in 2000 held managerial and professional occupations. At the lower end, more Hispanic females worked in factories and other industrial places as operators, fabricators, and laborers than non-Hispanic females.

Unemployment rates were greater for Hispanics than for the white population. In March 2000, 6.8 percent of Hispanics were unemployed compared to 3.4 percent of non-Hispanic whites. Within the Hispanic population, Puerto Ricans had the highest unemployment rate at 8.1 percent, followed by Mexicans at 7.0 percent, Cubans at 5.8 percent, and Central and South Americans at 5.1 percent.

Because many Hispanics have not had the opportunity to get as much education as non-Hispanics, it is not surprising that they earn less income than non-Hispanics. While 23.3 percent of Hispanics earned $35,000 or more, 49.3 percent of non-Hispanic whites earned $35,000 or more in 2000. In 1998, Hispanic females had a median income of $10,862, while that figure for non-Hispanic white women was $14,617.

In terms of jobs, Mexican Americans, Puerto Ricans, and Cuban Americans all have a large number of men working in skilled and semiskilled occupations. About 50 percent of all Mexican American men and 43 percent of Cuban and Puerto Rican men hold skilled or semiskilled jobs. In managerial, professional, sales, and administration, however, there is a large gap between Cuban Americans and the other two groups. There are far more Cuban Americans working as managers, professionals, salespeople, and administrators than there are Puerto Rican or Mexican Americans. Among women, more Cuban Americans work and they have higher job status.

Poverty

More Hispanic than non-Hispanic families live in poverty (lacking enough money to meet the needs of daily life). According to the 2000 U.S. Census income figures, 22.8 percent of all Hispanic families were classified as living in poverty, compared with 7.7 percent of non-Hispanic families. Among

Full-Time, Year-Round Workers With Annual Earnings $35,000 or More by Detailed Hispanic Origin: 1999

(In percent)[1]

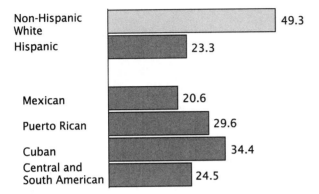

Non-Hispanic White — 49.3
Hispanic — 23.3
Mexican — 20.6
Puerto Rican — 29.6
Cuban — 34.4
Central and South American — 24.5

[1]Each bar represents the percent of individuals, of the specified origin, who earned more than $35,000 for full-time, year-round work. Data for other Hispanics not shown.
Source: U.S. Census Bureau, Current Population Survey, March 2000.

People Living Below the Poverty Level by Detailed Hispanic Origin: 1999

(In percent)[1]

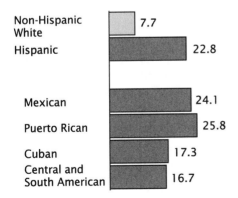

Non-Hispanic White — 7.7
Hispanic — 22.8
Mexican — 24.1
Puerto Rican — 25.8
Cuban — 17.3
Central and South American — 16.7

[1]Each bar represents the percent of individuals, of the specified origin, who were living in poverty. Data for other Hispanics not shown.
Source: U.S. Census Bureau, Current Population Survey, March 2000.

105

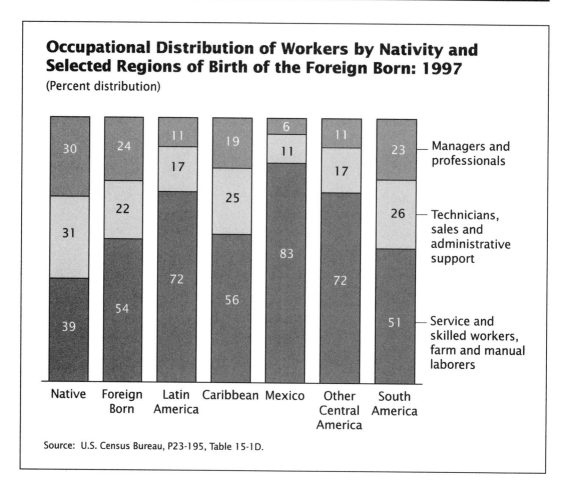

Occupational Distribution of Workers by Nativity and Selected Regions of Birth of the Foreign Born: 1997

(Percent distribution)

Source: U.S. Census Bureau, P23-195, Table 15-1D.

Hispanic children under the age of 18, 30.3 percent were living in poverty, compared to 9.4 percent of non-Hispanic white children. Puerto Ricans and Mexicans were more likely to be living in poverty than Cubans and Central and South Americans.

Central and South Americans and Other Hispanics

Central Americans make up 4.8 percent and South Americans 3.8 percent of the total Hispanic population in the United States. These figures, however, are misleading because in the 2000 Census, another 17.3 percent of Hispanics did not answer the question about the country they or their ancestors came from. This group falls into the category of "other Hispanics."

Generally, Central and South Americans and other Hispanics living in the United States tend to be more like Cuban Americans than like Puerto Rican or Mexican Americans. They are often more educated and have more professional and better-paying jobs. More have come from middle-class backgrounds in their country of origin.

Counting Hispanic Americans

The various Hispanic American communities have many similarities—Spanish heritage, culture, and language—and a shared immigration experience. For this reason the U.S. Census Bureau has grouped together Mexican Americans, Puerto Rican Americans, Cuban Americans, and the others described above for a long time. Hispanics have been identified and counted as a group since 1850. Over the years, however, the criteria for identifying Hispanics have changed. At one time or another, categories such as foreign birth or parentage, Spanish mother tongue, Spanish speaking, Spanish surname, and Spanish heritage have been used.

Today, the Census Bureau uses a self-identification method for ethnic background. Persons are asked if they are of Spanish or Hispanic origin. If they answer yes, they are then asked to identify themselves as Mexican, Mexican American, Chicano, Puerto Rican, Cuban, or other Spanish/Hispanic origin.

The U.S. government wants to identify Hispanics and other groups so that it can use this information to make policies that serve the needs of all Americans. However, in counting Hispanics, it is very likely that the information gathered is not accurate. There is a large number of undocumented Hispanic immigrants. These "illegal aliens," as they are often called, are difficult for the Census Bureau to count. Therefore, no one really knows how many are now living in the United States. Estimates of their number have ranged from half a million to 12 million. The census estimates of approximately 8 million illegal immigrants living in the United States in 2000 were unexpectedly high. In 1990 the figure was 3.5 million. Nearly half of the immigrants who entered the United States since 1990, approximately 3.9 million, came here from Mexico.

Despite its limitations, the U.S. Census Bureau is generally regarded as the best source for certain kinds of information about Hispanic Americans and their relationship to non-Hispanic Americans.

The Hispanic Population and Its Growth

In 2000 Hispanics numbered approximately 35.3 million people, composing 12.6 percent of the total U.S. population of 281 million. The Hispanic population is growing at a faster rate than the non-Hispanic population. Between 1980 and 1990, the Hispanic population increased by 53 percent. The non-Hispanic population grew by only 6.7 percent. Between 1990 and 2000 the Hispanic population grew by 58 percent. If the number of undocumented Hispanic immigrants could be accurately counted, the census numbers for the Hispanic population and its growth rate would be greater.

In 1996, the U.S. Census Bureau predicted that Latinos and Asians would account for more than half the growth in the population of the United States every year for at least fifty years. The result is, and will continue to be, a great and ongoing change in the ethnicity of the United States. While the rate of general population growth will shrink over the next fifty years, the rate of growth of the Hispanic population will actually increase. By the year 2050, the Hispanic population is predicted to make up 24.5 percent of the total population, making the Hispanic population almost half the size of

Telemarketers performing market research on Hispanic customers. *Reproduced by permission of AP/Wide World Photos.*

the non-Hispanic white population. Even without immigration, the Hispanic population would be the fastest growing because it is younger and has a higher fertility rate than other U.S. groups.

The large numbers and rapid growth of the Hispanic population are already making major differences in the way the United States views its Hispanic citizens. Businesses are now looking for new ways to get His-panic American consumers to buy their products. Politicians are looking for the Hispanic vote. Sports teams want Hispanic fans. The Spanish language is accepted as an important second language in a wide variety of places. The imbalance in Hispanic Americans' income and education level, their underrepresentation in the media, and the discrimination that has plagued them throughout the national history will certainly be strongly affected by these new changes.

8

The Pillars of Hispanic American Society

Family and Religion

WORDS TO KNOW

altar: a special table for religious things that serves as a place for prayer.

Catholicism: the beliefs and practices of the Christian church led by the Pope in Rome, Italy.

family: the nuclear family is made up of the children and parents living together in the same house. An extended family includes children, parents, and other relatives, such as grandparents, aunts, or uncles, usually living together in the same house. *La familia* is the Spanish word used by Hispanics to refer to the extended family.

feast: a large meal prepared to celebrate a special day.

folk religion: the beliefs and spiritual practices that grow out of the lives of people.

godparents: a man and woman who accept responsibility for helping parents raise a child. They usually accept the responsibility in a religious ceremony.

kinship: the relationship a person has with her or his relatives.

pilgrimage: a journey to a religious place.

pillar: a support that is very important to holding up something.

Protestantism: the beliefs and practices of many Christian churches not led by the Pope, including Baptists, Methodists, Presbyterians, and others.

role: the part that a person plays in a play, in the family, or in society.

Like American society in general, Hispanic society is greatly influenced by the social institutions of the family and religion. Hispanic Americans may be even more deeply committed to these institutions because of their heritage and their immigrant experience. The Spanish civilization that settled in the New World depended on the family and religion for its strength. Spanish settlers in the New World could not have survived without them. Hispanic immigrants to the United States have relied on them for help in difficult times. Truly, the family and religion are two pillars of Hispanic society.

The Hispanic Family

Hispanic Americans have come to the United States from a variety of different countries. They have settled in large groups in cities on both the East and West Coasts. Rural pockets of Hispanics dot every state of the union. Once in the United States these groups have adapted to their new home in a variety of different ways. The United States has one of the most diverse populations of Spanish speakers in the world. Even so, these diverse groups have relied on a common social institution in order to adapt to the culture and environment of the United States. This social unit has been crucial to the survival and success of Hispanics in their new home. The institution is the family. Hispanic Americans, no matter where they originated or where they settled, place special emphasis, sentiment, and value on the family.

For each Hispanic group that has settled in the United States—Mexicans, Puerto Ricans, Cubans, Dominicans, Salvadorans, and the others—the family has provided the practical, financial, moral, and social support necessary for immigration and settlement. For newly arrived Hispanics, family members already in the United States have been essential in helping the newcomers find housing, friends, and employment. They have also helped the newcomers adjust in other ways to the new environment. Family connections in the home country have also helped. By keeping in contact, new immigrants have had a safety net in difficult times or in emergencies.

Characteristics of the Hispanic Family

The concept of family among Hispanic Americans refers to more than just the nuclear family, a man and woman with their children in one household. The Hispanic family, *la familia,* is understood to mean an extended family. It includes the nuclear family and relatives of both the father and the mother. Grandparents, aunts, uncles, and cousins are important and active members of la familia. In addition, any blood relative that can be identified through family names and records is important to la familia. Each person has a role in the family. In turn, the extended family offers a framework of support to help every member.

Family Roles

The traditional Hispanic family is led by the father. The ideal father is a strong male figure. He is ultimately responsible for the well-being of all individuals under his roof. The concept of *machismo* is closely related to the role of the father as family leader. Machismo requires men to be strong, aggressive, masculine, and willing to make decisions. This responsibility and machismo has prompted many Hispanic men to travel alone

A family celebrates a birthday. *Reproduced by permission of the Corbis Corporation (Bellevue).*

to the United States in order to provide for their families. Many others brought their families with them to give them a better home.

For many years, the traditional role of the adult female of a Hispanic family was to be a wife and a mother. Her responsibilities were in the private world of the home, not the public world. Her main function was to have and raise her husband's children. Training for the role began early. In childhood, girls helped with the housework and cared for the other children. Girls were expected to serve the males in her family. When they grew up, they had a responsibility first to their fathers and then to their husbands. In this tradition, selflessness was a high quality for a Hispanic woman.

The stereotypical role of the Hispanic woman has changed a great deal under the pressures of immigration and fitting into American society and modern life. Nowa-

HISPANA

STATE ● WOMEN'S ● CONFERENCE

NOVEMBER ● 21 ● 1987 ● DALLAS ● TEXAS
HOSTED BY
MEXICAN AMERICAN LEGAL DEFENSE AND EDUCATION FUND, INC
SPONSORED BY
ANHEUSER-BUSCH COMPANIES, INC.

BUD LIGHT   Rainbo

Poster advertising a Hispanic women's conference in Dallas, Texas, in 1987. *Reproduced by permission of Arte Público Press.*

days, women are not just responsible for child rearing and household chores. Many Hispanic women lead their families. There is a very high percentage of woman-headed households. This is especially true among Puerto Ricans in New York. A high percentage of women in all Hispanic American groups have jobs and are the primary household wage earners. Even in more traditional families, the father often shares the leadership with the mother.

In the early 1970s, after many Hispanics had joined the struggle for equality in the United States promoted by the civil rights movement, groups of Hispanic women nationwide slowly began their own movement for liberation from traditional roles in which they were often cast as inferiors. The Chicana movement, particularly strong in the Southwest, urged women to examine their roles within the family and within the society. Organizations developed around the country to aid Hispanic women in areas such as birth control, education, and employment.

Probably because of their strong traditional role within the family, Hispanic women were somewhat slower to get into the labor force than were white and black women. In 1999, 55.9 percent of Hispanic women participated in the labor force; black women had a labor force participation rate of 63.5 percent and white women participated at 59.6 percent. Although there is still a gap, Hispanic women have been catching up to the labor force participation rate of other women in the United States.

The entry of large numbers of women into the work force has affected the Hispanic family. Women now have a great deal of responsibility in the public world to add to their duties at home. In some families home and work duties are shared equally between husband and wife. In others, the traditional roles have not changed. In those cases, husbands do not take on any new household duties even though their wives have added jobs. Working women have also affected the authority roles within the Hispanic family. Now more than ever, Hispanic American women direct family action and take part in important decisions, including those that involve money.

The role of children in the traditional Hispanic family can best be described by the proverb: "Children are to be seen but not heard." Children, especially those of new immigrants, are expected to serve their elders and generally show the respect (*respeto*) of their culture values. However, in the United States children's roles have changed drastically. An American education and mixing with people outside the family has introduced Hispanic children to different family roles and relationships. Also, among new immigrants, children often need to take a leadership role. They become the link between their parents and the new culture. They are comfortable in both the Hispanic and mainstream worlds. So, they conduct business, negotiate, and translate Spanish and English on their parents' behalf.

Extending Family Ties

Hispanic culture has also developed social patterns that strengthen family ties and extend them beyond the circle of blood relatives. The Catholic religion has had a very strong influence on this aspect of the Hispanic family. When a Hispanic child is baptized, godparents (*padrinos*) are carefully selected by the parents. These padrinos have special responsibilities toward the godson (*ahijado*) or goddaughter (*ahijada*). For example, godparents have traditionally been expected to take on the parental role if the parents were to die. The godchild, in return, is expected to give special respect and attention to padrinos and to care for them in their old age.

However, the strongest relationship in godparenthood (*compadrazgo*) is the one between the child's parents and the godparents. These four call each other *compadres* (literally "coparents"). Compadres are expected to help one another, to care for one another in times of need, and to be readily and unconditionally available in times of crisis. In the Hispanic immigrant experience, compadres perform the same services as blood relatives. They provide shelter to newcomers, access to jobs, and a secure base from which immigrants can take steps toward adapting to their new environment.

In addition to compadrazgo, Hispanic Americans extend their families in other ways. Immigrants, especially Mexicans, include in their extended family people originally from the same village or region. In some cases they include those with similar immigrant experiences into their family networks. A feeling of kinship (*parentesco*) is established with these people. These relationships further increase the support group in the United States. They strengthen lines of communication between this new place and the hometown or region. Parentesco is common among early immigrants to the United States, especially those who come primarily from rural backgrounds. Kinship terms are often used to express this relationship. Uncle (*tío*), aunt (*tía*), and cousin (*primo* or *prima*) are common.

Trust (*confianza*) is of particular importance to both the institutions of compadrazgo and parentesco among Hispanics in the United States. It is the basis of the relationships between people in many spheres of social activity. To have confianza with an individual is not just to regard that person with trust. It also signifies a relationship of special feeling and importance. It involves respect and intimacy. Trust developed in friendship can, for example, lead to a godparent relationship and to expressing kinship to people who are not blood relatives.

Marriage

Marriage also serves to extend the family network. Among Hispanics in the United States, marriage practices vary a great deal. The type of marriage depends upon the origins of the bride and groom and the conditions in which they find themselves in the United States. Common practices include the church wedding (*matrimonio por la iglesia*), the civil marriage (*matrimonio por ley*), and the free union (*union libre*). Church weddings carry more prestige among people with wealth and high social status. Free unions allow new immigrants to quickly establish family ties. For the most part, Hispanics in the United States have continued to marry within their own groups. That is, Mexicans have tended to marry Mexicans, Puerto Ricans have tended to marry Puerto Ricans, and so on. Intermarriage between groups and between Hispanics and Anglo-Americans is increasing, especially among the children of immigrants, and is quite common among people of Hispanic origin who have been in the country for several generations.

La Familia in the United States

Among all Hispanics some form of extended family has been the tradition. The ideal extended family includes children, their parents, grandparents, aunts, and uncles. Many members of this kind of family live together under one roof and share economic and social activities. Although extended families do exist among Hispanics in the United States, they are no longer the preferred type of family. Later settlers and people born in the United States tend to favor nuclear families in separate households. When the extended family does live together in the same household, it is generally a temporary stage soon after arrival in the United States. During this time newcomers need support in adjusting and finding their way in a new environment. The extended family provides this support. Once the newcomers have established themselves, they tend to adopt the nuclear family norm of the general population: one father, one mother, and children together in one house.

In the United States in the early 2000s, the number of traditional nuclear families in general has been decreasing. A study by the *Washington Post* after the U.S. Census of 2000 found that the two-parents-plus-children family accounted for only about one-fifth of white or black households, a significant drop from earlier trends. However, couples with children represent one-third of Hispanic and Asian households. While mainstream American culture has increasingly adopted alternative lifestyles, with households formed by single parents, people who live alone, people who live with roommates, and couples who never have children, Hispanics are much more likely to be living in a traditional family situation. Hispanics who have recently arrived in the United States from other countries are the most likely of all to live in a nuclear family.

La familia is characterized by family ties extended through blood relations, godparenthood, feelings of kinship, trust, and marriage. It gives Hispanic society a solid structure. It also builds the social networks necessary to allow Hispanics to adjust and

The Armijo family celebrates the Christmas holiday at their Santa Fe, New Mexico, home. *Reproduced by permission of the Corbis Corporation (Bellevue).*

adapt to living in the United States. The typical Hispanic family is changing as generations are born in the United States. Families are shifting from an extended to a nuclear structure. Even so, family ties remain. They are simply expressed in new ways, ways related to life in the United States. Although somewhat Americanized, la familia continues to be a central thread in the social fabric of Hispanic American culture.

The Religions of Hispanic Americans

Hispanic Americans are very religious as a group. They have kept their faith through difficult times, in their homelands and their new homes. Religious expression is still a part of everyday life. Hispanics are quick to say *"Gracias a Dios"* (Thanks be to God) and *"Si Dios quiere"* (God willing). They commonly call upon God, the Virgin Mary, and the saints in their daily activities. They are predominantly Christians and Catholics. In 2000, surveys showed that 70 percent of U.S. Hispanics are Catholic, 22 percent are Protestant, and 8 percent are "other." This last figure includes Jews, Jehovah's Witnesses, Mormons, and various folk religions.

In the Beginning

The year 1492 is a very important date in the religious history of Hispanic Americans.

First, it marks the beginning of Catholicism as the dominant religion in Spain. In January 1492 the armies of Queen Isabella and King Ferdinand captured Granada in southern Spain. Their victory forced the Islamic Moors from the Iberian Peninsula once and for all. In April of that year, the king and queen began a process to unite their land under one religion, Catholicism. They announced that Jews had until July to give up their religion. If they refused, they would be forced to leave Spain. An estimated 140,000 Jews chose to leave. From 1492 on Spain would be united under the Catholic cross.

The year 1492 was also the year Catholicism came to the New World with Spanish explorer Christopher Columbus. The Spanish *conquistadors* that followed were filled with the religious fervor of their day. They wanted more than new lands and treasures for their king and queen. Their religion had triumphed over the Moorish infidels (people who were not Catholic). Now, they wanted to bring it to the native people they found in this New World. During the first two hundred years of European settlement in the Americas, Spain was the Roman Catholic Church's greatest champion.

Unlike most English explorers and settlers, the Spaniards who came to the New World believed that Native Americans were made in God's image. They had a soul. The Spaniards believed that it was their religious duty to convert the Native Americans to Catholicism. In order to spread the Spanish religion to these people, the Spanish usually destroyed the Native Americans' idols and temples. In their place the Spanish put crosses and shrines in honor of the Virgin Mary. Hernan Cortés, the conqueror of Mexico, saw his mission not just in political and economic terms. He saw it as a religious crusade.

As Spanish explorers pushed north into areas now in the United States, Catholic monks came right alongside them. Their goal was to convert the Native Americans to Catholicism and teach them Spanish ways. They built missions to be a center for their religious works. These missions became some of the first formal schools in the New World. The monks first taught the Native Americans Spanish. After that came Catholic beliefs and practices as well as Spanish customs and laws. They also included European techniques in raising livestock, farming, construction, and furniture making.

The Spanish wars against the Islamic Moors served to unite the nation and its people under the Catholic cross. When native-born Spaniards came to the New World, they brought their strong Catholic faith with them. It continued to be a crucial part of the daily lives of *criollos*, Spaniards born in the New World. And finally, because of the efforts of Spanish monks, many Native Americans were converted to Catholicism. At times Native Americans were forced to practice the religion against their will and were also forced to give up public celebrations of their own religions. But when Spaniards and Native Americans mixed to create the *mestizos*, they often already had religion in common.

Hispanic Catholicism

Hispanic Americans have preserved the religious traditions of their ancestors and arriving immigrants reinforce (make stronger) a strong Catholic faith. There are, in the early 2000s, approximately 21 million

An image of Our Lady of Guadalupe on tour from Mexico in Houston, Texas, 1992. *Reproduced by permission of the Texas Catholic Herald.*

U.S. Hispanic Catholics, and they make up about 35 percent of all Catholics in the United States. Hispanics accounted for 71 percent of the Catholic Church's growth over the past forty years. Hispanics are very loyal to the church, particularly recently arrived immigrants, who often find the U.S. culture strange and not very friendly. The Catholic Church often gives them the support and comfort they cannot find elsewhere as immigrants.

Perhaps because priests were not available in the remote areas of Spanish Ameri-

ca, the family and the home have traditionally been at the center of Hispanic religious practices. In the home, religion is often the concern of Hispanic women. A grandmother or some other elderly female usually sees to it that children learn their religious lessons and practices. Women have taken on the role of being the guardians of the spiritual well-being and salvation of their men. Many Hispanic girls mark their fifteenth birthdays (*quinceañera*) with a special prayer service to remind them that they must be good Christian wives and mothers. These tradi-

OUR LADY OF GUADALUPE

Juan Diego was a Native American from near Mexico City who had been converted to Catholicism. In the early morning hours of December 9, 1531, he was on his way to mass when he was surprised by beautiful singing voices. He went toward them and found a brown woman surrounded by a brilliant light. She told him in his native language, Nahuatl, that she was the Virgin Mary. She appeared to Juan Diego several more times. Eventually, she told him that she wanted a temple to be built on the hill at nearby Tepeyac. There, she would be able to defend the people who lived in the area. She would free them from their misery. Juan Diego told Archbishop Zumárraga of the Virgin's request. At first, he did not believe the story. But, the Virgin performed a miracle to convince him. She told Juan Diego to gather roses from a bush that normally did not bloom in the winter. He should wrap the roses in a cloak and take them to the archbishop. When Juan Diego opened the cloak before the archbishop, the roses fell before him. On the cloak where the roses had been was an image of the Virgin Mary. This image can be seen today in the basilica of Our Lady of Guadalupe in Mexico City.

The miracle of Our Lady of Guadalupe offered Native American Catholics a link between their old culture and their new one. The brown Virgin surrounded by light, flowers, and nature combined symbols from Native American and Spanish religions. She promised to protect these conquered people in their own language. Later, the Native American and Spanish cultures mixed to form Mexican culture. Our Lady of Guadalupe became one of the central figures in the Catholic religion of that new culture. She has continued to be important to Hispanics in the United States.

tions change, to varying degrees, to suit modern family and work roles.

In the Hispanic home, it is common to find a place that serves as an altar. This altar helps the Hispanic woman fulfill her responsibility as the spiritual caretaker of her family. She creates her family's unique altar by gathering symbols of the spiritual forces on which she depends. The altar might be a religious picture surrounded by candles on a small table. It could be a statuette of a saint, of the Virgin Mary, or of Jesus along with a vase of flowers on a television set. It may also be quite elaborate, an approximation of a church altar. If so, it would have several religious images, hand-embroidered cloths, candles, incense, holy water, and other Roman Catholic sacred objects.

One strong characteristic of Hispanic American Catholicism is its deep respect for the Virgin Mary in all her forms. Mexican Americans identify with Our Lady of Guadalupe and with Our Lady of San Juan de los Lagos. Puerto Ricans identify with Our Lady of Providencia, Cubans with La Caridad de Cobre, and Dominicans with Altagracia. For Hispanic men the Virgin Mary represents the understanding mother who helps and forgives her troubled sons. For Hispanic women she sympathizes with their difficulties on earth as a mother, sister, or daughter. Hispanic women especially identify with Our Lady of Sorrows (Dolores), the Virgin suffering for her son.

Each Hispanic group also traditionally identifies with a particular image of Christ. For Guatemalans there is El Cristo Negro de Esquipulas (The Black Christ of Esquipulas). For Colombians there is El Señor de los Milagros (The Lord of Miracles). For Salvadorans there is Cristo El Salvador (Christ the Savior). The cult of the Sacred Heart of Jesus is universally popular. In this image Jesus suffers because of his human love for people. All of these cults usually focus on a bleeding, wounded Christ. In this way Hispanics seem to stress the dead rather than the resurrected Christ, a characteristic that disappoints many Hispanic religious leaders.

Processions, pilgrimages, and other events are an important part of Hispanic religious expression. In the United States, feasts are often followed by a solemn mass, then some form of merriment. A procession around the church grounds may follow. Larger processions are mounted and take to the streets to celebrate Our Lady of Guadalupe in the Southwest and La Caridad del Cobre in Miami.

Wherever large groups of Mexican Americans live, they regularly organize pilgrimages to the shrine of Our Lady of Guadalupe in Mexico City. Hispanic Americans in the U.S. Southwest also organize pilgrimages to the shrine of Our Lady of San Juan de los Lagos in Jalisco, Mexico. Since colonial times pilgrims have sought the healing powers of an image of the Immaculate Conception at this shrine. A large shrine to the Virgin Mary in the Texas border town of San Juan attracts many Hispanic Americans. A shrine to La Caridad de Cobre was built in the 1960s with funds collected from Cuban exiles. This shrine, which faces Biscayne Bay in Coral Gables, Florida, attracts Cuban American pilgrims from all over the United States.

For each pilgrimage the faithful challenge themselves with a vow they must fulfill. For instance, some pilgrims make the final part of the journey to a shrine on their knees. Mexican Americans and some Central Americans still practice the *ex-voto*. In this tradition the pilgrim gives presents to a saint in gratitude for a favor granted by the saint. Colonial ex-votos were often primitive drawings on tin or wood. They depicted the miracle performed by the saint and often included a written explanation. Modern ex-votos can be photographs, bridal wreaths, baby shoes, or letters of gratitude. In many cases they are the traditional *milagrito*. This is a charm made out of tin, silver, or gold and shaped in the form of an arm, a leg, a

Children at a Christmas posada in Houston, Texas, 1988. *Reproduced by permission of Texas Catholic Herald.*

baby, or a house. Other ex-votos include crutches, leg braces, eyeglasses, and other such devices that are no longer needed thanks to the miracle performed by the saint. This practice is popular in places such as the magnificent shrine in San Juan, Texas, and the quaint Sanctuary of Chimayo in Chimayo, New Mexico.

Hispanic Americans have continued to observe their traditional religious holy days and devotions. Ash Wednesday draws large crowds to Catholic churches in Mexican American neighborhoods. The feast of Our Lady of Guadalupe on December 12 also draws many Mexican Americans to church. This is a celebration of new hope. The par-

ticipants shower the Virgin Mary with flowers, and mariachi groups sing the traditional *Las Mañanitas* (Morning Songs) at the break of dawn.

Popular among Mexican Americans is the traditional *posada,* which dates back to colonial days. This is a novena, or nine-day devotion, that ends on Christmas Eve. During its nine nights, a different neighborhood family serves as host for the posada. Their neighbors reenact Mary and Joseph's search for a place to stay in Bethlehem. They knock at the hosts' door, singing a traditional hymn and asking for shelter. They are repeatedly refused. Finally, an innkeeper allows them into a home. The participants say a rosary, or special prayer. Then, everyone enjoys refreshments. Some Mexican American communities also present the *Pastorela* during the Christmas season. This folk play which reenacts the adoration of the shepherds also dates back to colonial times.

In northern New Mexico, a special brotherhood of Hispanic Americans continues to observe its Holy Week traditions during the Easter season. These men gather in the *moradas,* or secret meeting places. There, they inflict pain on one another to remind themselves of the pain Christ felt in his final days. They commemorate the death of Christ on Good Friday. Then, they observe *tinieblas.* In the completely dark morada, traditional wood and metal noisemakers are used to conjure up the sounds of the horrors of hell.

The Catholic Church among Hispanic Americans has shown some signs of change in recent years. In the United States and around the world, forms of evangelical Christianity are becoming very popular. Perhaps in response the Roman Catholic Church has seen a charismatic renewal movement. This movement focuses less on the saints and the Virgin and more on worship of the Holy Spirit. In the United States, it has attracted a large following among Hispanic Catholics.

Hispanic Protestants

Soon after the United States took control of the Southwest from Mexico, Anglo-Protestant ministers traveled to this region to try to convert Hispanic Catholics to Protestantism. Protestant churches in the United States were interested in spreading their religion to the Southwest. They also

A Hispanic family attending Protestant services. *Reproduced by permission of the Texas Catholic Herald.*

wanted to use Protestant Hispanics to spread the religion to Mexico and other Latin American countries. One example of this was Alejo Hernández, a Catholic priest who converted to the Methodist faith. He was ordained deacon in Corpus Christi, Texas, in 1871. Shortly thereafter he was sent to Mexico City as a missionary.

In the second half of the 1800s, the number of Hispanic Protestants grew in Texas and the Southwest. The early Hispanic churches were controlled by Anglos. Hispanics were not encouraged to make their own decisions or establish their own institutions. The Hispanic culture was not included as part of the religion. Rather, Hispanic Protestants were expected to adapt to the Anglo-Protestant culture. Hispanic church leaders were trained because they could more easily work with the Hispanic community.

In 1898 after the end of the Spanish-American War, Protestant missionaries descended upon Cuba and Puerto Rico. Some of the missionaries had been born in Cuba or Puerto Rico and converted as exiles in the United States. In the Caribbean they were somewhat successful at converting the people to their religion. One argument they made was that Catholicism was the religion of the oppressive Spanish. Protestantism was the religion of a new order.

Conversion carried a high price for Hispanics who chose Protestantism. In choosing Protestantism Hispanics had to give up a large part of their identity. Catholicism had been very closely tied together with their Hispanic culture. Protestantism forced them to accept Anglo culture, to Americanize.

By the 1930s a Spanish-speaking Protestant clergy was emerging. The biggest problem for Hispanics and for the American churches was how to integrate Hispanic churches into the church structure. Hispanics who wanted to keep their culture and language feared being absorbed into an Anglo majority. In places where Hispanic churches accepted mainstream church leadership, the Hispanic culture and language suffered in church life. For example, when the Latin American Conference of Southern California merged with Anglo conferences, Hispanic church members went elsewhere. This and other cases have caused Hispanic membership in highly structured Protestant denominations to level off or drop.

The most successful Hispanic Protestant churches have been those that have remained independent. Good examples of this are the Methodist churches in Texas and New Mexico that have come together in the Rio Grande Conference. This group dates from the early 1930s. At that time Alfredo Náñez, the first Hispanic graduate of Southern Methodist University in Dallas, Texas, and Francisco Ramos were selected elders of the Texas American Conference. In 1939 it became the Rio Grande Conference. It is a powerful group of churches that to this day has remained independent from the larger Methodist Church.

Southern Baptist and Pentecostal churches also appeal to Hispanic Protestants. These denominations are less structured than some others. They allow individual congregations to make their own decisions. For this reason Hispanic membership in these churches has continued to grow during the early twenty-first century.

Today, Pentecostalism is sweeping Central and South America. It is also growing by leaps and bounds among U.S. Hispanics. Its small, community churches give Hispanics a feeling of belonging. It also allows Hispanic converts room to express their religious feeling. Pentecostalism does not accept all of the Catholic traditions (processions and other public devotions) but its emotional form of worship is familiar to Hispanics from the Catholic background. The Catholic saints and Virgin Mary (protectors and healers) are replaced for Hispanic Pentecostals by the healing powers of the Holy Spirit.

During the era of activism in the 1960s, Hispanic Protestants tended to stay on the sidelines. Exceptions were Reies Tijerina and Rudolfo "Corky" González. Tijerina was a Pentecostal minister who fought for the rights of New Mexicans to recover land taken from their ancestors. González was a former boxer and Presbyterian leader. He fought for Mexican American rights and served jail time for his activism. He was also an early Chicano poet. He wrote the important epic poem *I Am Joaquín / Yo Soy Joaquín.*

Folk Religions among Hispanics

Folk religions have always coexisted with mainstream religions despite efforts by Christian leaders to get rid of them. These cults include herbal healing, magic, communication with the dead, and spiritual healing based on African traditions. In some cases Hispanic Americans follow only the rituals of the folk religion. More often, however, they use the folk religions to supplement their Christianity. In some cases Hispanics have combined the folk religions with Christianity to create a new, uniquely Hispanic religion.

Folk Healing

Herb shops known as *yerberías* by Mexican Americans and *botánicas* by Hispanics from the Caribbean are an important part of many Hispanic communities. They offer not only medicinal plants but also many products recommended by spiritualists and faith healers. *Yerberos* are herb specialists. They know the medicinal qualities of plants and use them to cure physical ills. They claim that the roots, leaves, and seeds of many herbs can cure any illness from snakebites and infertility to arthritis and kidney stones.

Juanita Alvárez dispenses charms, candles, herbs, and perfumed oils at her East Los Angeles, California, shop Botanica Cristo Rey, 1991. *Reproduced by permission of AP/Wide World Photos.*

Curanderos are also folk healers. But, these healers can cure both physical and spiritual ills. They can also remedy just about any human condition by using the forces of good and evil. To bring about a cure, curanderos use medicinal plants, eggs, candles, spells, perfumes, prayers, incense, holy water, religious images, and other things. Curanderos can perform many services. They can remove a spell that is making a person physically ill. They can make an unfaithful husband return to his wife. They can help someone have good luck in business or gambling. They can prepare special amulets, oils, and charms. Most curanderos practice both white and black magic to do good. However, some curanderos use the tools of their trade to do harm to others. These evil curanderos are technically witches. A man is a *brujo* and a woman is a *bruja*.

Spiritism and Spiritualism

Some folk religions practiced by Hispanic Americans involve communicating with the spirits of dead people. Spiritism is one. It was developed by Alan Kardec in France in the 1800s. By the 1860s it had reached Latin America. Spiritists communicate with the dead through mediums (people who act as a channel of communication between the earthly world and the world of spirits). Through these communications spiritists seek guidance, advice, and supernatural revelations. Spiritists believe that they have access to the spirits of famous people, such as Napoleon, Moctezuma, and Cleopatra. Even so, they more often work through ordinary spirits, such as a black slave, a great-grandmother, or a fisherman. These spirits usually perform services that relate to their personalities when alive. A favorite among Hispanic American spiritists is Pancho Villa. This Mexican bandit and revolutionary known for his hot temper is called upon to chase away all evil spirits.

Another folk religion that involves the spirits of the dead is Spiritualism. Spiritualism as practiced by Hispanics was developed in Mexico during the 1800s. The people who believe in Spiritualism are usually practicing Catholics. They believe that they are channels or *cajas* (boxes) for great religious figures. They use the powers of the spirits to heal. Among Mexican Americans, mediums often serve as channels for two late Spiritualists, Don Pedrito Jaramillo, a curandero from Falfurrias, Texas, and the Niño Fidencio, from Nuevo León, Mexico, a village outside Monterrey. Today, there is a popular movement in the Catholic Church to make these two healers saints. Others, especially followers of Fidencio, have created separate cults. They display Catholic images of Our Lady of Guadalupe and the Sacred Heart of Jesus with Fidencio's face where the face of the Virgin Mary or Jesus Christ would normally appear.

Santería

Santería, sometimes called *santerismo,* is a folk religion that was first developed in the Caribbean Islands. It is based on beliefs and rituals brought by Yoruba slaves from West Africa to Cuba and Puerto Rico. To these African traditions, Santería has added elements of Hispanic Catholicism. African slaves were often forced to accept Catholicism by their masters. Even so they continued to worship their African gods, only disguised as Christian saints. A less complex form of Santería is practiced by people from the Dominican Republic. It is a modified form of Haitian voodoo, an African-based religion often associated with witchcraft. Today, the centers of Santería are Miami, Tampa, New York, and San Juan, Puerto Rico. But, in the United States this religious cult has spread beyond the Cuban and Puerto Rican communities to people of other national origins. It is influencing and being influenced by Mexican American curanderismo.

Santería is a cult of the *orishas* (gods), who control the forces of nature. The ruler of all these spiritual forces is Olofin, God the Creator. The most popular of these gods are *Las Siete Potencias* (the Seven Powerful Spirits). They are often shown on candles and icons. Olofin's son is Obatala. Obatala is vengeful, powerful, and indifferent. His worshipers wear white. He is worshiped through the Catholic images of Our Lady of Mercy and Christ. Some Mexican Americans worship Obatala through the image of Our Lady of San Juan. Chango is the godess of war, the snake, the storm, and thunder. Her color is red, the color of blood. She is called upon through the image of Saint Barbara. Babaluaye is the god of healing. He is portrayed as a leper on crutches, often with two dogs. He is represented by Saint Lazarus. Ogun is a wild man of the forest who controls things made out of iron. He wears the guise of John the Baptist. Ochun is the goddess of love. She is seen as Our Lady of la Caridad del Cobre. Yemaya rules the waters. She is Our Lady of Regla. Orula can see the future. He is Saint Francis of Assisi.

Santeros and babalaos are the healers and witches of Santería. Santeros are the devotees of the different gods. After a rigorous initiation, they become the son or daughter of a particular orisha. As such, they have special powers. In their house santeros keep a container in which their orisha lives. In the United States, it is usually an expensive soup tureen in the orisha's favorite color. The santero wears the orisha's color and builds this god an elaborate altar. The santero also celebrates the feast day of the Catholic saint associated with the orisha. The priests and priestesses of Santería are in charge of the public worship of the orishas.

A babalao looks on as a santero says a prayer to Chango, a chief Santería god at a church in Hialeah, Florida, 1995. *Reproduced by permission of AP/Wide World Photos.*

The babalaos understand the supernatural powers by a system they learn after many years of study. They use the Rosary of Ifa (a god) to decide which god or orisha is affecting a person's life. This rosary is usually 16 cowrie shells, mango seeds, or pieces of coconut. The babalao throws the 16 shells to make one of a possible 256 patterns. Each pattern calls for a specific verse that the babalao recites from memory. He then interprets the verse for the client.

Once the problem is clear, the babalao offers a solution. The solution usually means pleasing the orisha by making a sacrifice. The sacrifice varies. Different gods like different gifts. Some like food, perfumes, or ornaments. Some gods demand animal sacrifices. To please Obatala, for example, a white hen or dove must be sacrificed. At the end the client pays the babalao for the divination and the sacrifice.

There are three *reglas,* or ways to practice Santería. The regla Obatala described above is the most widespread. The regla Lucumi is similar to the regla Obatala, but it has less mixing of African and Christian saints. The third way is the regla Mayombera or Palo Mayombé. It mixes rituals from the Congo in central Africa with spiritism, or the cult of the dead. It works more with the *ngangas* (spirits of the dead) than with the orishas. In this way it is similar to Haitian voodoo. The *mayomberos* who practice this religion are feared as powerful magicians. They can exorcise evil spirits, cast spells, and make amulets. A person may choose to consult a babalao to determine the nature of his or her problem and then go to a mayombero for the solution or cure.

9

Hispanic Americans on the Job and at School

FACT FOCUS

- The number of Hispanic workers in the United States is growing faster than any other group.
- Soon after Texas, New Mexico, Arizona, and California joined the United States, Hispanics living in those areas began to lose their land. Over time, they began to work for wages on other land or in the cities.
- Hispanics have come to the United States to work since colonial times. American society has accepted Hispanic workers during good economic times and rejected them during hard times.
- Spanish monks started the first schools in the U.S. Southwest. These mission schools were to teach Native Americans the Spanish language, religion, and culture.
- In the 1600s and 1700s, Spanish children in the Southwest were originally taught at home and on the job in their community. Under Mexican rule, frontier schools were started to help preserve the Spanish culture.
- In the 1800s and early 1900s, American public schools focused on teaching Hispanic children the English language and American culture. For the most part, these schools were segregated.
- Since the 1960s, Hispanic children have been able to study the Spanish language and Hispanic culture in bilingual/bicultural programs. In recent years, however, these programs have lost support and have even been banned in California.
- Today in U.S. public schools, Hispanic American children often get a poorer quality of education than other children.

WORDS TO KNOW

agriculture: the knowledge and practice of farming, raising plants and animals for food.

bilingual/bicultural education: in the United States, usually learning and teaching in both English and Spanish about both Anglo and Hispanic cultures.

entrepreneur: a person who takes responsibility for a business.

formal education: learning and teaching that takes place in a school. Informal education takes place at home or in the community.

industry: the work done by businesses and factories.

labor force: the group of people working in a country or other place.

migrant worker: a person who moves from one place to another following the jobs.

segregation: separating people in schools and other public places because of their race or culture.

skilled professionals: someone who works at a job that requires special training or education.

undocumented immigrant: a person who lives or works in the United States who is not a citizen of the United States and who does not have permission to stay in the country.

unskilled worker: a person who works at a job that does not require special training or education.

Nowhere have the difficulties of being a minority in American society been more apparent for Hispanics than on the job and at school. Ever since the first Hispanics found themselves on American soil, they have fought for equal opportunities in the workplace and in the classroom. They have faced discrimination based on color, culture, language, and income. At times they have been forced to accept their situation, but at others they have moved to make changes. They have acted through social, legal, and political channels.

In the 2000s, the rapidly growing Hispanic population is receiving new attention from American businesses and schools. Hispanics form a huge market within the U.S. economy: American businesses want to sell to them. They represent a large voting group and will be electing more and more representatives to local, state, and federal government positions, who will meet the Hispanic community's needs. While there have been rulings in many states banning bilingual education (teaching in both Spanish and English), today many non-Hispanic people are finding it useful to learn the Spanish language to accommodate their clients and customers. Still, even with a great number of advantages gained by the growing population and years of struggle, discrimination still exists. Many Hispanic children go to schools that are segregated (apart from the rest). Education and income levels of Hispanics are not equal to those of non-Hispanics.

Hispanics on the Job

Hispanics had been farming, ranching, and working in their *pueblos* (towns) in the

Southwest for over two hundred years when the United States acquired the territories they were living in from Mexico. Since that time millions of Hispanics have come from Mexico, the Caribbean, and Central and South America. They have come for many reasons, some political, some religious, and some economic. They have come to find a better life for themselves and their families. They have come to work. And work they have. Hispanics labor in agriculture and industry. They own their own businesses and employ others. They are highly educated professionals in science, law, education, and other fields. They are also public servants in government organizations and politics.

Hispanics in the U.S. Work Force

The number of Hispanics in the U.S. labor force is growing at a fast rate. In fact the Hispanic American work force is growing faster than any other major group. The U.S. Department of Labor studies show that between 1998 and 2008 Hispanic labor force growth should increase by 37 percent. In 1980 Hispanics made up about 6.1 percent of the nation's work force. By 1990, they were at 9 percent and in the early 2000s Hispanics make up about 11 percent of the work force. Hispanic males work more than other groups. In 2000, 80.4 percent of Hispanic men were either working or looking for work, compared to 74.3 non-Hispanic white men. Hispanic women had a 56.6 percent presence in the workforce.

Hispanics work more but basically make less money than other U.S. groups, largely because they have been employed at less professional or skilled jobs. In 1999 whites were three times more likely to earn $50,000 or more per year than were Hispanics. Hispanics were more likely to live in poverty than non-Hispanic whites as well.

The year 2000 brought the highest median (point at the middle; the average) income for Hispanics and African Americans ever recorded. The median Hispanic income in 2000 was $33,400, compared to $31,800 in 1999, an increase in one year of 5.3 percent. The median income for whites in 2000 was $44,200. In 1999 Hispanic men earned 61.6 percent of what white men earned; Hispanic women earned 52.1 percent of what non-Hispanic white women earned. Cubans had the highest family income and Puerto Ricans had the lowest.

In 2000, 22.8 percent of all Hispanic families were classified as living in poverty, compared with 7.7 percent of non-Hispanic families. Among Hispanic children under the age of 18, 30.3 percent were living in poverty, compared to 9.4 percent of non-Hispanic white children. Puerto Ricans and Mexicans were more likely to be living in poverty than Cubans and Central and South Americans.

Generally, Hispanics made steady gains in income during the 1990s and 2000s. The downturns in the U.S. economy, however, hit the Hispanic population particularly hard. They are usually the first to lose work in a crisis. After the terrorist attacks on the World Trade Center in New York City and the Pentagon in Washington, D.C., on September 11, 2001, Hispanics were laid off nationwide at a higher proportion than other groups and the level of unemployment among Hispanics was more than 2 percentage points higher than the rate of the country as a whole.

Mexican miners in the early 1900s. *Reproduced courtesy of the Arizona Historical Society Library.*

A Brief History of Hispanic Americans at Work

From the late 1500s to 1848, Hispanics lived and worked in the Southwest under Spanish, then Mexican rule. These people were farmers and ranchers. Most of them held small plots of land on which they grew and raised the food they needed. To meet additional needs, they often worked for others in their free time. After the Mexican War made the Southwest part of the United States, many of these Hispanic farmers began to lose their land. Without land, a majority became wage laborers. They worked as field hands, cowboys, railroad workers, ditchdiggers, and miners. Over time Mexican Americans moved more and more to American cities. There, they found jobs in manufacturing and services.

When Cubans immigrated to south Florida in the late 1800s, they went to work primarily in the tobacco industry. Some owned tobacco fields and some worked the fields. Others found jobs in Florida's cigar factories.

A new phase in the history of Hispanic Americans on the job began around the turn

Puerto Rican garment workers in New York City. *Reproduced by permission of Arte Público Press.*

of the twentieth century. At this time employers in the American Southwest began to go to Mexican border towns to recruit workers. Soon afterward midwestern employers were using the same approach. Labor contractors and other recruiters brought Mexican workers into the United States to do unskilled and low-paying work. Other Mexicans followed on their own.

Mexico in the early twentieth century offered difficult working conditions. Pay was low and unemployment was high. The United States seemed attractive. It offered many jobs, and wages were high compared to Mexico. This disparity between the United States and Mexico has continued throughout the century. Today, an unskilled worker in the United States can earn almost ten times more than he or she can earn in Mexico. But, there is a price. Food, rent, and other living expenses are higher in the United States.

In the early 1900s, Mexicans were primarily recruited to work on farms, on railroads, and in mines. Smaller numbers found jobs in manufacturing and as maids or other

Southern Pacific Railroad workers during World War II in Tucson, Arizona. *Reproduced courtesy of the Arizona Historical Society Library.*

domestic servants. Mexican immigrant families often worked as a single unit in cotton, sugar beet, fruit, and vegetable planting, cultivating, and harvesting. Adults worked in mining, manufacturing, and the services. Child labor laws limited the employment of children. Cities in the Southwest and the Midwest eventually attracted large groups of Mexican workers. They were available year round to do unskilled and low-paying work. Most of the work was seasonal, so Mexican workers changed employers often and suffered from unemployment.

After the United States won control over Puerto Rico in the Spanish-American War of 1898, more and more Puerto Rican workers started to immigrate. Large U.S. corporations forced many small farmers off their land. Facing wage labor in the fields or unemployment, many came to the mainland in search of better opportunities. Many traveled to New York City to work in the clothing industry and other low-paying industrial and service jobs.

Working conditions for all American workers got worse during the Great Depres-

THE BRACERO PROGRAM

The term *bracero* comes from the Spanish word for arm, *brazo*. It was originally used to refer to day laborers. In 1942, after the United States entered World War II, there was a labor shortage in the country. Braceros were brought into the United States to work on farms and railroads. For decades after the war, braceros were still important to the farm harvest in the Southwest and Midwest. They helped pick sugar beets, cotton, pickles, tomatoes, and other vegetables. The United States and Mexico made a number of labor agreements between 1942 and 1964 that became known as the Bracero Program.

Other programs also brought Puerto Rican workers to the United States during and after the war. In 1944, the Puerto Rican government started Operation Bootstrap. This program sought to reduce unemployment on the island by attracting industry. It also invited labor recruiters to Puerto Rico and arranged with airlines to offer cheap flights to New York City. There and in other cities, Puerto Ricans went to work in manufacturing and services. Some Puerto Ricans were recruited to work on farms from Florida to New England. They harvested fruits and vegetables and worked in canneries. During the heyday of Operation Bootstrap, 100,000 Puerto Rican workers came to the United States each year.

sion of the 1930s. They were especially bad for Mexican workers. In cities in the Southwest and Midwest, they were singled out and fired or laid off. Immigration from Mexico stopped, and many immigrants returned to their original homes. In some places, however, Mexican Americans did not choose to return. They were forced out. Local governments and businesses started programs to convince the English-speaking public that Hispanics were taking jobs away from Americans. Actually, most Mexicans had already lost their jobs. These programs came to an end when Franklin D. Roosevelt became

president and the Democrats took control of Congress in 1933. Unlike the Republicans, the Democrats did not believe that Mexican workers had caused the Depression.

In 1940 and 1941, World War II in Europe stimulated the American economy. The need for workers rose sharply. American farms and businesses wanted workers from Mexico. However, at this time the Mexican government opposed these efforts. It was worried that Mexican workers would be forced out of work as soon as the war ended, repeating the Depression experience.

Field workers in the Bracero Program. *Reproduced courtesy of the Library of Congress.*

To solve the problem, the U.S. and Mexican governments agreed to set up a formal recruiting program to protect the Mexican workers. The program included guaranteed minimum wages and other protections. It also included a plan to fairly return the workers to Mexico when their contracts expired. This program, the Mexican Labor Agreement, was popularly called the Bracero Program.

A third phase of Hispanic labor migration to the United States began in the 1960s. The Bracero Program, which had started in 1944, ended in 1964. Mexican immigration decreased for a couple of years. Then, Mexican workers resumed coming to the United States under the guidelines of other immigra-

tion laws. Puerto Ricans, who had been American citizens since 1917, faced no immigration barriers. They continued to come to the mainland, but there was often an equal number of workers returning to the island.

Perhaps the most important feature of this third phase has been that it has included workers from many more Latin American countries. A large wave of Cubans immigrated to the United States after the 1959 Cuban Revolution. Recent political, social, and economic problems in Central and South America have encouraged many from these countries to travel to the United States. Unlike the majority of Mexican and Puerto Rican workers, who were unskilled, many of these new arrivals have been skilled professionals and business owners. The major exception was the Cubans who came during the Mariel Boat Lift of the 1980s. Many of these poor and ill-prepared immigrants are still struggling to join the American work force.

Current Issues in Hispanic Labor

Migrant Farm Labor

Every year, the United States depends on migrant farm workers to plant and harvest its fruit and vegetable crops during the harvest season. There are two kinds of migrant farm workers: seasonal farm workers who live and work in a local community during the winter and then migrate to work on farms in the spring and summer months; and migrant farm workers, who travel all year from farm to farm to work. For both groups, working and living conditions can be harsh and dangerous. Despite programs to organize and address the needs of migrant workers, they still suffer from unemployment, low pay, and poor working conditions. Their working lives give them few chances for education and often leave them with serious illnesses. Few people in the community or in politics want to bring the migrant farm worker's plight before the public. They are outsiders to the local community. They are often separated by ethnic and language barriers, so they are rarely involved in making policy decisions.

Some progress was made in addressing migrant concerns during the 1960s and 1970s, especially in places where large groups of migrants were American citizens. More recently, however, employers have got-

UNDOCUMENTED WORKERS, NOT ILLEGAL ALIENS

Many people have come to the United States to work without the proper immigration papers. These people are commonly called "illegal aliens." In 1974, the International Labor Organization decided that it would be better and more accurate to call these people "undocumented workers." "Illegal" has a negative value and suggests that the people are criminals. It is against civil laws to immigrate without papers, but it is not a criminal offense. Some undocumented workers enter the United States without the proper papers. Others enter under temporary permits and stay beyond the limits of the permits.

ten around these measures by hiring noncitizens to replace citizens. Along the East Coast, they have recruited from Caribbean countries such as the Dominican Republic and supplemented with Mexicans and Central Americans. In other parts of the country, employers have gone to Mexico and Central America for their recruits. Many of these migrants now come to the United States legally under the guidelines of the H-2 Program of the Immigration and Nationality Act of 1952. Increasingly, other migrant workers come illegally. These "illegal aliens" are more accurately called "undocumented

Workers at a maquiladora plant in Metamoros, Mexico, 1993. *Reproduced by permission of Archive Photos, Inc.*

workers." Their presence continues to pose problems for American communities.

Although many federal programs were put into place to help migrant workers, in the 1990s and 2000s it is clear that they live and work under the worst conditions of any group of workers in the United States. A National Agricultural Worker Survey (NAWS) examined the lives of migrant workers in 1989. It found that out of about 5 million people who work some or all of the year on one of the United States's 800,000 farms that hire labor, about 840,000 could be classified as migrant farm workers. Of these, 94 percent were Hispanic; 80 percent were born in Mexico; 52 percent were married and had children; 59 percent were

working in the United States without their families present; 82 percent were men; 67 percent were undocumented workers. Although migrant workers make more money than they could in their homes, they do not make very much by U.S. standards. Their children are often at a disadvantage in getting an education. The health of migrant workers has been shown to be much poorer than that of the rest of the population.

The Maquiladoras and NAFTA

Since the end of the Bracero Program in 1965, Mexico and the United States have cooperated on a program to address unemployment in northern Mexico. The Mexican government has also hoped that this program would raise the standard of living for its people living along the U.S. border. Under this program American companies have built *maquiladoras* (assembly plants) along the U.S.-Mexican borders. In these plants they use cheap Mexican labor to put together products bound for American markets. The assembled goods are then sent across the border free of duties or tariffs to a "twin plant" on the U.S. side. Here, the manufacturing process is completed and the products are shipped to American consumers.

In the early years of the maquiladora program, about two-thirds of the assembled products were electric and electronic goods. When the program expanded in the 1970s and 1980s, the range of products expanded rapidly. By 1987 electric and electronic goods were only about 35 percent of the total. Textiles, clothing, and shoes represented 18 percent, and furniture made up 10 percent. Transportation equipment (including car motors) was 9 percent. Other goods represented 28 percent.

The scale of production in maquiladoras also grew impressively during the 1970s and 1980s. In 1966 there were 57 plants with about 4,000 workers. By 1979 there were about 540 plants with 120,000 workers, and by 1986 there were 844 plants employing 242,000 workers. In 1990 there were more than 1,000 plants employing about 450,000 workers. With the passage of the North American Free Trade Agreement (NAFTA) in 1994, taxes and customs fees were nearly eliminated, so that corporate profits from the inexpensive labor in Mexico were even higher. In 2000 there were 3,800 plants with more than one million workers.

Despite its impressive numbers, the maquiladora program has not lived up to its original goals. It was designed to reduce unemployment among male Mexicans in border towns. However, 85 percent of the maquiladora work force is and has been female, mostly teenage women. There has also been a great deal of job turnover. In sum, the program has not offered steady work for unemployed men. Some of the manufacturing plants have been called sweat shops, meaning that they work their employees very hard with low wages and poor working conditions. In 2000 people worked in the maquiladoras for as little as 50 cents an hour. The program has also extended beyond its original 12.5-mile strip near the border. Since 1972 assembly plants have been allowed throughout northern and central Mexico.

Many in Mexico and the United States are concerned that the maquiladora program and the North American Free Trade Agreement will do harm to the people, society, and environment of Mexico. Others point out that Mexico's cheap labor and poor protection for workers will make it more difficult for working-class Americans, including Hispanic Americans, to improve their conditions.

Hispanic Americans in Business

Like the Hispanic population itself, the number of Hispanic-owned businesses has grown rapidly during the 1990s and into the twenty-first century. The U.S. Census analysis of business in 1997 (issued in 2001) reported that U.S. Hispanics owned 1.2 million nonfarm businesses that year and employed 1.3 million people. Together, these businesses generated $183.6 billion. This is an estimated growth since 1992 of 30 percent. Overall during that period the rate of growth in U.S. businesses was only about 6.8 percent.

California, Texas, Florida, and New York had the majority of Hispanic businesses in 1997. California had 336,405 Hispanic-owned businesses with a revenue of $52 billion, which comprised 28 percent of Hispanic-owned businesses. Texas had 240,396 Hispanic-owned businesses, Florida had 193,902, and New York had 104,189. The top five cities for Hispanic-owned businesses were Los Angeles, California; Miami, Florida; New York, New York; and Houston and San Antonio, Texas.

Most of these businesses are small businesses with few employees and little in income. Many are operated only part time. Hispanic business owners tend to be dynamic young entrepreneurs. When compared to

Workers packaging tortillas in a factory in San Jose, California, 1979. *Reproduced by permission of the Corbis Corporation (Bellevue).*

nonminority business owners, a larger percentage of Hispanics are running their first business. They have less overall education and less managerial experience. Finally, they are more likely to hire other Hispanics and minorities than nonminority employers.

Things are changing in the U.S. business world because of the boom in the Hispanic population. Business experts estimate that in the year 2000 U.S. Hispanic consumers spent $454 billion and that by 2006 they will spend $634 billion in one year. Many U.S. businesses are at work learning about the different Hispanic groups and what they want to buy. They are also making sure that their employees speak Spanish and can accommodate the needs of Spanish-speak-

ers. The Spanish-language media—television, press, radio, and even Internet providers—has grown huge. This gives Hispanic workers more opportunity to work in mainstream U.S. business or to establish businesses of their own within this rapidly growing section of the U.S. economy.

Hispanic-owned businesses make up a sector of the U.S. economy that will continue to grow in number and productivity. Business ownership will be a career option for a growing number of Hispanic Americans.

Hispanic Americans in Politics

Hispanic Americans have been a part of public service and politics in the United States since the beginning. However, they have had little success at the national level. In 1822 Joseph Marion Hernández became the first Hispanic elected to the U.S. Congress. He represented Florida and the Whig Party. No other Hispanic held national office for the next thirty years. In the entire nineteenth century, only eleven Hispanics were elected to Congress. Nine were from New Mexico, one was from California, and Congressman Hernández was from Florida. From 1900 to the 1950s, a total of fifteen Hispanics served in Congress. Five came from New Mexico, two from Louisiana, and eight were nonvoting representatives from Puerto Rico.

Since the 1960s the number of Hispanic Americans elected to Congress has been steadily increasing. In 1991 there were thirteen Hispanics serving in Congress, and in 2002 there were eighteen. They represented five states: California, Texas, New York, Arizona, Illinois, and New Jersey. Nonvot-

Representatives Linda Sanchez and Loretta Sanchez, the first sisters to serve in the U.S. Congress together, 2002. *Reproduced by permission of AP/Wide World Photos.*

ing representatives came from Puerto Rico, Guam, and the U.S. Virgin Islands.

Since 1976 the Hispanic members of Congress have worked together through the Congressional Hispanic Caucus. The goal of the caucus is to raise awareness of issues affecting Hispanics and to bring solutions before the legislature. It monitors the bills considered by the House and the Senate as well as the policies of the executive branch and legal decisions of the judicial branch. The caucus also includes dues-paying mem-

bers of Congress who are not of Hispanic descent. All in all the caucus includes members from 20 states, Puerto Rico, Guam, and the U.S. Virgin Islands.

There has not been a Hispanic American candidate elected to the U.S. Senate since 1970. In that year New Mexico Democrat Joseph Manuel Montoya won his second and last term. Senator Montoya served from 1964 to 1977. The only other Hispanic American to be elected to the Senate was New Mexico Democrat Dennis Chávez. He

Joseph Manuel Montoya. *Reproduced by permission of the Corbis Corporation (Bellevue).*

served from 1935 to 1962. Both senators Chávez and Montoya served as members of the U.S. House of Representatives before being elected to the Senate.

Over the last century, the majority of Hispanic Americans in local political offices lived in the Southwest, southern Florida, and New York City. Since the 1960s Hispanic candidates have had success in other parts of the country. One reason is that the Hispanic population has grown across the country. Another reason is the Voting Rights Act of 1965. This law helped eliminate obstacles to minority voting. With these and other changes, Hispanics have made their greatest strides forward at the town and city level of government.

The number of Hispanics voted into office at the state and city level has risen more rapidly at the turn of the twentieth century than in the past. In 1998 California elected Cruz Bustamante to be the state's lieutenant governor, the first Hispanic to be elected to a statewide office since 1871. The mayor of San Jose and the sheriff of Los Angeles, both elected in 1998, were Hispanic. That year Colorado elected a Hispanic attorney general, Massachusetts elected three Hispanics to the state House, and Wisconsin elected a Hispanic to its state House.

During the presidential elections in 2000, candidates Al Gore (Democrat) and George W. Bush (Republican) both courted the Hispanic vote. The majority of the Hispanic population lives in five states, California, New York, Florida, Texas, and Illinois, that are central to a presidential election. More than 8 million Hispanics were registered to vote in 2000.

In 2001 Hispanics made gains in mayoral elections nationwide. San Antonio, Texas, elected Ed Garza as mayor. Hartford, Connecticut, and Austin, Texas, elected first-ever Hispanic mayors; Democrat Eddie Perez, a native of Puerto Rico and president of a local community group, won in Hartford, and former city councilman Gus Garcia was elected mayor of Austin. In the democratic primary elections for the governor of Texas in 2002, two Hispanics ran against each other. Former attorney general Dan Morales ran against Laredo businessman Tony Sanchez. They held a much-publicized debate in the Spanish language, which was televised throughout the state. Tony Sanchez won the democratic primaries.

The number of Hispanic Americans in politics is growing. This is due primarily to the fact that Hispanic voters have been going to the polls in increasing numbers. However, in order to increase representation at the national level, obstacles still must be overcome. Poverty, lack of education, language, and fear of drawing attention still keep many eligible voters from registering. Beyond this, the Hispanic community is very diverse and not likely to vote as a bloc. For example, the Cuban Americans in Florida are very conservative as a whole, and more likely to vote Republican than the Mexican Americans in Texas or California. There are issues, however, that are uniting many groups, such as reform in immigration and bilingual education. Many non-Hispanic politicians now recognize the potential power of this large minority group. For this reason, they are now working with Hispanic politicians to make positive changes.

The Education of Hispanic Americans

During the first three hundred years of Spanish exploration and settlement in the New World, most children were educated informally. There were few schools. Most children learned at home and by working in the community. Formal learning, or schooling, did not take hold in society until the 1800s. This was about the same time that Hispanics began to come to the United States. In the United States, schools were first set up for white, Anglo-American children. Hispanic children were not allowed to attend these schools. Eventually, a variety of public, private, and parochial (church) schools were built for Hispanic children. Many of these schools were not very good. There was no college for Hispanics.

Eddie Perez, mayor of Hartford, Connecticut. *Reproduced by permission of AP/Wide World Photos.*

In the twentieth century, public education became the primary form of schooling for the Hispanic community. Until 1965 Hispanics continued to attend segregated schools that were often of poor quality. Since 1965 Hispanics have continued to get their education from public schools. However, since that time segregation has not been legal.

Even with the changes, Hispanic American children do not get the same education as other American children. Schools in Hispanic communities still often lack resources. A full range of educational opportunities is not always available. The diversity of the Hispanic population in terms of national origin and socioeconomic background often makes solutions difficult to find.

Education during the Spanish and Mexican Periods, 1540–1848

From 1540 to 1821, education in what is now the American Southwest and California was directed by the Spanish Crown, the Catholic Church, and the Spanish settlers. At that time Spanish children learned three things. They learned how to make a living, how to take care of a household, and how to satisfy personal needs. This education did not take place in schools, however. Most Spanish children were taught at home and on the job in their villages and towns. Some learned to read from available books, but much of the learning involved practical skills. Children also learned through storytelling, plays, and traveling puppet shows. In the parish churches, they learned about Spanish politics and culture, the Catholic religion, and morals.

During this period of Spanish control, monks established the first schools in the Southwest. However, these mission schools were for the Native Americans of the area, not for the Spaniards. These schools were built to teach the Spanish language and culture as well as the Catholic religion to the native people. After learning the language, Native Americans learned about Spanish customs and laws. They learned to dress in the Spanish style. They learned to raise livestock and farm like the Europeans. Many learned building and furniture-making skills. Most important to the monks, however, was religious education. Native Americans learned Catholic beliefs, prayers, and religious rituals.

Mission schools served many purposes. One goal was certainly to help improve Native American living conditions. Even so, the education of Native Americans probably served the Spanish more than it did the native people. The Catholic Church was able to replace the original Native American religions and assert control over a new population. The Spanish language and culture replaced the Native American language and culture. Native Americans who accepted Spanish ways were easier to get along with. They usually did not resist Spanish settlement or attack Spanish settlers.

During the late 1700s and early 1800s, the family, village, and parish church continued to educate Spanish settlers. However, during this same period, mission schools for Native Americans became less important. The number of Spanish settlers was growing and the focus turned to serving them. In areas where settlers were concentrated in large groups, they began to build frontier schools.

The power of missions among the Native Americans and growing population of mixed-race *mestizos* decreased even more when Mexico gained its independence in 1821. The founders of Mexico believed that everyone, including Native Americans, were equal. They acted to put an end to distinctions based on race or class. They also moved to reduce the power of the Catholic Church. The new government believed that the church had acquired too much land and wealth. It also found that the church oppressed Native Americans. Government institutions replaced religious ones. Public schools were one of these new institutions.

Most of the people who lived in the frontier had had little contact with Spain or

Mexico City, the centers of their culture. For this reason the new frontier public schools tried to preserve Spanish and Mexican political, economic, and cultural values. They also focused on teaching basic reading, writing, and arithmetic skills. Spanish and Mexican governors in Texas, New Mexico, and California worked hard to build a strong public school system in their areas. Even so, most settlers were used to educating their children at home. For this reason, even though the number of schools grew, most children were still educated in traditional ways.

At home on the ranch and in the *pueblos* (towns), families taught their children values and traditions. These included obedience, respect, political values, religious beliefs, and cultural traditions. Children also learned survival skills. In the household they learned how to cook, wash clothing, and make candles, soap, cloth, and wine. On the farm or ranch, they learned how to plant crops, raise cattle and sheep, and make tools and other useful items. In church they learned religious values and customs.

The Education of Hispanics in the United States

When the United States took control of the Southwest, it introduced new political, economic, cultural, and social institutions. Anglo ideals began to replace Hispanic ideals. At home Hispanic families continued to educate their children in the Spanish language and Hispanic culture. But, the school became a place to teach Hispanic children Anglo-American ways. This was especially true in schools built by the state and Protestant churches. As time went by, it also became true in private schools and those built by the Catholic Church. By Americanizing Hispanic children, school leaders felt they were better preparing the youngsters to fit into society. The problem was that they threatened to destroy the Hispanic culture and leave Hispanics outsiders in an Anglo society.

The Early Years of Public Schools

American public schools established in the late 1800s sought to reach all children living in an area. However, racial discrimination and political problems in the American Southwest slowed this process among Hispanics. By 1900 the education of Hispanic Americans was clearly inferior to that of other Americans. There were four major reasons for this: (1) Hispanic children did not have equal access to public schools; (2) Hispanic children could only attend segregated schools; (3) Hispanics were not involved in making decisions about their schools; and (4) Hispanic cultural and language needs were not addressed.

The first schools in the American Southwest were built for white Anglo-American children. Discrimination and indifference blocked Hispanic children from attending these schools. In some places Anglo parents and local politicians simply would not allow Hispanics to go to these schools. In other places schools were built near Anglo neighborhoods and far from Hispanic neighborhoods. Without transportation Hispanic children found it difficult to reach the school. When Hispanics were able to overcome these obstacles, they were forced to study a foreign culture in a foreign language.

Schools were finally made available to Hispanics in California in the 1850s. Texas

The fourth grade class at the Drachman School in Tucson, Arizona, c. 1913. *Reproduced courtesy of the Arizona Historical Society Library.*

provided public schools for Hispanic children living in cities in the 1860s and for those living in the country in the 1880s. New Mexico and Arizona did not provide any schools for Hispanic children until 1872. Most of these schools were in segregated school systems. In segregated systems some schools were for only white Anglo children and others were for only Hispanic children. In some cases the segregation was caused by settlement patterns. White Anglos tended to live together and so did Hispanics. Neighborhood schools attracted only one group. In other cases school officials used race to separate children. In these communities, no matter where they lived, white Anglo children were sent to white Anglo schools and Hispanic children were sent to Hispanic schools.

By 1900 because Anglo Americans were increasingly in the majority, they could force segregation on Hispanic Americans. They could also dominate the decision-making process for schools. In the early years of American rule in the Southwest, Hispanics had served on school boards and as school superintendents. However, in the late 1800s, Anglos passed laws to make it difficult for Hispanic Americans to vote and serve in public positions. Anglo school leaders gave little effort to hiring Hispanic teachers and administrators. Eventually, even in areas where Hispanics were in the majority, the teachers, administrators, and school board members were almost all Anglos.

Under Anglo domination Hispanic public schools set out to Americanize Hispanic children. They taught Anglo-American political, social, and moral values in English. Eventually, Hispanic cultural traditions, Catholic values, and the Spanish language were completely excluded from schools. The stated purpose of these policies was that they would help Hispanic children better enter and succeed in mainstream society. However, they also served to suggest that the dominant culture was superior and the Hispanic culture inferior.

The Education of Hispanics in the Twenty-First Century

In the twentieth century, public schooling has become the main source of education for all Americans, including Hispanic Americans. At the same time, public education for Hispanic Americans has continued to suffer from the problems of the previous century. Changes in access, segregation, the number of Hispanic decision makers, and the focus on Anglo-American goals have come slowly and with difficulty. The slow progress has left many Hispanic children poorly served by their schools and poorly prepared for success in society.

In the 1900s more and more Mexican American children were able to go to public school. This increased access was due in large part to some changes in their community. Mexican Americans began to move to the cities in large numbers. Once there they were able to find stable jobs. As they learned more about public education, they wanted it more for their children.

Proof of increased access can be seen in statistics from this period. In New Mexico in 1900, for example, less than 50 percent of Hispanic children between the ages of five and seventeen attended public schools. By 1930 attendance had increased to 74 percent. In Texas during the same period, Hispanic attendance in schools grew from 18 percent to 50 percent. After World War II this trend continued. By 1980 over 91 percent of school-aged Hispanic children were enrolled in public schools. There were still gaps, however, especially in areas with large numbers of undocumented workers.

Hispanic children did gain access to schools during this period, but for much of the twentieth century their schools have been separate and unequal. The segregation of schools began in the mid-1800s, but it expanded during the 1900s. Before the 1930s segregation grew primarily within existing communities in the Southwest. By the 1950s the practice had spread to the entire country. At first it was confined to elementary schools, because there were few Hispanic children who wanted to attend high school. Later, as the number of Hispanic Americans in high school grew, segregated high schools were built. Since the 1960s, laws have made segregation based on race illegal. However, because Hispanic

Nora Bustios teaches at the J. F. Oyster Bilingual Elementary School in Washington, D.C., 2002.
Reproduced by permission of AP/Wide World Photos.

Americans often live in close-knit communities in large cities, their children continue to find themselves in separate schools. Even as the twenty-first century begins, Hispanics are more likely to be in separate schools than any other ethnic group.

In most cases Hispanic schools in the era of segregation were inferior to schools for Anglos. Buildings were often older and in disrepair. Equipment was poor or lacking. The tax money spent to educate each student was much lower than for the average Anglo student. Finally, teachers in these schools were often poorly trained, had inadequate qualifications, and had less experience than in other schools. In some districts only new teachers or those who received low ratings were sent to Hispanic schools.

Another serious problem faced by Hispanic American school children was discrimination. On a personal level, Hispanic students encountered discrimination from Anglo students, teachers, and administrators. Hispanic students also faced discrimination in testing and tracking policies. Tests used to determine the learning skills and disabilities of Hispanic American students were usually in English. They were also biased toward mainstream American culture. For these reasons many Hispanic children were incorrectly labeled "retarded" or "learning disabled." Others were directed away from college prep

A Latino Outreach student learns about fractions using a computer program at Langston Chapel Elementary School in Statesboro, Georgia, 2001. Latino Outreach is a Georgia Southern University program that uses college students to help teach Hispanic children English. *Reproduced by permission of AP/Wide World Photos.*

classes toward vocational and general classes. These practices in elementary and high schools created large gaps between Hispanic and Anglo educational achievement.

The education of Hispanic Americans in the twentieth century also suffered because of a focus on Americanizing these students. The curriculum for Hispanic children originally focused on the three Rs, reading, writing, and arithmetic. It also included some socialization. However, in the early 1900s, this began to change. By 1930 the curriculum for Hispanic elementary schools emphasized the three Cs, the common American culture, American civics, and command of English. In high schools the

curriculum focused on vocational and other practical studies. Americanizing Hispanic students became more important than educating them.

During the era of protest in the 1960s, Hispanics began to react against policies that gave no value to their culture and native language. They fought for a bilingual/bicultural curriculum for their school children. In 1974 the U.S. Congress passed the Equal Educational Opportunity Act. This law sought to assure equality in public schools by making available education in Spanish to Hispanic students who had limited English skills. The Supreme Court and the president also took action to allow American children

147

to study in their native language and to get help in learning English. Many state governments soon added laws to support bilingual/bicultural education.

On June 2, 1998, California voters passed Proposition 227, which banned bilingual classroom education and English as a second language (ESL) programs, replacing them with a one-year intensive English immersion program for students with limited abilities in English. Although the proposition passed by a majority of voters, a solid majority of Hispanic voters voted against it. A federal judge denied challenges to the proposition in July of that year, and 227 went into effect in California schools in August.

Hispanics have a higher dropout rate than any other group in the United States. In 1997, about 25 percent of Hispanic students dropped out of school compared to 13.4 percent of black students and 7.6 percent of white students. By 2000 Hispanic girls were dropping out at a rate of 26 percent, while Hispanic boys were dropping out at an alarming rate of 31 percent. The proportion of students who were born outside of the United States who drop out of school is far higher than the dropout rate of Hispanic students who were born in the country. Many educators and parents are concerned that students with poor English skills are left out in school. They do not have equal access to the education as English-speaking students do and many give up. The people who defend the English-only classrooms say they think it is the only way that these students will learn the language and go on to succeed in this country. The debate continues well into the early 2000s.

In higher education, anti-affirmative action (policies aiming to increase opportunity for minorities and women) rulings have caused colleges and universities throughout the nation to change their admissions programs (how they decide who will be admitted to the school). The matter of affirmative action in college admissions went through the courts for several years around the turn of the century. In the summer of 2002 the U.S. Court of Appeals upheld the right of the University of Michigan to use affirmative action policies in its admissions.

Generally, Hispanics are increasingly prosperous and well-educated in the early 2000s although, for a variety of reasons, not at the level of other groups in the United States. With increased voting power due to the increase in Hispanic population and opportunities due to the huge market of Hispanic consumers being targeted by businesses, the next decade should bring about significant improvements in access to education and jobs for U.S. Hispanic people.

10

The Languages of Hispanic Americans

FACT FOCUS

- The Spanish language has been and continues to be one of the most important unifying factors for Hispanic Americans. Yet, even though most Hispanic American communities speak Spanish, there are many different varieties of the Spanish language among them.
- Mexican-Spanish has the largest number of speakers within the Hispanic American population. Next in order are the Spanish dialects of Puerto Rico, Cuba, and Central America.
- Mexican Spanish contains many Native American words. This Spanish has been spoken in what is now the United States for over 350 years.
- The Spanish spoken by Central American immigrants varies a great deal. Some speak a Spanish similar to Mexican Spanish. Some speak a Spanish similar to Caribbean Spanish. Others speak another distinct form of Spanish.
- Caribbean Spanish can be recognized by its pronunciation. Caribbean-Spanish speakers are known for swallowing their final consonants.
- Hispanics tend to hold onto Spanish longer than other immigrant groups hold onto their languages. This may be because many Hispanics want to preserve their culture through their language.
- A majority of Hispanics born or raised in the United States speak English. It is either their native or second language.
- Within the Hispanic community, there is a special form of English known as Hispanic English.
- Many Hispanic Americans can speak both Spanish and English easily. These bilinguals can switch back and forth between the languages without problems.

WORDS TO KNOW

bilingual: speaking two languages easily.

code-switching: when a bilingual person changes from one language to another in the same conversation or even the same sentence.

fluent: speaking a language easily, without hesitation.

native language: the first language that a child learns, usually at home from her or his parents.

standard English: the variety of English accepted as correct by most English speakers. It is usually the English heard on television and radio and seen in newspapers.

One of the key cultural elements that brings together the Hispanic population of the United States is the Spanish language. Spanish was first brought to the New World by Columbus's men. It soon spread to become the common language of traders and settlers in Spanish America. It was used by native Spaniards and *criollos* (Spaniards born in the New World). It also became the language of *mestizos* (those of mixed Spanish and Native American heritage) and *mulattoes* (those of mixed Spanish and African heritage). Eventually, just as the Spanish people were changed by contact with the Native American people and land, so was the language. In some places it stayed close to the native Spanish born in Spain. In other places it became more of a criollo Spanish, a new Spanish born in a New World. In yet other places, it mixed with Native American or African languages to become a mestizo or mulatto Spanish. Today, most Hispanics speak Spanish, but many varieties of that language.

Varieties of Spanish

The variety of Spanish spoken by a particular Hispanic American community depends on the community's origin and its surroundings in the United States. Each immigrant group has brought along its own regional form of Spanish. When immigrants from the same country and social class decide to live in the same neighborhood, they use and preserve their own regional forms of Spanish. New immigrants follow the same pattern and the regional Spanish community grows.

Most of the Hispanics living in rural areas of the United States come from rural areas of Mexico. For this reason a rural Mexican form of Spanish is common in American farm and ranch communities. In cities many diverse Hispanic groups live near one another. Here a variety of Spanish language forms compete to be the dominant form. Usually, the largest and most economically powerful Hispanic group sets the common language. In the Southwest and some midwestern cities, Mexican American Spanish is the common language. In South Florida, Cuban American Spanish dominates. In most northeastern cities, it is Puerto Rican Spanish. In Chicago there is no clear dominant form of Spanish. Instead, Hispanics speak several varieties of Spanish.

The forms of Spanish spoken in the United States are (from the largest community down) Mexican, Puerto Rican, Cuban, and

Central American. Among Central American immigrants to the United States, Nicaraguans and Salvadorans are the most numerous. Another group, the Dominican population of New York City, is rapidly growing. Dominican Spanish is similar to Puerto Rican Spanish. Even so, speakers of each can identify differences. Large numbers of Colombians are found in Miami, New York City, and elsewhere.

There are also several other small but close-knit Spanish-speaking groups in the United States. Their Spanish does not fit under the four main Spanish-speaking groups. These other Spanish speakers include Sephardic (Jewish) Spanish speakers in New York, Miami, and other cities. Also included are the *Isleños* of southeastern Louisiana, descendants of Canary Island settlers who arrived in the late 1700s, and the pre-Castro Cubans (those who left Cuban before Fidel Castro's revolution of 1959) of Key West and Tampa.

Mexican Spanish

Mexican Spanish has been spoken in what is now the United States for over 350 years. New varieties of Mexican Spanish came to the United States as the country expanded west. Still more varieties have come in the twentieth century with Mexican immigration. Each new group has brought differences to this form of Spanish. Overall, however, the similarities have held the language together as Mexican Spanish.

Old Spanish Forms in the United States

Spanish speakers settled in New Mexico in the 1600s, shortly after Juan de Oñate's

expedition traveled there. They have lived there ever since. When Mexico won its independence from Spain, the lives of these Spanish speakers hardly changed. When the region became U.S. territory after the Mexican War, there were again few changes. Spanish remained the dominant language in New Mexico and Colorado until large groups of English-speaking settlers pushed west in the 1800s. Even today, however, it is possible to find speakers of seventeenth-century Spanish spoken in these two states.

Descendants of the earliest Spanish settlers in New Mexico and Colorado came to refer to themselves as "Spaniards." They rejected labels such as "Mexican," "Latin," and "Chicano." In its purest form, the speech of these "Spaniards" provides a window to the past. They offer a taste of the language of Spanish settlers during the era of exploration and conquest. The speakers of this old Spanish use words and expressions that have disappeared from other varieties of Spanish. They also use fewer Native American words than does modern Mexican Spanish.

There is another group of U.S. Spanish speakers that is little known and that is rapidly disappearing. It represents a later form of Mexican Spanish. Long before Texas joined the United States, mestizo (mixed race) soldiers from Mexico were sent to eastern Texas. They were to fortify the border between Texas and the French territory of Louisiana. In the early 1700s, Spain set up outposts at Los Aes (present-day San Augustine, Texas), at Nacogdoches, Texas, and at Los Adaes, near modern-day Robeline, Louisiana. By the 1750s these settlements were well established and the settlers knew no other home.

Spain had settled eastern Texas to create a buffer zone between French settlements in Louisiana and Spanish settlements in Mexico. In a 1763 treaty, however, the French gave Louisiana to Spain. The buffer zone was no longer needed, and the settlers were called back to San Antonio, Texas. They protested but most were forced to return to Texas. Once there they were treated poorly and given bad land. Immediately, they began to plan a return trip to the only home they had known. Many settlers managed to move back to eastern Texas. They founded the town of Nacogdoches in 1779 at the site of an old Spanish mission. The French reclaimed Louisiana in 1800, and the United States purchased the Louisiana Territory in 1803. Through both changes the Spanish settlers remained.

When Mexico won independence from Spain in 1821, only three large Spanish-speaking settlements remained in Texas: San Antonio, Bahía del Espíritu Santo (Goliad), and Nacogdoches. A large wave of English speakers would soon flood Texas and overwhelm the Spanish settlements. Despite this flood of English speakers, tiny pockets of Spanish-speaking residents survived. A tiny settlement near Zwolle, Louisiana, bears the name Ebarb, a name shared by some residents. Ebarb is an English version of Ybarbo. Antonio Gil Ybarbo was the leader of the settlers who returned to their homes in this area more than two hundred years ago.

Today, their small communities can be found deep in the pine woods of northern Louisiana and eastern Texas. Their old variety of Spanish captures the rustic life they have led in this part of the United States.

Two generations ago there were still people who only spoke this form of Spanish living in rural northwestern Louisiana. A generation ago the number of Spanish speakers in these communities was still high. Currently, however, only a handful of the oldest residents speak Spanish.

The Language of Mexican Immigrants

Additional groups of Mexican Spanish speakers became part of the United States after the Mexican War in the 1840s when Texas and the Southwest became a part of the United States. The speech of these first Hispanic Americans represented the northern Mexican form of Spanish. Even with the new U.S. border, migration back and forth from Mexico continued. Until the turn of the twentieth century, the Spanish spoken in the southwestern United States was identical to that of Mexico.

The U.S.-Mexican border began to tighten up during the first decades of the 1900s. This created a separation between Mexicans and Mexican Americans. Separation often leads to language change. The gap between Mexican Spanish speakers in each country was widened in the 1930s. At that time American farms and businesses recruited workers from central and southern areas of Mexico. Workers came from Guanajuato, Michoacán, and Guerrero. They spoke a different form of Mexican Spanish. This early program attracted more central and southern Mexicans to come to the United States to work as migrant workers. Many of these Mexicans settled in northern cities such as Chicago, Detroit, Milwaukee, and Cleveland. Because of these patterns of immigration, Mexican Americans in the northern

United States speak the Spanish of southern Mexico. Mexican Americans in the southern United States speak the Spanish of northern Mexico.

Early Mexican immigrants to the American Southwest settled on farms and ranches far from the cities. However, during the mid-1900s a growing number of northern Mexicans moved to cities in the American Southwest. Here, an urban form of their language began to evolve. The newcomers created new words and revived old ones to express their views on their new home. Among these were negative terms for their new neighbors. One such word was *pocho,* a very negative word used to label a Mexican born in the United States. Pochos were people who had lost their Mexican identity in the American setting. The old Spanish word *gabacho,* once used for the French, was revived to label Americans. Another old word *bolillo,* a type of white bread, was also used for Americans.

Mexicans and Mexican Americans began to use the word *chicano* to refer to themselves. This was an old colonial word from the time when *México* was pronounced "Méshico" and *mexicano* was pronounced "meshicano." In Mexico, chicano carries a negative value. In the United States, while it is not accepted by some, it is worn like a badge of honor by others. Today, the term chicano is most often used by groups who helped define the chicano identity, especially social and political activists.

Within Mexico there are many regional dialects, just as there are with English in the United States. In the United States, however, Mexican Spanish forms show the greatest differences between urban and rural

areas. The pronunciation of Mexican Spanish in the United States reflects the northern and southern Mexican dialects.

The vocabulary of Mexican Spanish differs from textbook versions of Spanish. Over a period of four hundred years, the original Spanish that came to Mexico has mixed with and absorbed a large number of Native American words. Most of these Native American words come from Nahuatl, a language of the Aztecs. They refer to plants and animals found in rural areas of Mexico or to tools and objects used in rustic life. In the United States some of these words are replaced by English words or just not used. Nahuatl words that have become a part of general Spanish are *tomate, aguacate, chocolate,* and *chile.* These same words have become the English words tomato, avocado, chocolate, and chili (the type of pepper).

Central American Spanish

People often refer to Central America as if it were a single country. Indeed, five of these countries, Guatemala, El Salvador, Honduras, Nicaragua, and Costa Rica, were united for a brief time. After gaining independence from Spain in the 1820s, these five tiny countries formed the Central American Union. They hoped to become a regional power. The union was never really successful, and it was dissolved once and for all in 1854. Since then the countries have gone their own ways.

Even during the colonial period there were clear differences in the Spanish spoken in the various regions of Central America. These differences were not only to do with geography. For instance, the Spanish of Costa Rica in the south is most similar to the Spanish of Guatemala in the north. Guatemalan Spanish also resembles the Spanish of Mexico's Yucatán region. Both regions have been influenced by their Mayan heritage. Honduran and Salvadoran Spanish blend together smoothly, but they differ from Guatemalan Spanish. Nicaraguan Spanish is also rather different. In addition, Costa Rican Spanish bears little resemblance to the Spanish of its neighbor Panama. Panama used to be a province of Colombia. Today, it is known for speech similar to Colombia's coastal areas.

In the United States, the Spanish spoken by Central American immigrants reflects their social and economic backgrounds, their native country, and its history. With Nicaraguans the speech of the middle and professional class sets the standard. In many ways the pronunciation of Nicaraguan Spanish is similar to that of Cuban and Puerto Rican Spanish. Each of these groups often does not pronounce final consonants. In several other ways, though, Nicaraguan speech differs from the speech of Cubans and Puerto Ricans. These differences create the unique accent of the *nicas,* as Nicaraguans sometimes call themselves.

Most Salvadorans in the United States have come from the poorest social groups with little formal education. Few get additional education in the United States. For this reason the Salvadoran Spanish found in the United States has many of the words and grammar features of the poor and uneducated. Salvadoran Spanish is closer to Mexican Spanish than to the varieties of Caribbean Spanish. This is due in part to similar histories. Salvadoran and Mexicans share many

vocabulary items from the Native American languages Nahuatl and Mayan.

All Central Americans share a pronoun that is strange to other Spanish speakers in the United States. The informal form of "you" in most varieties of Spanish is *tú. Tú* is used in certain social situations, usually among friends or peers, and for children. Central Americans use the plural and more formal *vos* instead. This pronoun has its own verb form. Some Central Americans in the United States consciously avoid using *vos* with other Hispanics. They may want to hide their origin or to avoid misunderstandings. Others cling to this word precisely because of its strong regional identity.

Spanish of Caribbean Origin

Puerto Ricans, Cubans, and Dominicans can easily identify their own form of Spanish. Still, outsiders see more similarities than differences among these Caribbean Spanish language varieties. Pronunciation is the single most important unifying factor. Caribbeans are known for "swallowing" the final consonants of words. This slurring of final sounds also gives the impression that Caribbean Spanish is spoken faster than other varieties. One typical example is the final "s." The final "s" is clearly pronounced in most Mexican and Central American forms of Spanish. In the Caribbean, however, it sounds more like an English "h."

Most of the other unique features of Caribbean Spanish are related to vocabulary. They usually identify everyday items in the island cultures. Some words such as *ají* (hot or sweet pepper), *maní* (peanut), and *caimán* (alligator) have spread to other

Spanish-speaking countries. Others are used only by Caribbeans. Several words are unique to Puerto Rico. Most come from food items and cultural practices. Puerto Ricans eat *habichuelas* (pink beans) or *gandules* (greenish brown beans) with rice. A *jíbaro* is a "hillbilly" from the central mountains of the island. In the past the term was used negatively to describe rustics who failed to adapt to city customs. Now because of a Puerto Rican cultural revival, *jíbaro* is used with respect.

Cuban Spanish also contains many local words. Similar to the Puerto Rican *jíbaro,* Cubans have the *guajiro,* a country dweller. The popular Cuban song "Guantanamera" immortalizes the *guajiro.* In the Cuban American community, a well-known food item is the *sandwich cubano* and a popular drink is the *café cubano,* a tiny cup of espresso with a lot of sugar.

Holding onto Spanish

Hispanics have tended to hold on to their traditional language longer than other ethnic groups in the United States. There are several reasons for this. One is that the first Hispanics did not choose to join English-speaking America. The original Mexican Americans did not move to the United States. They were caught in a tide of westward expansion. They soon found themselves outnumbered by English-speaking newcomers. Many Mexicans who did immigrate to the Southwest kept in close contact with their homeland. This contact encouraged them to keep Spanish alive.

Many Hispanics have held on to Spanish because they believed that their stay in the United States would be temporary. These include many exiles from political and social problems. During the 1960s and 1970s, many Cuban professionals came to the United States to escape the Castro regime. These "temporary" exiles insisted that their children learn and use Spanish. They were confident that they would soon return to Cuba. Now, more than forty years after the Cuban Revolution, young Cuban Americans continue to learn and use Spanish. They use Spanish more often and English less often than any other Hispanic group.

The Nicaraguan community in the United States is similar to the Cuban community. The Sandinista Revolution of 1979 brought several hundred thousand Nicaraguans to the United States. Most of these exiles were from the professional and middle classes. Like the Cuban exiles, these Nicaraguans planned to return to their homeland. Thus, although their children learn English in school, they also speak Spanish.

Among Salvadorans the situation is different. Most come from the rural poor. In the United States, they tend to live and work in Spanish-speaking neighborhoods. They tend to work at jobs that do not require learning English. Even so, young Salvadorans who go to school often shift to English faster than the young people of other Hispanic groups. They usually have their parents' support.

Spanish in the United States

According to the U.S. Census of 2000, the United States is more multilingual (speaking more than one language) today than it has been for a century. Spanish speakers in the nation, who grew by more

Bilingual aisles at the Tianguis market in Montebello, California, 1987. *Reproduced by permission of AP/Wide World Photos.*

than 50 percent from 1990 to 2000, account for most of the change. Nearly 27 million Hispanics in the United States over the age of five speak Spanish; 86 percent of U.S. Hispanics say Spanish is their first language. An estimated one out of every ten people in the nation speaks Spanish, and the United States has the fifth largest Spanish-speaking population in the world.

The traditional immigration patterns of the United States from the past century—when immigrants mainly from Europe entered the country and usually lost the use of their native languages within a generation—do not seem to apply to the Hispanic community in the United States. Rather than replacing the Spanish language for English, U.S. Hispanics appear to be bringing Spanish into the mainstream culture in a way that is unique in U.S. history.

In the early 2000s, businesses are becoming bilingual; politicians up to the level of president are speaking in Spanish to court the ever-growing Hispanic vote. Spanish-language television, radio, Internet sites, and press are booming. ATM machines and many corporate voice mail systems throughout the nation are increasingly multilingual. Studies have found that a majority of Hispanic people regard the preservation of their language as a high priority.

Spanish lives in many forms in the United States. It is on the lips of new immigrants and longtime residents. It is the language of daily activities among the Mexican Americans of the Southwest, the Puerto Ricans of New York City, and the Cubans of Miami. It is the community language and a part of the foundation of Hispanic culture. More and more, the value of the Hispanic culture and its language has prompted non-Hispanics to learn Spanish. Large numbers of non-Hispanics in New York City, south Florida, and the Southwest have learned Spanish. The language is no longer the exclusive property of Hispanics.

Hispanics in English-Speaking America

English Use among Hispanics

The majority of Hispanic Americans speak English to some extent. Those born or raised in the United States speak English fluently. Some use it as a home language. Others use it as a strong second language. Arrivals from Spanish-speaking countries also learn English. How much English they learn depends on several factors. How old are they when they arrive? How much English have they already studied? How important is English at home or work? Do children in their family bring English home from school?

Hispanic children may grow up speaking standard American English. Or, like those who learn the language when they are older, they may speak a variety called Hispanic English. Second-language learners who learn English as teenagers or adults usually have an accent. This is often true no matter how fluent they become. Even in bilingual communities where most children learn English in childhood, there is often a slight accent or special style to the English. When the speaker is Hispanic this accent and style is called Hispanic English.

There are several reasons why children born in the United States might speak a form of Hispanic English. In large bilingual communities, Hispanic English may be the form that they hear most often. The more they hear and use Hispanic English, the stronger it becomes in the community. Like other ethnic groups, Hispanics can hold onto their accents for many generations. The accents usually fade only after the ethnic community mixes into the mainstream society. The mixing includes people marrying outside the group and children going to schools with children from other groups.

Over the years the mainstream American society has viewed Hispanic English negatively. They have judged it a form that needs to be corrected. More recently linguists have studied Hispanic English and how it is used. They have found that it serves a valuable role in keeping the Hispanic community together.

The shift from Spanish to English affects all Hispanic groups in the United States. A change in language affects their culture. By holding on to an accent in their English, Hispanics can resist being pulled completely into the American melting pot. They can keep some of their Hispanic identity.

According to research, many Hispanics change from standard English to Hispanic English when they go from a mainstream community to a Hispanic community. Activists and politicians have found that they are more successful when they use Hispanic English in the neighborhoods. Teachers and community leaders debate the value of Hispanic English. Some feel that it is a barrier to economic and social advancement. Others believe that society should become more accepting of different language forms.

Whether Hispanic or standard English, Hispanic Americans use their English more as they begin to spend more time in the mainstream society. As they live and work with non-Hispanics, English becomes more important. Eventually, for some, Spanish becomes a less important part of their Hispanic identity. They speak English in most of their activities, even though they may still hang on strongly to their Hispanic identity. Among some older members of the Hispanic community, the switch to English is seen as a failure, a loss of culture. But those who believe in social integration (assimilation, or blending into the mainstream society) see the switch as a positive action.

Bilingualism

Hispanics in the United States face a choice. Their heritage is Spanish-speaking. Their environment is English-speaking.

Actress and director Carmen Zapata, shown here portraying Isabela la Católica in *Moments to Be Remembered,* was the founder and director of the Bilingual Foundation for the Arts in Los Angeles. *Reproduced by permission of Arte Público Press.*

Which language do they choose: Spanish, English, or both? To choose Spanish is to limit themselves to Hispanic communities. To choose English is to risk losing part of their Hispanic heritage. Bilingualism, or speaking both languages easily, is the answer for some generations of Hispanics. These bilingual Hispanic Americans move easily from Spanish to English and back, depending upon the situation. They are also bicultural. They feel comfortable in the Hispanic culture and the mainstream American culture. This bilingual/bicultural segment of the Hispanic community is large and it gives the Hispanic population some unique qualities.

The shift from Spanish to English among Hispanic Americans follows a common pattern. New immigrants tend to move to city neighborhoods or country areas where there are already Hispanic communities. There, they learn some English, but they can usually get by with Spanish. In isolated rural areas and strong, Spanish-speaking urban neighborhoods, Hispanics can retain their native language for a long time. In areas with more contact with outsiders, the children of newcomers may use both languages fairly easily. This bilingualism may persist for one or several generations, depending on conditions.

The length of this bilingual period is decreasing for many immigrant groups. Ethnic neighborhoods are not as tight as before. There are more marriages between different ethnic groups. The power of English-language radio, television, and other media also speed up the shift to English. In many cases only one generation is truly bilingual. The newcomers use primarily the native language and their grandchildren use primarily English. Only the second generation easily uses both.

Switching Languages

Bilinguals have the valuable ability to communicate comfortably in two worlds. They can choose the language appropriate to a situation. In a Hispanic community among Spanish speakers discussing Hispanic topics, they can converse in Spanish. In a mainstream setting among English speakers discussing general topics, they can interact in English.

In the large Hispanic bilingual community a unique phenomenon occurs. In a conversation of fluent bilinguals, speakers

Shoppers looking for bargains along Broadway in downtown Los Angeles, 2001. New immigrants tend to move to areas where there are already Hispanic communities. *Reproduced by permission of AP/Wide World Photos.*

often switch rapidly from one language to another and then back. Linguists call this code-switching. Here, "code" refers to the language. One type of language switch occurs at a logical break in the conversation. For example, a speaker switches from Spanish to English when answering the phone or welcoming someone new to the conversation. These switches are not always conscious, but they are almost always short and informal. They serve to establish solidarity and intimacy with other bilingual speakers.

In the United States, a common case of code-switching is using Spanish phrases in the middle of a conversation in English. In these situations English is used as a neutral, standard language. It is spoken by everyone and carries no ethnic value. Spanish is the "special" language that is used to express Hispanic cultural solidarity.

The most striking type of language shifting is the switch in the middle of a sentence. This occurs in many bilingual conversations. The speaker begins a sentence in Spanish and finishes in English or vice versa. Such combinations baffle outsiders. Spanish speakers do not understand the English half of the conversation. English speakers do not understand the Spanish half. Foreign-language learners get lost at the switch. Some observers see this type of switching as evidence that both languages are weak in the bilingual. The solution, they claim, is to drop the weakened Spanish so

Rolando Hinojosa. *Reproduced by permission of Arte Público Press.*

the speaker can at least learn to speak English correctly. Shifting languages in the middle of the sentence has been called "Spanglish" or *pocho*. These words have had negative values in the past. Code switching among Hispanic Americans has been criticized. However, it is actually a natural phenomenon. It occurs in many bilingual communities throughout the world. For instance, Gibraltar is a British possession on the southern tip of Spain. Here, Spanish-English bilinguals switch languages in the same way as Hispanic Americans.

After speaking, Hispanic bilinguals may not remember where they switched languages. They may not even remember switching at all. This is not evidence of confusion. It is not a sign that bilinguals cannot keep the two languages apart. They can and do. Proof is that bilinguals do not switch with

people who are not bilingual. Bilinguals just make use of all the tools available to them in a conversation. When they switch, both the Spanish and English parts of the sentence are grammatically correct. When a switch would break grammar rules, they do not switch. So, in the end the transition from one language to another is smooth. Each half of the sentence is acceptable in that language.

Researchers do not yet understand why bilinguals switch in the middle of a sentence. At times they cannot find the word they need in one language so they switch to the other. Sometimes a name triggers the switch. The switch then pulls the rest of the sentence into the new language.

Bilingual language switching is not only a way of speaking. It is also a way of writing. The use of Spanish-English switches is increasing in literature by bilingual writers. It is most often used in poetry because of its focus on language, but it is also found in novels and stories about the life of Hispanic Americans. Rolando Hinojosa is one of the best-known novelists to use language switching. *Mi querido Rafa* is an example. Many important poets and playwrights also use language switching to capture the real language of the Hispanic American community.

During the 1990s, some parts of the United States tried to forcibly put a stop to the widespread use of the Spanish language in the country. These people formed "English-only" organizations and got legislation passed in many states that proclaimed English to be the nation's only language. The people of California voted for an end to bilingual education in the public schools that had been aimed at helping children who spoke other languages to learn.

But the reality is that the Spanish language has already taken hold in many parts of the nation. The use of Spanglish, too, is gaining new legitimacy and serves as a reflection of the mix of people and cultures within the United States. Spanglish is a fitting language for the border culture that exists in Texas, Arizona, New Mexico, and California, where the two cultures, U.S. and Mexican, have always exchanged ways of life. It is just as prevalent in southern Florida, where Cuban and Puerto Rican Spanish meets southern American English. In some schools, Hispanic children are taught to write freely with a mixture of both English and Spanish. Some educators believe this helps them to become more fluent in both languages and more able to express themselves in general. In Albuquerque, New Mexico, one radio station has welcomed Spanglish by changing to a completely bilingual format. The radio announcers switch back and forth randomly between Spanish and English without translating either one.

A U.S. Form of Spanish

It is often asked if there is a uniquely "U.S." variety of Spanish. In general the answer is no. Spanish in the United States continues to be influenced by the speaker's country of origin: Mexican, Puerto Rican, Cuban, or others. Even in cities where more than one large Hispanic group is found, one form of Spanish usually dominates. In a few cities, such as Chicago, more than one variety of Spanish can be found on radio and television. But, even here, the media Spanish has little effect on the Spanish spoken in neighborhoods.

The lack of a unique U.S. Spanish variety is not negative. Spanish in the United States is increasing. More people are speaking Spanish and they are speaking more varieties. U.S. Spanish is, more than ever, closely tied both to the international Spanish-speaking community and to American society and culture. What is unique is the use of Spanish and English together by bilinguals. This finds its highest form of expression in bilingual literature. Having the choice of two languages, U.S. Spanish speakers control a rich storehouse of language. This ability to wrap together the language of their Spanish heritage and the language of their American environment is uniquely Hispanic American.

11

Hispanic American Literature

FACT FOCUS

- Hispanic American literature is as diverse as the groups that produce it. It has many styles, concerns, and languages. It is published in Spanish, English, and bilingual editions.
- Hispanic literature has been written on American soil since 1598. A soldier among the first settlers of New Mexico wrote the epic poem *La conquista de la Nueva México* (The Conquest of New Mexico).
- In the late 1800s and early 1900s, Spanish-language newspapers helped publish a great deal of Hispanic literature. They included works in their papers and put out books through their publishing houses.
- Writers in the Chicano movement gave new life to Hispanic literature in the 1960s. They challenged society to make changes.
- Unlike the writers who stayed on the island, Puerto Rican writers in New York usually came from working-class families. These writers have become known as Nuyoricans.

Like the people who have written it, Hispanic American literature has a long history. It includes the written and oral traditions of the people who settled the Southwest, long before this territory became part of the United States. It includes the writings of early explorers of the North American continent. It includes the works of Spanish-speaking immigrants and exiles who have made the United States their home. Hispanic American literature reflects the diverse ethnic and national origins of Hispanics in the United States. It offers a window into the history and culture of Spain, Mexico, and the Caribbean, as well as Central and South America. It reflects the Spanish, Native American, and African legacies of Hispanic Americans. Finally, Hispanic American literature shows the linguistic diversity of the Hispanic people. It has been written and published in Spanish, English, and even bilingual editions.

The Colonial Period

The roots of Hispanic American literature were planted north of the Rio Grande over

WORDS TO KNOW

autobiography: a true story that someone writes about her or his life.

Chicano movement: a group of twentieth-century Mexican American writers and activists who celebrated their culture and historical background in their works.

crónica: a local newspaper column that makes fun of the people and customs of the area.

folk ballad: a poem or song that tells a story. It is created by average people and based on their lives.

novel: a long story about fictional characters and events.

Nuyorican literature: the novels, poetry, and other writings of Puerto Ricans who were born or raised in New York City.

oral tradition: storytelling using the spoken word.

---

diaries, and letters right up until the Southwest became a part of the United States after the Mexican War in 1846. The Spanish written tradition came to the American Northeast in 1654. This is the year that Spanish Sephardic Jews founded a colony in New Amsterdam (present-day New York).

Spanish soldiers, colonists, and missionaries also brought the Spanish oral tradition to the Southwest. They staged dramas, sang songs and ballads, and recited poetry. Some of these can still be heard in New Mexico and the Southwest. Unfortunately, much of the early literature and oral tradition from the colonial period has been lost. What has not been lost has not been collected or studied. For this reason there is still much to be learned about the early Hispanic literature in the United States.

Nineteenth-Century Hispanic American Literature

The Southwest

The period between the Mexican War and 1900 saw a flourishing of Hispanic literature in the United States. In the Southwest, Mexican Americans turned to literature to preserve their culture. They read it to keep informed and to provide thought. They also read it for entertainment. In turn the literature brought unity to the Mexican American community. It helped people face the growing influence of Anglo-American culture in their areas. During this period many Spanish-language newspapers began publishing in Texas, New Mexico, Arizona, and California. In addition to news and information, these papers also printed short stories, poems, essays, and even novels. One impor-

two decades before the landing of the Mayflower at Plymouth Rock. In 1598 Juan de Oñate led an expedition of colonists up from central Mexico into what is today New Mexico. This expedition brought Hispanic culture to the land that is now the United States. It was also the beginning of a written and oral tradition in a European language, Spanish. One of the soldiers on Oñate's expedition, Gaspar Pérez de Villagrá, wrote the epic poem *La conquista de la Nueva México* (The Conquest of New Mexico). Later, missionaries and colonists continued to write. They wrote historical chronicles, tant Hispanic American novel of this time was *Las aventuras de Joaquín Murieta* (The Adventures of Joaquín Murieta). This novel about the legendary California social bandit was published in 1881 by the Santa Barbara newspaper *La gaceta.*

During the latter part of the 1800s, many Mexican American writers were published in book form. In Southern California Pilar Ruiz de Burton wrote about the shift in power and wealth from Hispanics to Anglos. Her English-language novel *The Squatter and the Don* was published in 1881. In New Mexico, Manuel M. Salazar wrote about romantic adventure. His *La historia de un caminante, o Gervacio y Aurora* (The History of a Traveler on Foot, or Gervacio and Aurora) was also published in 1881. This novel creates a colorful picture of the farm life in New Mexico at this time. Another New Mexican, Eusebio Chacón, published two important short novels in 1892. They were *El hijo de la tempestad* (Child of the Storm) and *Tras la tormenta la calma* (The Calm after the Storm). Miguel Antonio Otero was one of New Mexico's governors and an important writer. His autobiography, published in 1935, captures Hispanic life in the Southwest during the late 1800s. This work, *My Life on the Frontier,* was written in English.

The Mexican American poetry of the nineteenth century was primarily about love and the rural landscape. It appeared regularly in the Spanish-language newspapers of the Southwest. Among the most popular of these poets were E. Montalván from Texas, Felipe Maximiliano Chacón and Julio Flores from New Mexico, and Dantés from California. Very few of these poets ever collected their works into books.

RECENT EFFORTS TO RECOVER HISTORIC WRITINGS

In 1992, Hispanic scholar Nicolás Kanellos established the Recovering the U.S. Literary Heritage Project, in which a group of scholars and researchers searched the North American continent to find the writings of U.S. Hispanics that have been lost or ignored. For ten years they searched libraries and archives and collected many unknown, as well as well-known, U.S. Hispanic writings from the 1500s to the 1900s. In 2001 the results were published in *Herencia: An Anthology of Hispanic Literature of the United States.* It presents four centuries of Hispanic writing, translated into English where necessary, from all the different Hispanic groups, beginning with Alvar Núñez Cabeza de Vaca's (1490–1560) account of his explorations of the New World. The recovery project continues its search for lost literary works by U.S. Hispanics and its efforts to make these works available to the reading public.

One of the most popular literary forms to develop among Mexican Americans during this time was the *corrido.* The Mexican cor-

Eusebio Chacón. *Reproduced by permission of the Miguel A. Otero Collection, Special Collections, General Library, University of New Mexico.*

rido was a folk ballad related to the romance, which Spanish colonists had introduced to the New World. These ballads told the stories of bandits such as Joaquín Murieta, Aniceto Pizaña, and even Billy the Kid. And, through these stories, Mexican American writers helped establish an identity for their people. The corrido continued to increase in popularity into the twentieth century. It was often used to record the history of the great Mexican immigrations and labor struggles in the early 1900s.

New York

Nineteenth-century New York was also home to a flourishing of Hispanic American literature. Again, the newspapers played a key role in printing and publicizing this literature. In New York at this time, the majority of Hispanic writers were Spanish and Cuban. Spanish-language newspapers published from the 1820s to the 1860s offered news of the homeland, political commentary, poetry, short stories, essays, and even excerpts of plays. One poet who had work published at this time was Miguel Teurbe Tolón. He was born in the United States and educated in Cuba. He eventually joined the Cuban exiles in New York working for Cuban independence. A Mexican poet, Anastacio Ochoa y Acuña, had his work published in book form. His *Poesías de un mexicano* (Poems of a Mexican) appeared in 1828.

In the late 1800s, newspaper, magazine, and book publishing began to expand. The reasons for the growth included immigration and political problems on several Caribbean islands. The population of Hispanic writers grew to include Puerto Ricans and Dominicans. Some of Puerto Rico's most important literary and revolutionary figures published essays, letters, diaries, poems, and short stories in New York during these years. They included Eugenio María de Hostos, Ramón Emeterio Betances, Lola Rodríguez de Tió, and Sotero Figueroa. The Puerto Rican revolutionary leader and poet Francisco González "Pachín" Marín also wrote during this period. In one of his works, he sketches New York from the point of view of a disappointed immigrant. This essay marks the beginning of Hispanic literature about the immigrant experience.

The Cuban patriot and writer José Martí was also writing in New York at this time. He wrote numerous essays and other writings about his life in New York and the United States. Martí became an important international literary figure in the nineteenth century. Today, his writings are studied throughout the world in Latin American literature classes. In addition to his literary works, Martí worked for Cuban independence. (He was killed in 1895 leading the revolution that freed Cuba from Spain.) Many of the books written by Cubans in New York also dealt with the Cuban independence struggle. One example was Luis García Pérez's *El grito de Yara* (The Shout at Yara), published in 1879. Another was Desiderio Fajardo Ortiz's *La fuga de Evangelina* (The Escape of Evangelina), published in 1898. This tells the story of the Cuban heroine Evangelina Cossío. She escaped from a Spanish jail on Cuba and fled to New York. There she helped organize the independence movement.

Lola Rodríguez de Tío. *Reproduced by permission of Arte Público Press.*

Early Twentieth-Century Hispanic American Literature

The Southwest

The turn of the century brought record immigration from Mexico to the Southwest and the Midwest. This was due in large part to the events leading up to and during the Mexican Revolution of 1910. Working-class Mexicans came to the United States and so did educated professionals and the wealthy. These new immigrants mixed with the Hispanic Americans already in these regions and revived their Spanish-language literature. They also added their own mark. Many of the publishers of this era were well-educated political refugees. They hoped to return to Mexico, so they created an ideology of a Mexican community in exile. This ideology was called *México de afuera* (Mexico on the outside).

San Antonio and Los Angeles soon had daily newspapers in Spanish. San Antonio boasted *La prensa* (The Press) and Los Angeles, *La opinión* (The Opinion) and *El heraldo de México* (The Mexican Herald). Some of the most talented writers from Mexico, Spain, and Latin America earned their living as reporters, columnists, and critics at these newspapers. Among these were Miguel Arce, Esteban Escalante, Gabriel Navarro, Teodoro Torres, and Daniel Venegas. In addition to their journalism, they wrote hundreds of books of poetry, essays, and novels. Many of these books were published by the newspapers.

DANIEL VENEGAS

Daniel Venegas influenced modern Chicano literature through one of his novels. *Las aventuras de Don Chipote* (The Adventures of Don Chipote) was published in 1928. *Don Chipote* is a novel of immigration and protest. It is the humorous story of a Mexican immigrant. He travels through the Southwest looking for the mythic streets of gold that the United States offers to immigrants. Instead, he finds himself working here and there at odd jobs. He suffers at the hands of criminals, officials, and his bosses. He does not find the streets of gold.

In addition to the publishing houses owned by the newspapers, there were many smaller publishers in San Antonio and Los Angeles. Many of the novels published by these houses were novels of the Mexican Revolution. The novels in this genre focused on the events and people of that moment in Mexican history. In the United States, the refugees who wrote these novels were very conservative. They usually criticized the revolution and Mexican politicians. These, they believed, were the reason for their exile. Mariano Azuela has become the most famous of these writers. He wrote *Los de abajo* (The Underdogs). This novel was a masterpiece that laid the foundation for modern Mexican literature. It was first published in parts in 1915 in the El Paso, Texas, newspaper El paso del norte *(The Northern Pass)*. The newspaper later published the novel in book form.

One of the most important literary forms that developed in the newspapers at this time was *la crónica* (chronicle). It was a short column that poked fun at the local scene. It was the chronicler's *(cronista)* job to promote Mexican culture and the Spanish language. These writers mocked Hispanics who mixed Spanish and English. They criticized Hispanic women for taking on the customs of American women. These included short hair, short skirts, and smoking. Their hope was to keep alive the goal of returning to Mexico. Among the most important cronistas of this period were Benjamín Padilla and Julio Arce, who wrote under the name Jorge Ulica.

The Great Depression in the United States was very hard on the Hispanic people and culture of the Southwest. Mexican Americans were forced back to Mexico in large numbers. Some writers began to write in English to better publicize the Hispanic experience of the Depression. Américo Paredes wrote his novel *George Washington Gómez* during this time. The Franciscan monk Fray Angelico Chávez also began to publish his poetry and stories during the Depression. His poetry was based on his religious life. His stories were based on New Mexican folklore. In the two decades after the Depression, some Mexican Americans published their stories in mainstream English-language magazines. These included Robert Hernán Torres and Josephina Niggli. Even so, Mexican American literature faded somewhat until the 1960s.

The Northeast

In New York the period from 1900 to the Great Depression also saw increased immigration and mixing of Hispanic groups. After the 1917 Jones Act made them citizens, Puerto Ricans could come to the United States more easily. In the late 1930s, many Spaniards came to flee the Spanish Civil War. Filled with political and artistic passions, these new immigrants joined the Cuban and Spanish writers already at New York's Hispanic newspapers. Their literary work soon followed.

The publishing of Spanish-language literature in the Northeast began to expand in the late teens and early twenties. One of the most important publishing houses was the Spanish American Publishing Company. It began issuing titles in the teens and continued through the fifties. It published a number of books on the theme of Hispanics in New York. One of these was Javier Lara's *En la metrópoli de dólar* (In the Metropolis of the Dollar), published in 1919. Some books were self-published by authors through local printers. One of the most interesting books to appear during these years, was a self-published immigrant novel written by the Venezuelan author Alirio Díaz Guerra. *Lucas Guevara,* published in 1917, is the story of a young man who comes to the city seeking his fortune. In the end, however, he is disappointed.

Hispanic writers in New York increased their activity during the late 1920s and early 1930s. To begin with, several special newspapers began to appear. The weekly *Gráfico* (Graphic) began publishing in 1927 to cover the growing interest in Hispanic theater in Manhattan and Brooklyn. This and other

Américo Paredes. *Reproduced by permission of Ralph Barrera.*

newspapers and magazines like it included poems, short stories, literary essays, and crónicas by the leading New York Hispanic writers. While Southwestern writers promoted the Mexican community in exile, New York writers often tried to create a *Trópico en Manhattan* (A Tropical [or Caribbean] Culture in Manhattan).

Unlike in the Southwest, the Hispanic community in New York continued to grow during and after the Great Depression. The lives of Puerto Rican workers and Spanish exiles from civil war were reflected in the new Hispanic newspapers that started. The stories of these immigrants took the form of autobiographical sketches, anecdotes, and short stories. Within the last thirty years, many of these writings have been

Cover of the first issue of the newspaper *Gráfico*. Reproduced by permission of Arte Público Press.

collected into books as a way of saving this piece of Hispanic history and culture. *The Memoirs of Bernardo Vega* and Jesús Colón's *A Puerto Rican in New York* are two important collections.

Alongside the writing in newspapers emerged a Hispanic oral tradition and scripts written for the theater. Some poems and stories were not written down, but they were shared in the family and in community gatherings. Much of this oral tradition has been lost. However, some of the spoken lyric and narrative poetry of the Caribbean people has been preserved in their songs. It can be found in the recorded music of

Rafael Hernández, Pedro Flores, and Ramito. The oral tradition and culture of this time was also preserved in published plays from the Hispanic theater. This dramatic literature was especially important in the Puerto Rican community. Important playwrights from this period included Gonzalo O'Neill, Luis Muñoz-Rivera, Lola Rodriguez de Tió, and Vicente Palés.

World War II to the Present

Chicano Literature

The year 1943 was the beginning of a new period in Mexican American history and culture. At this time Mexican Americans began to recognize that they no longer belonged to Mexico and they did not yet belong to the United States. They began to assert their own unique identity. Young Mexican Americans marked their identity in their clothing, speech, and music. Many wore baggy pants and a feathered, wide-brimmed hat. This outfit was known as a "zoot suit."

Young community leaders took this seed of a new Mexican American identity and began to shape it into the Chicano movement. This movement toward change was a spark to Mexican American writers. During the 1960s Chicano writers led the renaissance in Hispanic literature. The Chicano literature of the 1960s questioned the commonly accepted truths. It drew attention to the inequality faced by Mexican Americans in the Southwest and elsewhere.

Young writers lent their voices to the political, economic, and educational struggles of that decade. Their writings were often used to inspire social and political

Alurista. *Reproduced by permission of Arte Público Press.*

Rodolfo "Corky" Gonzalez. *Reproduced by permission of the Corbis Corporation (Bellevue).*

action. They read at meetings, boycotts, and protest marches. The most successful of these writer/speakers were those who tapped into the Hispanic oral tradition. Abelardo Delgado, Ricardo Sánchez, and Alurista (Alberto Urista) informed and inspired workers and students through their powerful poetry presentations.

The most important literary work of this period provided the foot soldiers in the Chicano movement a sense of their history, mission, and identity. It was the epic poem *I Am Joaquín/Yo Soy Joaquín* by Rodolfo "Corky" González, an ex-boxer and Presbyterian leader. The short, bilingual pamphlet

edition of the poem spread widely through the Chicano community. It was passed from hand to hand in neighborhoods. It was read at rallies. It was dramatized by street theaters and even produced as a slide show.

The grass roots organizations and cultural movements created a new interest in publishing small community and workers' newspapers and magazines. In 1967 *El grito* was launched. This influential Chicano literary magazine gave a start to some of the most important writers in Chicano literature. This magazine and its publishing house, Editorial Quinto Sol, also helped define Chicano literature. This was done by choosing to print those works they felt were the best examples of Chicano culture, language, themes, and styles. The 1968 anthol-

Denise Chávez. *Reproduced by permission of Arte Público Press.*

Gary Soto. *Reproduced by permission of Gary Soto.*

ogy *El espejo/The Mirror,* published by Editorial Quinto Sol, featured the writing of Alurista, Tomás Rivera, Miguel Méndez, and Rolando Hinojosa.

By the end of the 1970s, most of the Chicano literary magazines and publishers had disappeared. In 1973, however, a new Hispanic magazine called *Revista Chicano-Riqueña* (Chicano-Rican Review) appeared. This magazine, edited by Nicolás Kanellos and Luis Dávila, developed a following among academics in American universities. In 1979 Kanellos founded Arte Público Press, which quickly took a leading role in publishing the works of Hispanic women writers. During the 1980s, Arte Público published books of poetry by San Antonio poets Evangelina Vigil and Angela de Hoyos. It published the Chicago poets and prose writers Ana Castillo and Sandra Cisneros. It also published Los Angeles short story writer Helena María Viramontes and New Mexico novelist and playwright Denise Chávez. These writers produced some of the best-selling and most reviewed Chicano books of the decade.

The most recent generation of Chicano writers has begun to make inroads into the mainstream American literary scene. Some of these writers no longer speak or write in Spanish. Some no longer derive their inspiration from the oral tradition and political action of the Chicano movement. One poet

A poet, supported by drummers, reads during a poetry slam at the Nuyorican Poets' Café in New York City, 1995. *Reproduced by permission of AP/Wide World Photos.*

in this group is Gary Soto. His poetry is finely crafted, down-to-earth, and rigorous. It is inspired by the life of the common workingman in the fields and factories. Noted poet and novelist Ana Castillo is considered one of the primary writers of the movement, and remains popular in the twenty-first century. Sandra Cisneros's important 1984 novel *The House on Mango Street* is still widely read in schools in the 2000s.

Today, there are more and more opportunities for Chicano writers and students in university settings. With the help of specialized scholars and publishers, Chicano literature has built a strong foundation on American campuses.

Nuyorican Literature

Puerto Rican writing in New York emerged in the late nineteenth century. But, it was not until well into the twentieth century that this literature established itself. Puerto Rican writing began to spread beyond the Spanish-speaking public after World War II when more writers turned to English.

Most Puerto Rican writers who lived on the island were a part of the social elite. They were well educated and many worked

Nicholasa Mohr. *Reproduced by permission of Larry Racioppo.*

as university professors. Puerto Rican writers in New York, known as Nuyoricans, were different. They usually came from the working class. Their parents had come to the city to work in services and manufacturing. The writers were then raised in a bilingual and bicultural setting. When they turned to writing, many chose to write bilingual poetry. Others chose to write prose, usually in English. Because of their Hispanic American experience in New York, their writing had a variety of influences. It was influenced by folk and popular traditions such as traveling poets, storytellers, and salsa music composers, as well as the culture and commerce of New York City.

The real growth in Puerto Rican literature came in the late 1960s and early 1970s. At this time Nuyoricans began to gain better access to education. There was also a movement to raise awareness of Puerto Rican culture. A group of poet-playwrights at the Nuyorican Poets' Café on the Lower East Side of New York began to define Nuyorican literature through their works. Included in this group were Miguel Algarín, Lucky Cienfuegos, Tato Laviera, and Miguel Piñero. One aspect of this literature was its description of prison life. Two of the members of the café group had begun their writing careers while in prison. Other aspects of the writing included its cultivation of Afro-Caribbean traditions and its avant-garde quality.

The first generation of Nuyorican writers was dominated by poets. These writers built on the Spanish and African oral traditions that had come together on their home island. They improved their art by giving numerous public readings. Among the best performers of Nuyorican poetry were Victor Hernández Cruz, Tato Laviera, Miguel Piñero, and Miguel Algarín. Influenced by popular music and street culture, poets such as Hernández Cruz produced what was called bilingual jazz poetry. One of the few women's voices heard in this generation was that of Sandra María Esteves. She was very active in calling for women's rights, African Americans' rights, and the independence of Puerto Rico.

The best known Nuyorican novelist of the 1970s and 1980s was Nicholasa Mohr. Her novels include *Nilda* (1973), *El Bronx Remembered* (1975), *In Nueva York* (1977), *Felita* (1979), and *Going Home* (1986). She wrote an acclaimed children's book in 1995 and in 1997 published a collection of seven short stories, *A Matter of Pride and Other Stories.* All of these were published in hardcover and paperback editions by major commercial publishers. For this reason her books have reached a wide audience of mainstream American readers. They have won such awards as the *New York Times* Outstanding Book of the Year, the *School Library Journal* Best Children's Book, and many others. In 1997 she was a Hispanic Heritage Award Honoree.

Another very popular Puerto Rican writer at the turn of the twenty-first century is Esmeralda Santiago, whose *When I Was Puerto Rican* and *Almost a Woman* describe her experiences as a child in growing up in Puerto Rico and then in the United States.

Cuban American Literature

Cuban American literature has developed in New York, New Jersey, and Miami over the last three decades. Older Cuban American writers who fled to the United States from Castro's Cuba brought with them their literary concerns. In the United States, many have added attacks on the Cuban Revolution. For these writers the exile novel became another weapon in their struggle to overthrow Castro. Even those who have avoided political attacks have looked back toward Cuba. They show a nostalgia for their homeland.

The younger generation of writers that has emerged is no longer preoccupied by exile. They no longer look back to the island for inspiration. Instead, they are looking forward to becoming a part of the English-language literary scene. They are looking forward to serving the intellectual and cultural needs of the Cuban and Hispanic American communities. These younger writers, Roberto Fernández, Iván Acosta,

JESÚS COLÓN

Jesús Colón was a newspaper columnist. A black Puerto Rican who was active in the Communist Party, Colón fought against racism and the oppression of workers. He also wrote about Puerto Rican culture. In 1961, he selected some of his columns and published them in the book *A Puerto Rican in New York.* This book offered insight into what it was like to be a minority in New York. It also presented Colón's social and political ideas. When it appeared in the 1960s, it helped influence the generation of Puerto Rican writers coming of age at that time in New York. This generation became known as the Nuyorican writers.

Virgil Suárez, and Oscar Hijuelos, for instance, have separated themselves from the older generation.

Oscar Hijuelos's novel *The Mambo Kings Play Songs of Love,* published in 1990, made history. It was the first novel by a Hispanic American writer to win the Pulitzer Prize (one of the highest honors in literature). It also marked the first time that a major publishing house, Simon and Schuster, had ever invested heavily in a novel by a Hispanic writer. The company brought the novel out at the top of its list and promoted it widely. Hijuelos went on to publish many more acclaimed novels,

Oscar Hijuelos. *Reproduced by permission of AP/Wide World Photos.*

including *The Fourteen Sisters of Emilio Montez O'Brien* in 1993, *Mr. Ives' Christmas* in 1995, *Empress of the Splendid Season* in 1999, and *A Simple Habana Melody (from when the world was good)* in 2002.

Mainstream Publishers of Spanish-Language and Hispanic-Themed Literature

In 1994 several large U.S. publishers opted to release Spanish-language titles for the first time. *El regalo,* a Spanish translation of Danielle Steele's novel *The Gift,* was released for Spanish readers by the major publishing company Dell. A spokesperson from Dell said that the Spanish-language release of this novel was more an experiment with Hispanic American consumers than a business venture. Bantam had tried several years earlier to publish a Judith Krantz novel, but did not find much interest among consumers.

A more successful effort at publishing a Spanish-language title in the United States was Doubleday's Spanish-language version of Laura Esquivel's 1990 novel *Like Water for Chocolate.* Penguin later published the Spanish version of Gabriel García Márquez's *Del amor y otros demonios* (Lovers and Other Demons). These sold well.

For many Hispanic American authors, it has been difficult to find major publishers for works that were considered to be of

RUDOLFO ANAYA

Rudolfo Anaya's *Bless Me, Ultima* is a novel about a boy's coming of age. It is written in a poetic and clear English. For this reason, it has reached more readers, especially non-Chicano readers, than any other Chicano literary work. In *Bless Me, Ultima,* Antonio must choose between his Spanish and Native American heritages, between a life as a rancher and a life as a farmer. He is guided in his choice by a folk healer, Ultima. She passes on many of her secrets and insights about life to Antonio. The author uses the romantic and picturesque New Mexico countryside to create this novel full of the mysteries and symbols of the Native American and Spanish cultures.

Rudolfo Anaya. *Reproduced by permission of AP/Wide World Photos.*

interest primarily to the Hispanic population of the United States. In the early 1970s, Rudolfo Anaya, an acclaimed writer and one of the leading figures of the Chicano movement, was rejected by many publishers when he tried to publish his first novel *Bless Me, Ultima*. In 1972 a Chicano publishing house in California published the book. It was an instant success and quickly won the prestigious Premio Quinto Sol Award, given annually to the best novel written by a Chicano. Anaya continued to produce novels, short stories, plays, poetry, and screenplays over the next two decades, focusing on Mexican American myths and culture. He has remained a profound presence in Chicano literature since the 1970s. But it wasn't until 1994 that Anaya received the recognition of a mainstream publisher. At that time he signed a contract with Warner Books to publish six of his books. As part of the deal, Warner agreed to publish paperback and hardcover editions of *Bless Me, Ultima* as well as a Spanish-language edition of the book. It was the first time Warner Books was to publish a Spanish-language book.

The United States has the fifth largest Spanish-speaking population in the world.

Cover of Laura Esquivel's novel *Like Water for Chocolate. Reproduced by permission of Doubleday, a division of Random House, Inc.*

Publishers have half-heartedly tried to break into the Spanish-language book market for years. Most publishers have established Hispanic imprints (separate names under which publishers publish a certain kind of book), but they have generally not done well because there was no effort put into marketing to Spanish-speaking consumers. This lack of success has translated into difficulty for Hispanic Americans to publish in the mainstream press, in English or Spanish.

The census figures for 2000 will almost certainly change this. In the future more Hispanic American and Latin American literature may be widely published in the United States. This should give all readers greater access to the literary movements of the Hispanic culture, greatly enriching American literature as a whole. This will also give Hispanic American writers more options for publication: mainstream or independent publishers; English-language, Spanish-language, or bilingual.

12

Hispanic American Cultural Expression

Theater, Music, and Art

FACT FOCUS

- Early Hispanic American theater combined Native American and Spanish religious traditions. Over time, plays became less religious.
- In 1598, the earliest Spanish settlers of New Mexico put on plays to entertain themselves. By the 1800s, theater groups from Mexico were touring the Southwest. Soon the Southwest had its own Hispanic theater.
- In the 1920s, Hispanic theater groups from Cuba, Spain, Mexico, and the Southwest regularly performed in New York City.
- In the 1920s, variety shows and musical comedies became more and more popular with the Hispanic working class.
- Hispanic music reflects the diversity of the people. Some began in Mexico, others in the Caribbean, still others in the United States.
- *Conjunto* music is played on the accordion, 12-string guitar, and drum. *Orquesta* music is played on the violin, guitar, and other instruments.
- Since the 1960s, Mexican Americans in the working class have made *música tropical/moderna* very popular. It is played on a keyboard, electric guitar, bass, and drums.
- *Salsa* music is known for its hot, spicy, Afro-Caribbean rhythms.
- New styles of Hispanic American music include Hispanic country and western, Latin pop, Latin jazz, and Latin rock.
- In 2000, the first annual Latin Grammy Awards show was presented, airing on television in 120 countries.
- The earliest Hispanic American art was the religious art of the mission churches in the American Southwest. Early Hispanic artists made sculptures and paintings of the saints.
- In the twentieth century, Hispanic painters and sculptors followed the styles current in American art.
- Into the twenty-first century, Hispanic artists brighten the urban landscape with murals, or large wall paintings.

WORDS TO KNOW

ballad: a song that tells a story.

conjunto: a style of Hispanic music first made popular in Texas and northern Mexico. It is sometimes called *música norteña*. Conjunto is also used to refer to the band that plays this music.

folk plays: plays created and presented by common people that are based on the lives of these people.

hybrid: a combination of two or more things to make something new and different.

mural: a large work of art painted onto a wall.

música tropical/moderna: the name given to the style of music now popular among Hispanic Americans. It includes fast and slow dance songs.

Theater, music, and art are all forms of cultural expression that the Hispanic American community has used to preserve its heritage and forge an identity. They have helped Hispanics cope with the difficulties of being a minority within the mainstream American culture. They have raised Hispanic spirits and entertained them. They have also served to communicate Hispanic American culture among members of the mainstream American culture. In recent years many Hispanic art forms have become extremely popular in American culture.

Hispanic American Theater

The roots of Hispanic theater in the United States reach back to the Spanish and Native American heritage of Hispanics. They include the dance-drama of Native Americans and the religious plays and pageants of medieval and Renaissance Spain. During the Spanish colonization of Mexico, Catholic missionaries used plays to help convert the native peoples of Mexico to Catholicism. Plays were later used to teach mestizo (those of mixed Spanish and Native American heritage) Mexicans the mysteries and rituals of the church. In the 1600s and 1700s, a hybrid religious theater developed. These plays combined the music, colors, flowers, masks, and languages that were a part of the native cultures with the stories of the Bible.

In Mexico and the American Southwest, these plays eventually moved farther and farther from their religious origins. In the end such plays were banned by the Catholic Church. They were not allowed on church grounds or in church festivals. Because of this separation from the church, such plays became part of the folk culture. The community put on the plays without the help and support of the church.

Hispanic Drama in the United States

In 1598 Spanish explorer Juan de Oñate led a group of Spanish colonists into what is today New Mexico. The colonists brought with them folk plays from Spain and Spanish America. In their camps Oñate's soldiers would entertain each other by making up plays based on their experiences on the journey. They also put on a popular Spanish folk play. *Moros y cristianos* was a heroic play about how the Spanish Christians defeated the Islamic Moors in northern Spain and drove them off the Iberian Peninsula. This play eventually spread throughout Spanish America. It has even been performed in the twentieth century in New Mexico. *Moros y cristianos* influenced many later Hispanic epic plays about war and conflict.

As early as the late 1700s, the Hispanic folk theater in the United States developed into a theater of professionals. This usually happened in areas with large Hispanic populations. At first, touring groups from Mexico traveled to California where they performed melodramas and musicals. In the mid-1800s regularly scheduled steamships made it easy for these groups to put on plays in San Diego, Los Angeles, and San Francisco. Eventually, professional theater troupes could be found in the Southwest, New York, Florida, and even the Midwest.

By the 1890s Mexican theater productions had greatly increased in the border states. Theater companies that had previously only toured in central Mexico began to extend their regular circuits into the United States. It became common for groups to tour from Laredo, San Antonio, and El Paso, Texas, to cities in New Mexico and Arizona, and on to Los Angeles and San Francisco. After the turn of the twentieth century, trains and cars allowed these companies to reach smaller cities. Between 1900 and 1930, many Mexican theater houses were built to provide stages for the traveling groups. Some smaller cities even had their own Mexican theater with a resident troupe of players. Mobile tent theaters, circus theaters, and makeshift groups took plays to small towns and rural areas on both sides of the Rio Grande.

Around the time of the Mexican Revolution in 1910, thousands of Mexican

---

WORDS TO KNOW

orquesta: the Spanish word for orchestra; it is the name of a style of Mexican American music organized around a violin and the ensemble that plays it.

playwright: a person who creates a play.

popular theater: the plays, musicals, and shows put on by theaters to attract the general public. Popular theater is concerned more with entertainment than art.

salsa: a style of music first made popular by Cubans of African heritage. It combines jazz and the rhythms of Cuban dance music.

sculpture: the art of making statues and other figures out of stone, plaster, wood, or metals.

shrine: a place that is important for religious reasons.

theater: the building where actors present plays. Theater is also used to refer to the plays and the business of putting on plays.

touring troupes: groups of actors that go from city to city to put on plays.

---

refugees settled in the Southwest and the Midwest. This influx of immigrants sparked an increase in theatrical activity. During the decades of revolution, many of Mexico's greatest dramatic artists and their companies came to the United States. They came to tour and take up temporary residence. However, some stayed permanently. These Hispanic groups and others already estab-

The California Theater in Los Angeles, California. *Reproduced by permission of Arte Público Press.*

lished in the United States toured cities in Florida, New York, the Midwest, and the Southwest. The most popular cities were San Antonio and Los Angeles. By the 1920s Hispanic theater had become big business.

Between 1922 and 1933, a group of successful Mexican playwrights emerged in Los Angeles. The four main figures in this group were Eduardo Carrillo (an actor), Adalberto Elías González (a novelist), Esteban V. Escalante (a journalist and director), and Gabriel Navarro (a poet, novelist, composer, and columnist). There were about twenty other Hispanic playwrights in Los Angeles who regularly had works staged by profes-

sional theaters. The serious full-length plays created by these authors showed the situation of Hispanics in California. The works drew upon the history of the Hispanic-Anglo struggle in California and presented their themes on a broad, epic scale. Examples included Carillo's *El proceso de Aurelio Pompa* (The Trial of Aurelio Pompa), Navarro's *Los emigrados* (The Emigrés), and González's *Los amores de Ramona* (The Loves of Ramona). This last play became one of the most successful of this era.

New York

The 1920s saw a rapid expansion of Hispanic theater in New York. At first touring

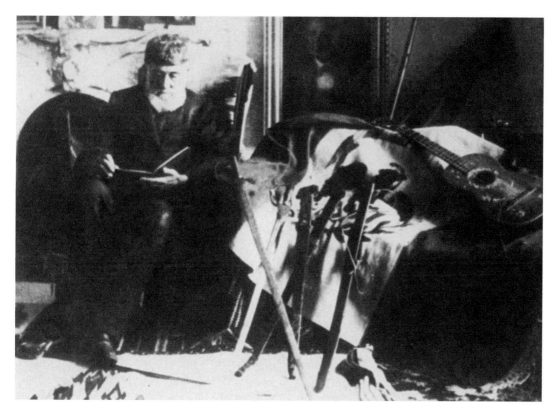

Don Antonio F. Coronel, who served as mayor of Los Angeles, was an early theater owner and impresario. *Reproduced courtesy of the Southwest Museum, Los Angeles, California.*

companies from Cuba, Spain, Mexico, and the Southwest came to meet the demand of the Hispanic community. These groups rented theaters for their runs. In 1922 the New York Hispanic community began to buy its own theaters. The first two Hispanic theater houses were the Dalys and the Apollo. After 1930 the Apollo no longer offered Hispanic theater. But, the San José/Variedades stepped in to replace it. In 1934 the core of the Hispanic theater moved to the Campoamor. It moved again in 1937, to El Teatro Hispano. El Teatro Hispano became the most important and long-lived Hispanic theater in New York.

In the 1930s Puerto Ricans joined other Hispanic Americans in the New York theater scene. Many of the Puerto Rican playwrights who emerged at this time wrote about social and political issues that affected their compatriots on the island and the mainland. These included the struggle of the working class and independence from the United States. The most important of the Puerto Rican playwrights was Gonzalo O'Neill. A successful businessman and patron of new immigrants, O'Neill also wrote poetry and plays. His play *Bajo una sola bandera* (Under Just One Flag) was an important inspiration to the Puerto Rican nationalist cause.

The García girls chorus line from the Carpa García tent show. *Reproduced by permission of Arte Público Press.*

The other Hispanic playwrights in New York during this era did not achieve the success of Southwestern playwrights. Even so, the Hispanic theater in New York performed an important role in the community. It helped unify the diverse Hispanic community, Cubans, Spaniards, Mexicans, and Puerto Ricans.

Popular Hispanic Theater

In the 1920s popular theater events began to compete with the more serious Hispanic theater. This was a time when working-class Hispanics were beginning to enjoy a more comfortable life. They had time and money and wanted entertainment. This was also a time when vaudeville was at its height.

Vaudeville was the original variety show. It included singing, dancing, circus and magic acts, as well as humorous skits. Musical comedy was also popular at this time. These types of American entertainment quickly found their way onto the Hispanic stage. They became more and more popular and gradually displaced the more serious theater.

The Mexican *revista* soon grew out of the early popular theater. This musical revue featured the character, music, language, and folklore of working-class Mexicans. Yet, even though these new productions had popular appeal, they continued to address important social themes. In the United States, revistas were typically used to express complaints against and poke fun at the U.S. and Mexican governments. They also contained a great deal of humor about the culture shock that recent immigrants experienced. During the Great Depression, many Anglos wanted to send Mexican Americans back to Mexico. The revistas stood up for Hispanic rights against this racist tide. They also cast sharp criticism at American culture.

The musical revue that became popular in New York during this time was not the Mexican revista. It was the *obra bufa cubana,* or Cuban blackface farce. This popular theater featured stereotyped Caribbean characters, Afro-Cuban song and dance, and slapstick comedy. Like the revistas, the obras bufas cubanas drew upon current events, politics, and local gossip. The most famous of all actors in these revues was Arquímides Pous. Pous always played the *negrito,* or character in blackface. He became famous for his social satire, especially his attacks on racism.

THE PELADO

The poorly dressed underdog, the *pelado* or *peladito,* was a common feature in the popular Hispanic theater of the 1920s to 1950s. This clown used the clothing and language of the poor to make theater audiences laugh. He also criticized upper-class society and the mainstream American culture. The Spanish actor Romualdo Tirado was the most famous pelado.

Don Fito, the Carpa García *peladito* from the Carpa García tent show. *Reproduced by permission of Arte Público Press.*

Recent Hispanic American Theater

During the Depression (1929–39) and World War II (1939–45), the Hispanic theater lost a great deal of its importance in the Hispanic community. Movies replaced live performances on many stages. Others suffered under financial burdens. Since World War II, there has been a gradual restoration of the theater in Hispanic communities throughout the United States.

In 1965 the modern Chicano theater movement was born. At that time playwright Luis Valdez left the San Francisco Mime Troupe to join labor leader César Chávez (1927–1993) in organizing farm workers in Delano, California, to fight for better working conditions and fair treatment. Valdez organized the workers into El Teatro Campesino to help raise funds and awareness for the grape boycott and farm worker strike. Valdez's labor theater grew to include small theater groups in communities and on college campuses. The goal of these groups was often to anger the audience into action. This *teatro chicano,* as it was called, included humor, folklore, and popular culture in a spiritual style. Valdez hoped to use these groups to spread a Chicano theater to both the urban and rural working-class Spanish-speaking populations.

Through the years Valdez has continued reaching out to the national audience. His breakthrough into the mainstream was the 1987 film *La Bamba,* the screen biography of Ritchie Valens, the 1950s Mexican American rock-and-roll singer, which he wrote and directed. Audiences across America learned not only about the tragically short life of Valens but also about the

Rosalba Rolon, an artistic director and one of the founders of the New York-based Hispanic theater Teatro Pregones, performs in the play "Los angeles se han fatigado," 2001. *Reproduced by permission of AP/Wide World Photos.*

Luis Valdez. *Reproduced by permission of Archive Photos, Inc.*

lifestyle and other elements of the Mexican American community.

Valdez's work with El Teatro Campesino continues into the 2000s. In 1994 the company produced Valdez's play *Bandido,* about the real life California outlaw Tiburcio Vasquez. Valdez portrays Vasquez (played by actor A Martinez in this production) as someone who turned to banditry to resist the domination of Anglos pouring into California in days of the Gold Rush of the mid-nineteenth century. Valdez believes that Vasquez's situation is still important to Mexican Americans today in giving them an opportunity to see the old West in a new way, without the stereotypes of Hispanic frontiersmen as bandits.

Since the 1960s Hispanic theater has included a wide variety of styles. Some theater groups have tried to influence working-class Hispanics to action. These groups have often sought out their audience, performing in the streets. Especially in New York, groups of similar-minded actors and directors have come together to produce works in their own style. These groups then cultivate their own audience. Many of these groups have their own theater houses today. Some of these are International Arts Relations (INTAR), Miriam Colón's Puerto Rican Traveling Theater, and Teatro Repertorio Español.

Many Hispanics in the 1990s and early 2000s are breaking through into mainstream

A scene from the Luis Valdez film *La Bamba,* starring Lou Diamond Phillips as Ritchie Valens and Esai Morales as his brother. *Reproduced by permission of the Kobal Collection.*

theater. One of the shining stars of screenwriting at the turn of the century was Josefina Lopez, who wrote her first play at the age of seventeen. Her play *Real Women Have Curves* about an overweight young Mexican American woman going to work in a garment factory was a success on stage for years before she could find someone to make it into a film. The film was finally made by Colombian director Patricia Cardoso and won the Sundance Film Festival's Audience Award in the dramatic competition.

Theater from all over Latin America, most often presented in Spanish, is becoming increasingly popular in the United States in the twenty-first century, among Hispanics, but among other groups as well. Every year from late May to mid-June the International Hispanic Theater Festival brings a multitude of Hispanic theater events, featuring U.S., Latin America, Caribbean, and European theater companies, to the El Carrusel Theater in Coral Gables, Florida. The theater company Reportorio Español in New York stages high quality Hispanic theater. Its playwrights and actors come from the many different Spanish-speaking countries. The plays are presented in Spanish, with simultaneous English translations.

Hispanic American Music

The music that has grown out of the Hispanic American culture takes many forms, reflecting the diversity of the Hispanic population. Among Mexican Americans of the Southwest, a number of musical styles have evolved. The most important of these are *música norteña, orquesta, música tropical/moderna, corrido,* and *canción-corrido.* Among Hispanic Americans of Caribbean descent, the most important musical style is salsa. Hispanic Americans have also combined their musical heritage with some modern American styles to create Hispanic country and western, Latin jazz, Latin rock, and Latin pop.

Mexican American Music

Conjunto and Orquesta Music. Mexican Americans in Texas helped to create two of the most important Hispanic musical creations. They are the musical styles associated with two types of bands common among Mexican Texans, or *tejanos.* The first is *música norteña.* Tejanos also call this music and the band that plays it *conjunto.* The other type of music is *orquesta tejana,* more commonly called just *orquesta.* Both of these musical styles emerged in the first half of the twentieth century. They were greatly influenced by the important social, cultural, and economic changes that were taking place in Texas at that time. Both conjunto and orquesta had become the dominant forms of music in Texas by the 1950s. Their influence had spread far beyond the Texas borders by the 1970s.

The heart of the conjunto is the accordion. This instrument was introduced in northern Mexico and Texas sometime during the mid-1800s. It was brought to these areas by either German, Czech, or Polish immigrants. In the conjunto this European instrument has come to be played in a very different style. The left-hand base-chord buttons are not used. Instead, this part of the music is played by the soul of the conjunto, an instrument called the *bajo sexto.* This type of twelve-string guitar originated in the Guanajuato-Michoacán area of Mexico. The rhythm for the conjunto is provided by the *tambora de rancho* (ranch drum). This drum was originally a primitive folk instrument made out of native materials. It was usually played with wooden mallets, their tips covered with cotton wrapped in goatskin. More modern versions are often used nowadays.

Prior to the 1970s, conjuntos played primarily in areas along the U.S.-Mexican border. Since that time their *música norteño* has spread to Washington, D.C., California, and the Midwest. It has also spread to Michoacán and Sinaloa in Mexico. In its expansion conjunto music has always represented a strong Mexican American working-class lifestyle. In this way it has helped to preserve Mexican American culture wherever it has taken root on American and Mexican soil.

The orquesta (orchestra) has evolved through three stages over the last century. The early examples of this musical ensemble were built around the violin. Another violin, a guitar, and other instruments were added if they were available, but often these were hard to come by. Despite the lack of resources, these orquestas were enlisted for all kinds of celebrations. These included weddings, birthdays, and festivals.

In the 1920s urban areas supported better-organized orquestas. These ensembles, called *orquestas típicas* (typical orchestras)

Steve Jordan playing an accordion at the Tejano Conjunto Festival in Texas. *Reproduced by permission of Al Rendon/Southwest Images.*

were still built around a violin. To this, orquestas added more violins, guitars, and any other instruments that were available. The size of the típica could vary from four or five musicians to as many as twenty. Many of these orquestas típicas displayed a romantic nationalism in their dress. They often wore *charro* (cowboy) outfits to capture some of the flavor of Mexican peasant life. Típicas were enlisted to play at many occasions, but they were especially suited for patriotic celebrations.

The 1930s saw the emergence of the third and most important type of orquesta. This orquesta was a version of the dance bands that were sweeping across the United States and Mexico. The major difference between these modern orquestas and the mainstream dance bands was in the attention orquestas gave to the growing biculturalism among Mexican Americans. These orquestas included music for Latin American dances such as the *danzón, bolero, guaracha,* and *rumba.* They also included music for American dances such as the boogie, swing, and fox-trot. When Mexican American orquestas in Texas added polka to the mix, the music became known as Tex-Mex. When this Tex-Mex was fused with American jazz

Mexican musicians in California in the 1890s. *Reproduced by permission of Arte Público Press.*

and rock, it came to be known as *La Onda Chicana* (The Chicano Wave).

By the mid-1980s, La Onda Chicana had lost much of its tradition. One sign of its changing nature came when orquestas began to replace the horns with synthesized keyboards. At first the keyboards tried to imitate the sound of the trumpets, saxophones, and trombones. Eventually, however, the keyboard players developed their own sound. This sound was closer in spirit to conjunto music.

Música Tropical/Moderna. Among the many Mexican immigrants who have come to the United States since the 1960s, the *música tropical/moderna* style has become the most popular. This Mexican working-class music evolved from the tropical music of the Caribbean coasts of South America and Mexico. It began to spread in Mexico about the same time that a large new wave of immigrants started to move north to the United States. Today, música tropical/moderna is the everyday music of many Hispanics in the American Southwest.

Música tropical was associated with the *cumbia.* This was a Colombian folk dance that evolved and spread throughout Latin America during the twentieth century. When it reached Mexico in the mid-1960s, it was taken up by the Mexican working class. At about this same time, a type of slow dance surged in popularity in Mexico. This Mexican *balada* was danced to *música romántica,* or *moderna.* Eventually, bands began to alternate between cumbia and balada music to please their audiences. The combination of the music for each dance became known as música tropical/moderna.

Xavier Cugat and his orchestra in the 1940s. *Reproduced by permission of Arte Público Press.*

While the dances and music were evolving, a four-instrument ensemble became the favorite dance band for the Mexican American working class. Soon, this type of band came to be associated with cumbia and balada music in Mexico and the American Southwest. The four instruments featured in a música tropical/moderna group are the keyboard, electric guitar, bass, and tap drums.

Vocal Music

Two important types of vocal music are the Mexican *corrido* (ballad) and the *canción-corrido,* a hybrid made between this ballad and the *canción* (song). These two types of songs occupy a special place in the musical life of Mexican Americans in the Southwest. They emerged as powerful tools for cultural expression in the years leading up to World War II. This was a particularly difficult time for Mexican Americans. They felt the Depression in their wallets and in greater discrimination from their Anglo neighbors. The lyrics of the corrido and canción-corrido gave them a forum to express their experiences. The songs also allowed the Mexican American community to share the burden and pull together to overcome it.

Caribbean Music

Salsa

Salsa is the Spanish word for "sauce." In music it refers to the hot, spicy rhythms of Afro-Caribbean music. This music has evolved by combining elements of Hispanic, African, and more recently, American music. There are actually a variety of types

Tito Puente and Celia Cruz performing in 1992. *Reproduced by permission of Jack Vartoogian.*

of salsa music, but the *son guaguancó* has been the most popular since the 1960s. In this style a song begins with a Hispanic flavor. The lyrics are organized in an ABA pattern, in which the first part is followed by a different second part, which is followed by a repeated first part. The musical background given by trumpets or trombones includes American jazz elements. This Hispanic section is followed by an African-style section. This section uses a call-and-response pattern. The solo and chorus keep alternating phrases.

Hispanic American salsa grew out of musical traditions in Cuba, but it has also been influenced by the music of Puerto Rico, the Dominican Republic, and the United States. In Cuba the African roots of salsa can be found in the music associated with the rituals of folk religions such as Santería. The rhythms and call and response were an important part of the worship of Afro-Cubans. The African influence on salsa has also come from the *bomba* and *plena* popular among Puerto Rican blacks. The bomba was a couples dance to music in the call-and-response pattern. The plena was street music that moved into Puerto Rican bars and nightclubs. The Hispanic roots of salsa can be found in the many varieties of dance music popular throughout Latin America. The two Cuban dance styles that most influenced salsa were the *rumba* and the *son*. After Hispanics brought early salsa music to the United States, it was further changed by American jazz.

Salsa continues to be an important part of Santería rituals. However, it has grown well beyond its religious role to become a cultural symbol for Hispanics of Caribbean descent. It has also spread to other Hispanic groups and the general American population. Important salsa musicians include Tito Rodríguez, Tito Puente, Machito, Willie Colón, and Eddie Palmieri. Salsa vocalists include Héctor Lavoe, Celia Cruz, Rubén Blades, and Marc Anthony.

Recent Hispanic American Hybrids

The late twentieth century saw some notable changes in the music of Hispanic Americans. Styles have mixed with one another to form new hybrids. In Texas there has been a dramatic mixing of conjunto music (música norteño) and orquesta music. The traditional orquesta virtually disappeared in the early 1990s. It has been replaced by groups that no longer have horn sections. Instead, these groups use electronic keyboards. At the same time, these orquestas have introduced the accordion from the conjunto. New groups such as Mazz and La Mafia have created a new sound that still reflects its Mexican-Texan roots.

Tejano music has also begun to borrow from American country and western music. Conjunto performers have forged a new sound that is spreading beyond Texas. The leaders of this new trend include Emilio Navaira and Roberto Pulido. It also includes the Texas Tornados, a group made up of vet-

Selena holding the Grammy Award she won for her album *Selena Live!*, 1994. *Reproduced by permission of the Corbis Corporation (Bellevue).*

eran musicians: Freddie Fender, Flaco Jimenez, and Doug Sahm.

But it was the Texas singer Selena who made tejano music known to the majority of U.S. households. Selena and her band performed *Tejano music-Mexican ranchera* style music, mixed sounds owing influence to pop, country and western, and Caribbean music. Selena modernized the traditional accordion-based Tejano or Tex-Mex music with country twangs, techno-pop beats, dance mixes, and international influences. Selena was only twenty-three years old when she was murdered by the former president of her fan club. By that time she had captured the hearts of young Chicanos from across the Southwest and young people throughout

Carlos Santana and Maná performing at the first Latin Grammy Awards, 2000. *Reproduced by permission of AP/Wide World Photos.*

Mexico. Because of their mourning, Selena was in the international headlines and her latest albums became best sellers.

Tejano music continued its explosive growth in the Southwest with top artists like Mazz, La Mafia, and Emilio playing the big city stadiums, like San Antonio's Alamodome, Houston's Astrodome, and Dallas's Texas Stadium. In fact, in February 1995, just before her death, Selena registered the highest ticket sales in history for the Astrodome during the Houston Livestock Show and Rodeo.

Rock en Español

Rock 'n' roll has mainly been sung in English in the past and those who tried it in differ-

ent languages didn't receive the attention that English-language singers did. But the Spanish-language world in the 1990s began to be heard with rock en Español. From the 1950s to the 1970s, many rock musicians in Spain and Latin America (as well as Latino players in the United States) merely imitated their Anglo-American counterparts. There were exceptions, from the early Chicano rock musician Ritchie Valens (1941–1959) through 1960s rocker Carlos Santana and Mexican American roots/rock band Los Lobos, though a lot of their music was in English.

That started to change during the 1980s, when musicians across Spain, Latin America, and the United States who had been raised on rock and bolero began mixing it

Gloria Estefan and the Miami Sound Machine performing at the first Latin Grammy Awards, 2000.
Reproduced by permission of AP/Wide World Photos.

all up and singing about things that mattered to them, in Spanish. In Mexico "los roqueros" flocked around such acts as El Tri, a smoky-voiced Mexican blues-rock band, and in Argentina they heard from Charly Garcia, a musical rebel with a cause.

In the early 1990s this movement became a force in the English-speaking world. Spanish folk-rock duo Duncan Dhu signed to Sire and teamed with Argentinian rocker Miguel Mateos for a small-scale U.S. tour that proved there was an audience outside their home countries. In Latin America a variety of rock bands began to flourish, including salsa/punk/*cumbia* Afropop band Maldita Vecindad (Mexico); alternative rock band Soda Stereo (Argentina); dreamy

rock band Caifanes (Mexico); electro-dance groove band Los Prisioneros (Chile); punk folklorico band Café (Mexico); punk-funk-ska band Los Fabulosos Cadillacs (Argentina); and the lightweight pop-reggae of Maná (Mexico). These rockers and many others began filling clubs and stadiums. This movement was helped along by the introduction of MTV Latino and, of course, the large and ever growing Spanish-speaking population in the United States.

By the mid- to late-1990s, rock en Español was becoming a hit in the United States, with performers such as Maria Fatal, Los Olvidados, King Chango, and Yeska. It has a Grammy category to itself, fanzines, and specialty record labels (Aztlan and Grita!).

Latin Pop

In the early 1990s Latin music expanded in the United States, experiencing increased record sales, a steady growth of Spanish-language radio stations, and newfound crossover success by several artists.

In Latin pop, excitement was created in the early 1990s by newcomers like the pop/dance/rap act the Barrio Boyzz, ballad singer Marcos Llunas, and children's pop group Roxie y Los Frijolitos. Banda is a brass-heavy (like marching bands) form, something like polkas and cumbias. Banda music gained a strong new foothold during the 1990s, particularly in California. It had been popular in the northern states of Mexico for more than twenty years, and the steady flow of Mexican immigrants from that area helped fuel the popularity of the music in southwestern California.

Grupo, the Spanish word for "group," describes musical bands, as opposed to solo artists. The styles of music covered by grupos varies, from pop ballads of Los Bukis or Los Temerarios, to the norteño/ranchera mix of Bronco or Los Tigres, to the Tejano polka/cumbia/ballad blend of La Mafia or Mazz.

Spanish-language pop albums began to draw mainstream attention in the United States when pop singer Gloria Estefan came out with albums evoking the tropical rhythms of her parents' generation in Cuba. The other largely successful crossover act was Los Lobos from East Los Angeles, which continued to produce cuts in Spanish and tour both Anglo and Latino nightclubs and concerts throughout the country.

Ricky Martin. *Reproduced by permission of David Atlas.*

In the late 1990s, Latin pop music exploded onto the U.S. music charts like never before. Ricky Martin's rise from stardom to superstardom reflected the new power of Hispanic music in the United States. In February 1999, at the forty-first Annual Grammy Awards ceremony, Martin danced onstage with a full Latin band and a hip-gyrating, stand-up-and-dance rendition of his hit "La Copa de la Vida." The performance "rocked the house," in presenter Jimmy Smits's words, and evidently had the same effect on television viewers across the nation. Martin won the Grammy for best Latin pop album that night, and his record sales skyrocketed.

Ibrahim Ferrer (center right), Compay Segundo (right), and other members of the Buena Vista Social Club acknowledge the audience during a performance at New York's Carnegie Hall, 1998. *Reproduced by permission of AP/Wide World Photos.*

Time magazine commented that "Martin's house-wrecking performance may be a turning point not just for him, but for all Latin pop in 1999."

Colombia-born singer and songwriter Shakira has been called the most influential voice in Latin pop rock in the early 2000s. Her stardom was launched with Spanish-language dance music albums with a Latin flair in the 1990s and gained momentum in America and worldwide in the 2000s. In 2002, her first English-language album *Laundry Service* was certified triple platinum.

Hispanic music was waiting to happen in the mainstream music scene of the United States at the turn of the twenty-first century. This was demonstrated by the remarkable "recovery" of the Cuban artists of the Buena Vista Social Club. In 1996 U.S. musician Ry Cooder, a devotee of traditional Cuban folk music, went to Cuba and located elderly traditional musicians who had long ago given up on music. With Cooder's assistance, singer Ibrahim Ferrer, guitarist and singer Compay Segundo, and pianist Ruben Gonzales quickly recorded an album as the Buena Vista Social Club. The album caught the attention of the nation, selling 1.5 million copies, and winning a Grammy Award for best Latin album. The group received further recognition when German filmmaker Wim Wenders released a documentary on the group, which chronicled the recording of the album in Havana, as well as live performances in Amsterdam and New York City. For many Americans, it was an introduction to traditional Cuban music.

On September 13, 2000, the Latin Academy of Recording Arts and Sciences, an association composed mainly of musicians, producers, engineers, and other members of the Latin music community, presented the first annual Latin Grammy Awards show. The inaugural show presented forty awards to various artists in many different categories. Veteran rocker Carlos Santana picked up three awards. Other awards went to producer Emilio Estefan, Mexican crooner Luis Miguel, Argentine rocker Fito Paez, Colombian singer Shakira, Dominican singer Juan Luis Guerra, and Mexican rock band Maná. Ibrahim Ferrer of the Buena Vista Social Club, in his seventies, was named the best new artist. Veteran salsa artist Celia Cruz won for best salsa performance. Some observers in the Hispanic music industry criticized the awards show, saying it discriminated against Mexican traditions and favored singers who performed in English. The awards show took place in Los Angeles and was broadcast on CBS. It aired in 120 countries.

Hispanic American Art

Religious Art

The earliest examples of Hispanic American art can be found in the mission churches of the American Southwest built during the seventeenth and eighteenth centuries.

The exteriors of these churches are adorned with many fine examples of sculpture. This early sculpture included images of important figures from the Catholic religion. It also included decorative architectural sculpture to add some interesting features to the flat facades of the missions.

Some of the mission churches also added painted decorations to their exteriors to enhance their appearance. This was especially true in missions that did not have enough money to add sculpture to their facades. An example of this type of painting can be found in San Antonio, Texas, on the facade of Nuestra Señora de la Purísma Concepción de Acuña Mission, built in 1755. On this church, the door, the tower bases, the belfries, and all the windows were painted to simulate stone masonry frames and belfry arches. Other church facades were painted in bright colors to simulate the tiles used on many churches in central Mexico. These churches wanted to recreate the dramatic effects of light and color found on tiled facades.

Inside these mission churches, unknown sculptors and painters focused on making holy images. These artists have come to be known as the *santeros,* or makers of saints' images. Their early sculptures were called *bultos.* Their paintings on large panels were called *retablos.* These traditions continued into the 1800s. In the late 1800s, however, plaster statues and inexpensive prints manufactured elsewhere replaced much of the locally produced religious art.

By the 1920s Hispanic communities in the Southwest had changed. They had been influenced by the mainstream American culture and the influx of exiles from the Mexican Revolution. Economic and cultural

Portal sculpture of St. Joachim on a San Antonio, Texas, church. *Reproduced by permission of Jacinto Quirarte.*

Nuestra Señora de la Purísma Concepción de Acuña Mission in San Antonio, Texas. *Reproduced by permission of Jacinto Quirarte.*

changes brought an end to traditional art for the church. Even so, the traditional arts were preserved and strengthened outside the church. Hispanics devoted to the saints and Our Lady of Guadalupe began to seek yard shrines and home altars. They turned to local artists to help them create private religious artworks. This private religious art has influenced contemporary santeros in New Mexico and Chicano *altaristas* (altar makers).

The yard shrines and home altars found in the barrios (neighborhoods) of the South- west are similar to the folk art produced in New Mexico. Yard shrines are called *capillas* (chapels) in San Antonio, *nichos* (niches) in Tucson, and *grutas* (grottoes) in Los Angeles. Along with home altars, these private shrines express the deeply held religious beliefs of the people who made them. They also express thanks to a saint or to the Virgin Mary for an answered prayer. The paintings and small sculptures included in shrines and altars represent the illness, malady, financial problem, accident, robbery, or enemy that inspired the prayer for help.

"Nicho," a yard shrine in Tucson, Arizona, by Theodora Sanchez, 1957. *Reproduced by permission of Jacinto Quirarte.*

Octavio Medellín's "Xtol." *Reproduced by permission of Jacinto Quirarte.*

Hispanic American Painters: The Twentieth-Century to the Present

From World War I through the 1950s, most Hispanic American artists were part of mainstream art in the United States. Some of these artists joined the regionalist movement that first developed during the 1930s. In regionalism artists turned away from the large cosmopolitan cities to rediscover the culture of neighborhoods, hometowns, and rural areas. Hispanic Americans often turned to their heritage and history for inspiration. They incorporated Native American, Spanish, Mexican, and Caribbean events and landscapes into their paintings. Others participated in the figurative movement. Figurative artists usually painted a single person in an interior or landscape. They often used an expressionistic style, seeking to depict emotions rather than reality.

Among the noted artists whose works are characteristic of this period are the Mexican American artists Octavio Medellín, Antonio García, José Aceves, and Edward Chávez. Other important Hispanic artists of the period are Francisco Luis Mora, born in Uruguay, and Carlos López, born in Cuba. Among the Spanish-born artists are José Moya del Pino and Xavier González.

Panorama of the Plains, a mural by Edward Chávez, 1942. *Reproduced by permission of Jacinto Quirarte.*

In the 1960s and 1970s, Hispanic artists continued to join the mainstream. Their work reflects the art current at that time. One sees figurative, abstract, pop, op, funk, destructive, and other contemporary forms. A number of these Hispanic artists have achieved national and international recognition. The Argentine American Mauricio Lansansky has become known for his prints. He has influenced a generation of printmakers through his work and his teaching in American universities. Venezuelan-born Marisol Escobar has become internationally famous for her sculptures of well-known personalities. These include President Lyndon Johnson and actor John Wayne. Fernando Botero is known for paintings that show big round people in satirical contexts. Botero was born in Colombia, but he now resides in New York City and in Paris.

Hispanic Muralists

Throughout the twentieth century, Hispanic artists have brightened the urban landscape with murals. These large paintings on an interior or exterior wall of a building have depicted the life and industry of the city. They have also shown the history and culture of the Hispanic people. Edward Chávez was one of the early Hispanic muralists. During the 1940s he painted murals in a realistic style for a number of

Judith Baca with youth assistants painting the mural *The Great Wall of Los Angeles,* 1976. *Reproduced by permission of Judith Baca/Social and Public Art Resource Center.*

post offices and government buildings in Colorado, Nebraska, and Wyoming.

More recently Chicano muralists have brought a great diversity of styles to this urban art form. Their goal has been to beautify the landscape, challenge viewers, and reflect the values of the local Hispanic community. They have also tried to continue the work of Mexican muralists from the 1920s through the 1950s.

Chicano murals are found in barrios throughout the Southwest, California, and the Great Lakes region. The number of murals varies from just a few in some cities, like Houston, to many hundreds in Los Angeles. They often show the complex political, social, and economic issues that Hispanics face every day. They are sometimes more important for these themes than for their artistic quality.

One of the most famous muralists at the beginning of the twenty-first century is Judith Baca. Her best-known work is *The Great Wall of Los Angeles,* a 13-foot high, half-mile long outdoor mural thought to be the longest mural in the world. In addition to her work as a muralist and painter, Baca helped found the Social and Public Art Resource Center (SPARC) in Los Angeles, California, an organization that fosters the development of Hispanic artists and has been responsible for more than a hundred new murals in the city of Los Angeles.

13

Hispanic Americans in the Media

| FACT FOCUS |

- The mainstream American media have usually shown stereotyped images of Hispanics.
- The most realistic images of Hispanic Americans have been offered by Hispanics themselves. Hispanic directors in Hollywood and Spanish-language newspapers, radio, and television have treated Hispanics more fairly.
- Today, there are hundreds of Spanish-language or bilingual newspapers and magazines in the United States.
- During the 1990s, Spanish-language radio experienced more growth than any other radio format and approached the level of listeners of some of the mainstream formats.
- The two major Hispanic television networks are Univisión and Telemundo. Between them in 2002 they had an average audience of about 3.7 million viewers.

Newspapers, magazines, films, radio, and television are sources for news, information, and entertainment. These media also show a society and its culture. The United States has had two different sources for news, information, and entertainment about and for Hispanic Americans: the mainstream American media and the Hispanic media. These two sources have given two different images of Hispanic American society and culture. For the most part, the mainstream American media have created and kept alive negative stereotypes of Hispanics. However, the Hispanic media have given a more balanced view of Hispanics. In this way they have better reflected Hispanic society and culture. The Hispanic media is growing rapidly in the early 2000s and is expected to be one of the first business areas to truly register the great increase in Hispanic population. At the turn of the twenty-first century Spanish-language and Hispan-

WORDS TO KNOW

media: newspapers, magazines, radio, television, films, and other sources for information and entertainment. The mainstream media are those whose audience includes all Americans. Hispanic media are directed at Americans who speak Spanish and who are interested in Hispanic culture.

network: a group of radio or television stations that produce shows to broadcast to a large audience.

stereotype: a common, but simplified and often untrue image of a person or group of people.

ic-oriented media were becoming giants in the United States.

Hispanics in the Mainstream Media

Newspapers

Mainstream newspapers were the first media to offer news, information, and images of Hispanics. For the most part, the images in nineteenth-century newspapers were negative. These newspapers often showed Hispanics as Mexican bandits. This stereotype may have helped Anglos to justify their part in the conflicts between Americans and Mexicans over Texas and the Southwest. Showing Hispanics as criminals made it easier for Anglo settlers to take their lands.

Even after these conflicts were over, the mainstream press still did not portray His-

panics fairly. Newspapers frequently focused on the negative aspects of Hispanic culture and ignored the positive ones. One of the worst examples of this happened during the 1940s. At this time there were social and economic tensions between Hispanics and Anglos in Los Angeles. These tensions eventually came to a boil in a major disturbance called the Zoot Suit Riots of 1943. Headlines and stories blamed Hispanics for the unrest and the city's problems.

In recent decades journalistic standards have helped decrease racism in newspapers. However, newspapers have continued to provide inadequate coverage of Hispanic issues and people. This is primarily because there are few Hispanic Americans working for mainstream newspapers.

Films

Newspapers were the first of the media to cover and offer images of Hispanics. However, newspapers usually influenced only readers in the local area. Films were different. Even early films reached a wider American audience. From the beginning, motion pictures have put stereotyped images of Hispanics on the silver screen.

Hispanics have been reduced to stereotypes in American films since the early days of silent movies. In the 1914 film *Bronco Billy and the Greaser,* the Mexican bandit stereotype moved from the newspaper to the movie theater. By the early 1920s, Hollywood had established at least six major Hispanic stereotypes. These were the bandit, the half-breed harlot, the male buffoon or clown, the female clown, the Latin lover, and the dark lady. From the 1920s until the 1940s, the majority of movies that included

Hispanic characters used one or more of these stereotypes.

During World War II (1939–45) Hollywood quickly changed this pattern. At the time the United States wanted Mexico and other Latin American countries to join with it against Germany and the German allies. To help build unity, Hollywood started to offer positive images of Hispanic Americans. Films that showed Hispanics in a more positive light included *Juarez,* a biography of the Mexican revolutionary Benito Juárez made in 1939. Walt Disney studios offered animated travel films such as *Saludos Amigos* (1943) and *The Three Caballeros* (1945). It was this era that saw the rise of such Hispanic stars as María Montez, Ricardo Montalbán, Fernando Lamas, and Carmen Miranda.

In the postwar period, two film genres regularly included Hispanic characters and issues, the *film noir* and the social melodrama. The film noir style offered dark, bleak films about betrayal. Those addressing Hispanic issues included Hollywood director Billy Wilder's 1951 film *Ace in the Hole,* Orson Welles's 1958 film *Touch of Evil,* and Ralph Nelson's 1962 film *Requiem for a Heavyweight.* All of these movies criticized the corruption in Anglo society. The social melodrama dealt directly with social problems. Herbert Biberman's 1954 film *Salt of the Earth* showed real-life gritty New Mexico miners who staged a strike. Joseph Losey's 1954 film *The Lawless* focused on Chicano issues. George Stevens's 1957 blockbuster *Giant,* which starred Rock Hudson, Elizabeth Taylor, and James Dean, criticized racism, the class system, and America's westward expansion.

María Montez. *Reproduced by permission of the Corbis Corporation (Bellevue).*

Since 1960 there have been two approaches to handling Hispanic stereotypes in movies. One approach has been to continue the stereotype. The other approach has been to counter the stereotype. The bandit stereotype can be found in several popular films during this period. Perhaps the most widely seen example is found in Steven Spielberg's 1981 film *Raiders of the Lost Ark.* In that movie's first fifteen minutes, the main character, Indiana Jones, is attacked by many Hispanic villains somewhere in South America in 1936. Another widely seen example of the bandit stereotype is found in *Romancing the Stone* (1984). Updated variations of the Hispanic bandit can be found in the young Puerto Rican toughs of the 1961 musical *West Side Story.*

The leader of the Sharks facing off with the Jets in the film *West Side Story. Reproduced by permission of Archive Photos, Inc.*

Even with these stereotypes, some positive images of Hispanic American culture have come from movies made since the 1960s. A number of talented Hispanics have started to work behind the camera. These Hispanic directors have seized the chance to counter the stereotypes. They have taken familiar Hollywood stories and given them an ethnic twist. In this way they have started to show a more multicultural America. León Ichaso's 1985 film *Crossover Dreams* offers a Hispanic version of the show biz success story. A New York salsa musician leaves behind the barrio in search of fame and fortune. Eventu-

ally, he returns to his neighborhood and its people. The movie critiques some of the ideas behind the American dream and celebrates traditional Hispanic values.

At the end of the 1990s, Latino pop culture, expressed by such artists as Ricky Martin and Jennifer Lopez, had created another kind of stereotype, although positive, of Hispanics, a Latin form of Hollywood glamor, sensual, glittering, and not very lifelike. Ichaso, among other filmmakers, countered this Latino boom image with his 2001 movie *Piñero* about the Puerto

Rican poet/playwright/outlaw Miguel Piñero who died in 1988. This great Nuyorican poet's work foreshadowed rap and hip hop of today, and his play *Short Eyes* won awards and was made into a movie, but Piñero was also a fiercely rebellious man. He had grown up tough on the streets of New York, had become addicted to heroin, and was constantly in trouble with the law. Piñero wrote about the street life in the 1970s at a time when most of America did not want to hear about it and much of his work has long gone out of print. As a film-maker Ichaso revived Piñero's poetry for his audience. The poetry reflects Piñero's street life but also the painful experience shared by many Puerto Ricans who immigrated from the island with the hope of finding a better world and then found themselves living in poverty in a strange, mean city.

Director Moctezuma Esparza helped revise the western movie by producing such films as *The Ballad of Gregorio Cortez* (1982). The movie tells the story of a Hispanic Texan who fled from prejudice and from the Texas Rangers (a group of rural law enforcers) around the turn of the twentieth century. The film counters the bandit stereotype.

The coming-to-America story from a Hispanic perspective can be found in Gregory Nava's *El Norte* (1984). This is the story of a brother and his sister fleeing political problems in their Central American homeland. It shows the danger and hope of their journey. Nava's 1995 film *My Family/Mi Familia* was the story of several generations of a Mexican American family from their life in Mexico to their life in East Los Angeles. It starred Edward James Olmos and Jennifer Lopez. In 1997 Nava's film *Selena* brought

A scene from the film *Selena,* in which Jennifer Lopez portrays the Tejano singer. *Reproduced by permission of AP/Wide World Photos.*

the name and music of the late Tejano music star to mainstream audiences.

Ramón Menéndez's 1988 film *Stand and Deliver,* the story of Jaime Escalante (played by Edward James Olmos), a courageous and innovative high school math teacher from East Los Angeles, also presents a positive view of the issues Hispanic Americans face in the United States.

Toward the end of the 1990s Moctezuma Esparza established a company that would develop movie theaters for Spanish-language movies in the United States. Other industry pioneers were following suit, hoping that the surge in the Hispanic population would revive the once-popular Hispanic cinema. At the end of the century, crowds at

Edward James Olmos (left) with Jaime Escalante on the set of *Stand and Deliver. Reproduced by permission of Archive Photos, Inc.*

Latino movie festivals were rapidly increasing. Many Hispanics who had grown up with neighborhood theaters that played Spanish-language movies expressed an interest, but there have not been distributors and theaters for Spanish-language and Hispanic-themed movies until recently.

For many Hispanics, though, the local mall is the place to see films, and Hollywood movies will be the main fare. The obvious underrepresentation of Hispanic people and themes in mainstream films in the twenty-first century remains a problem. For many years Hispanic actors have been urged to play down their ethnic backgrounds: Martin Sheen, for instance, changed his name from Estevez; Raquel Welch, born Jo-Raquel Tejada, dyed her hair blond for her breakthrough role; earlier, Rita Hayworth changed her name from Margarita Carmen Cansino. Most observers recognize that Hollywood needs to reflect the American population more realistically. In the 2001 Hollywood romantic comedy *Tortilla Soup,* starring Hector Elizondo, Jacqueline Obradors, Raquel Welch, Paul Rodriguez, and Elizabeth Peña, the ethnicity is embraced without becoming the theme of the movie.

What is of interest to Hispanic people may not always be Latino themes. Many Hispanic actors do not want to be cast only in roles for Latinos, and Hispanic audiences, particularly

A scene from the film *Tortilla Soup,* starring Hector Elizondo (standing), Raquel Welch, Paul Rodriguez, and Elizabeth Peña (from Elizondo's left to right). *Reproduced by permission of the Kobal Collection.*

of later generations, want to watch movies of diverse themes. Academy Award-winner Benicio del Toro observed in 2002, "I feel a great responsibility for being a Latino actor working in Hollywood.... The only thing that I ask is not to be solely seen as a Latino actor. The fact that my name is Benicio Del Toro should not imply that I must be thought of only as a Hispanic actor." In the 2000s there are many outstanding Hispanic actors who want to play challenging roles in mainstream films, whether or not they are Hispanic roles.

Television

Like film, television has shown many stereotyped images of Hispanics and a few positive images. In some ways television has actually been more critical of Hispanic culture and life. The situation is also worse in television because there have been fewer Hispanic actors and directors.

The first major Hispanic character on television was seen on *I Love Lucy* (CBS, 1951–61). Ricky Ricardo, Lucy's husband played by Desi Arnaz, was a hot-tempered Cuban bandleader. In most shows he played the Hispanic male buffoon stereotype. Other Hispanics who played clownish roles included José Jiménez, the bumbling Puerto Rican doorman on *The Danny Thomas Show* (NBC, 1953–71), and Sergeant García in the *Zorro* series (ABC, 1957–59). The

Benicio Del Toro in *Traffic. Reproduced by permission of the Kobal Collection.*

most recent Hispanic buffoon role on television was Chico (played by Freddie Prinze) in *Chico and the Man* (NBC, 1974–78).

The Hispanic bandit stereotype has also been used by television. It was common in the westerns of the 1950s and 1960s. Updated versions have also been used in urban cop shows such as *Dragnet* (NBC, 1951–59 and 1967–70). More recently the bandit has usually been seen as a drug dealer. Examples of the Hispanic drug dealer could be found on shows like *Hill Street Blues* (NBC, 1981–86) and *Miami Vice* (NBC, 1984–89).

In the 1990s Taco Bell found a popular star for its commercials: a Spanish-speaking chihuahua. Many Hispanic organizations found the commercials offensive and called for boycotts of the chain. Although the stereotypes were not as negative as in the Frito Bandito ads of the 1970s, many Hispanics believed that with so few other images of Latinos on television, representing the Mexican population and culture in the form of a little dog was degrading. Under pressure, the Taco Bell chain dropped the small dog from their commercials.

Mainstream television has included some Hispanic good guys. From *The Cisco Kid* and *Zorro* in the 1950s to more recent shows such as *CHiPs, Miami Vice,* and *L.A. Law,* there have been some positive Hispanic male figures. Actor Edward James Olmos's role as Lieutenant Martin Castillo in *Miami Vice* was one of the most positive Hispanic characters in television history. Olmos created a man of dignity and honor with quiet strength and great power. His role helped to somewhat balance the Latin American drug smuggler stereotype common on the show. Jimmy Smits's role as Hispanic attorney Victor Sifuentes on *L.A. Law* helped give that show some social awareness. Esai Morales appeared in many television series during the 1990s and early 2000s, including a role as Lieutenant Tony Rodriguez on *NYPD Blue*. Hector Elizondo played Dr. Phillip Watters on *Chicago Hope*. But in the early 2000s, many of the Hispanic roles on television portray maids or other unskilled workers and have no character or depth.

In 1999 Hispanics nationwide protested their underrepresentation on television. Studies showed that 63 percent of Latinos did not feel that television represented them accurately. Hispanic groups, such as the National Council of La Raza (NCLR), urged viewers to participate in a national brownout (large decrease in usage) of ABC, CBS, Fox, and NBC television networks the week of September 12, to coincide with Hispanic Heritage Week.

In 2000, the cable network Showtime came out with television's first Hispanic family drama, *Resurrection Boulevard,* a series about a working-class Mexican American family in East Los Angeles. Most of the roles in front of and behind the camera were filled by Hispanic people, making this a true milestone in TV. The cable network Nickelodeon then came out with several Hispanic-themed shows: *The Brothers Garcia, Taina,* and *Dora the Explorer.*

Jimmy Smits. *Reproduced by permission of AP/Wide World Photos.*

In 2000, CBS financed the pilot episode of a drama about a Mexican American family, created by filmmaker Gregory Nava. But, after financing it, CBS could not find a place for the show in its 2000–01 schedule. Finally, PBS picked up the show, which debuted in January 2002. The series stars Edward James Olmos, Raquel Welch, Sonia Braga, Esai Morales, and many others.

Olmos has been at the forefront of the efforts to make television more representative of the Hispanic population. After the series *American Family* aired, he observed that even with the few new Latino-themed shows coming out, Hispanics remain severely underrepresented on American television.

An edition of *La Prensa* newspaper. *Reproduced by permission of Latin Focus.*

The Hispanic Media

Hispanic Americans and their culture have been treated much more fairly in newspapers, magazines, film, radio, and television created specifically for Hispanics. From the 1800s border newspapers to the present Hispanic television networks, there have been media designed to inform and entertain Hispanic Americans. Most of these media have used the Spanish language, but many have also offered bilingual features. More recently some of these media have used only English. Some of the important Hispanic media have been owned by non-Hispanics, but many have been guided by Hispanic owners. No matter what the language or ownership, these media have shown Hispanics in a much more thorough and realistic way.

Hispanic Newspapers

The Spanish-language press within the United States started in 1808 in New Orleans, Louisiana. *El Misisipí* offered four pages of news and advertisements for Spanish-speaking immigrants. Over the next forty years, Mexican pioneers published dozens of Spanish-language newspapers throughout the American Southwest, which still belonged to Mexico. When Hispanics became part of the United States, they continued to produce Spanish-language newspapers. Over the years most of the newspapers produced for a Hispanic audience have continued to use Spanish. However, more recently, Hispanic newspapers have included English in bilingual editions. They have also targeted some Hispanics through English papers.

Hispanic press grew rapidly in the last decade of the twentieth century. The number of Hispanic newspapers in the United States grew by 55 percent, from 355 in 1990 to 550 in 2000. Hispanic magazines grew from 177 to 352. Some of the major Hispanic daily papers have been around for many years. *La Opinión* began publishing in Los Angeles on September 16, 1926. It features daily news, opinions, sports, entertainment, and advertising sections. It also includes special supplements for each of the weekdays and several Sunday supplements. In 2001 *La Opinión's* daily circulation average was 128,495 and it reached approximately 680,000 readers. It is one of the biggest Spanish-language newspapers in the United States, and in the city of Los Angeles it is second only to the *Los Angeles Times*.

El Diario-La Prensa began publishing in New York in the summer of 1963 after the merger of two newspapers, *La Prensa* and *El Diario de Nueva York*. *La Prensa* had originally begun publishing in 1913 and *El Diario* in 1948. *El Diario-La Prensa*'s current readership is primarily Puerto Rican. In addition to its regular daily features and weekday supplements, this newspaper includes reviews and opinions on literature, poetry, movies, and politics in its Saturday-Sunday edition. Its weekday circulation was 56,938 in 2001.

In 1998 a new Spanish-language newspaper, *Hoy* (Today), was established and it quickly came to rival *El Diario-La Prensa*. While the older paper catered to New York's large Puerto Rican population, *Hoy* went after the rapidly increasing Dominican, Mexican, Ecuadorean, and other Latin American population. In 2001 its weekday circulation was 65,768.

El Nuevo Herald started publishing in Miami on November 21, 1987. This paper was a new and expanded version of a Spanish-language insert that had been published in the *Miami Herald* since March 29, 1976. Unlike the Los Angeles and New York papers, *El Nuevo Herald* reaches most of its readers through home delivery and claims to be the Spanish-language newspaper with the highest circulation numbers in the continental United States. It is published by Knight Ridder Newspapers.

El Diario de las Américas was founded in Miami on July 4, 1953. It is the only Spanish-language daily that is owned and operated by Hispanics without Anglo partnerships. In 2002 its weekday circulation was 70,000 and its Sunday circulation was 73,000. Almost all of its papers are home delivered. This newspaper offers regular sections and

A cover of *Latina Style* magazine. *Reproduced by permission of Latin Focus.*

weekday supplements to its readers, many of whom are Cuban Americans.

There are many other U.S. newspapers in Spanish, including: *La Raza* of Chicago; *Dos Mundos* of Kansas City; *La Prensa* of San Diego (bilingual); *El Sol* of Arizona; *La Conexion* of North Carolina; *La Prensa* of San Antonio (bilingual); and many more.

Hispanic Magazines

Since before the turn of the century, publishers have produced a variety of Hispanic magazines. Of the current Spanish-language magazines, the oldest is *Temas*. It has been published monthly since November 1950 in New York City. It circulates over 110,000 copies per month. *Temas* includes articles

A cover of *Replica* magazine. *Reproduced courtesy of Replica Publications, Inc.*

on culture, current events, beauty, fashion, and home decorating. It also features interviews with people of interest to the Spanish-speaking populations of the United States. Another Spanish-language magazine is *Réplica,* founded in 1963. Its circulation is similar to that of *Temas.* From its base in Miami, this monthly magazine publishes articles on travel, fashion, sports, entertainment, and news events in Latin America and the Caribbean.

Unlike Spanish-language television and radio, which have become giant businesses as the twenty-first century gets under way, Spanish-language magazines have not been highly successful in the United States. This outlook changed in February 1998, when Time Inc. began publishing *People en Español.* By mid-2001 its circulation had increased by 70 percent to 356,000.

Two years earlier the remarkably young Mexican American entrepreneur Christy Haubegger created *Latina* magazine, the first bilingual magazine targeted exclusively to Hispanic women in the United States. Launched in 1996, *Latina*'s circulation had reached 239,000 in 2002. With the new census figures in view, many other publishing companies are looking at the possibilities in Spanish-language or bilingual magazines.

Three important English-language magazines for the Hispanic audience are *Hispanic, Hispanic Business,* and *Hispanic Link. Hispanic* published its first issue in April 1988. The focus of this magazine is on contemporary Hispanics, their achievements and contributions to American society. Its stories cover a broad range of topics. They include entertainment, education, business, sports, the arts, government, politics, and literature, as well as people and events in the news. In 2002 the circulation for this monthly was 260,000.

Hispanic Business is published in Santa Barbara, California. It started as a newsletter in 1979 and became a monthly magazine in 1982. Its circulation in 2001 was over 215,000. Special monthly topics include trends in the Hispanic media market, the Hispanic Business 500 (a list of the leading Hispanic-owned businesses), and Hispanics in mainstream entertainment. The third English-language magazine for Hispanics is *Hispanic Link.* Although it is actually a newsletter, it is still very influential. It offers a summary of the major issues and events for Hispanics related to education, immigration, business, politics, and the economy.

Two notable bilingual magazines for Hispanics are *Vista* and *Saludos Hispanos* (Regards, Hispanics). *Vista* started in September 1985 in Miami. It is a monthly insert to Sunday newspapers in cities with large Hispanic populations. It is included in 37 newspapers nationwide where there is a heavy Hispanic population. In 2002 its circulation was estimated at about 1.1 million copies, with a readership of 2.4 million people. *Vista* aims at informing, educating, and entertaining Hispanic American readers with stories that focus on Hispanic role models and their culture.

Hispanic Radio

Hispanic radio has been booming over the last ten years. The number of stations, companies, and organizations offering Spanish-language radio has grown at a great pace. So has the types of programming that they offer. Radio offers *rancheras* and *salsa,* two types of music that are very popular among Hispanic Americans. It also features Top 40, mariachi, *música norteña,* Tex-Mex, Mexican hits, adult contemporary, international hits, romantic, ballads, oldies, folk, regional, *boleros,* progressive *tejano, merengue,* rock en Español, and even bilingual contemporary hits.

Spanish-language radio programs from within the borders of the United States began as early as the 1920s. This was soon after the first radio broadcast of any type in the United States. In the mid-1920s some of the early English-language radio stations began selling time to Hispanic radio producers. One of the most well known pioneers of Spanish-language radio in California was Pedro J. González. González brought such shows as

Los Madrugadores, the group that played on Pedro J. González's radio program. *Reproduced by permission of Arte Público Press.*

Los Madrugadores (The Early Birds) to Los Angeles. The program was broadcast from 4:00 to 6:00 A.M. from KMPC. Because of the power of the station, it could be heard all over the Southwest as far away as Texas. Other programs common in the early years featured poetry, live drama, news, live programming, and advertising in Spanish.

From the 1950s to the 1970s, Hispanic radio was in transition. Instead of producers buying time on English-language stations, more began to run their own AM and FM stations. Many transmitted twenty-four hours a day. By the late 1960s, recordings had replaced the live singers and radio personalities. There was also less talk and more music. Since the 1970s Spanish-language radio has seen a great deal of growth. This expansion came especially in the late 1980s. In 1991 there were over one hundred AM and thirty-five FM radio stations that broadcast in Spanish full time. Many more AM and FM stations offered some Spanish programming.

Some of the Spanish-language radio stations produce everything they broadcast, including news and commercials. However, many stations buy some of their programs from other companies, such as news services and full-service providers. Among the major news service providers is Radio Noticias (News Radio). It began in 1983 as a division of United Press International (UPI). From Washington, D.C., it distributes news programs in Spanish to forty-two stations.

Other companies provide all the programming for Spanish-language radio stations. The largest of these is Cadena Radio Centro (CRC). It was founded in 1985 in Dallas, Texas. CRC provides news, music, talk shows, and special events in Spanish to local stations. Another full-service provider is the CBS Hispanic Radio Network. This special-events network was founded in 1990 by the Columbia Broadcasting System (CBS). It provides coverage of major sporting events such as the World Series and the Super Bowl. It also airs special cultural events of interest to Hispanics.

During the 1990s, Spanish-language radio experienced more growth than any other radio format. As Spanish-language radio approached the level of listeners of some of the mainstream formats, more businesses began to advertise on Spanish programs, infusing more money into the industry. The attention of the nation had been drawn. The National Football League (NFL) and the National Basketball Association

(NBA) began to broadcast games in Spanish through Hispanic broadcasting companies.

In the early 2000s, Spanish-language radio stations could be heard in almost every region of the United States. In cities with large populations of Hispanics, there were a wide variety of Hispanic stations to choose from. The news and other programming have allowed Hispanics to keep ties with their homelands and other Latin American countries. These radio stations have entertained Hispanics and are even, in the 2000s, bringing some Mexican musicians to American audiences. More important, however, they have helped bring together the Hispanic community in the United States.

In the summer of 2002, Univisión Communications, Inc., the largest Spanish-language media company, announced that it planned to buy Hispanic Broadcasting Corporation (HBC) for a whopping $3 billion. HBC has fifty-five Spanish-language radio stations and several of the number-one rated stations in the big Hispanic-populated cities, such as Los Angeles and Miami. Univisión already has about 80 percent of the large Spanish-language television audience and can use the radio stations it acquires to promote its TV stations. It can also use its TV stations to promote its radio stations. Most industry observers believed that, with the large new Hispanic market, this will mean vast growth in both industries.

Hispanic Television

Spanish-language television in the United States started soon after the earliest broadcasts in English. As with radio, Hispanic producers in the 1940s bought time from mainstream television stations. In the early days these producers bought a few hours of Spanish programming on stations in San Antonio and New York. The first Spanish-language television station in the United States soon followed. It was San Antonio's KCOR-TV. It began some evening programs in 1955. KCOR took advantage of the newly created ultra high frequency (UHF) band and broadcast on Channel 41. In the early days, it aired shows from 5:00 P.M. to midnight. About 50 percent of the shows were live variety and entertainment shows that featured Mexican performers.

In the early 2000s, Spanish-language television is one of the most booming industries in the United States. While television audiences nationwide have been shrinking, Hispanic audiences have been growing. The two major Hispanic networks are Univisión and Telemundo. Between them in 2002 they have an average audience of about 3.7 million viewers. They no longer rely on variety shows and old movies. They include drama, talk shows, comedy, news, the highly popular soap operas or *telenovelas,* investigative journalism, sports, contemporary movies, entertainment magazines, dance videos, and specials. In 2002, Spanish-language programs earned about $2 billion in advertising.

Univisión. Univisión Network is the largest Spanish-language television network in the United States, reaching an average of 1.7 million households each night in 2002. It is owned by Univisión Communications, Inc., the leading Spanish-language media company in the United States. Along with Univisión Network, the company's operations include Univisión Television Group, Galavisión, Univisión Music Group, and Univisión Online. Univisión's television

Cristina Saralegui. *Reproduced by permission of Arte Público Press.*

programming reaches more than 92 percent of Hispanic households. Univision.com is the premier Spanish-language Web site in the United States.

Univisión's programming includes a number of news and issues programs. The weeknight news program *Noticiero TV* often surpasses the "big three" network news programs in its audience size. It has a popular morning show, *Despierta América,* and a newsmagazine, *Primer Impacto.* *Cristina* is a talk show. Hosted by Cuban-born Cristina Saralegui, it is Univisión's version of *The Oprah Winfrey Show.* Its twenty-four-hour broadcast day also includes *telenovelas* (soap operas), which are a huge hit in many Hispanic homes. There are also variety shows, comedy

Cristian de la Fuente and Ricardo Molina, the stars of *Reyes y Rey,* a Telemundo series that reflects the Hispanic experience in the United States. *Reproduced by permission of Getty Images.*

Laura Bozzo, host of Telemundo's talk show *Laura en America. Reproduced by permission of the Corbis Corporation (Bellevue).*

shows, game shows, movies, sports, children's shows, religious shows, and specials.

Galavisión, the largest Spanish-language cable network in the United States, is owned by Univisión. Univisión plans the programming of the two networks so they do not compete with one another. Galavisión aims for the very large market of young U.S. Hispanics. Galavisión's twenty-four-hours-a-day line-up includes sports, music, bicultural shows, educational children's programming, news, novelas, variety, specials, and movies.

Univisión launched its second network, Telefutura, in January 2002. Telefutura reaches about 80 percent of U.S. Hispanic homes.

Telemundo. Telemundo is the second largest Hispanic television network in the United States. It was purchased by NBC for $2.7 billion in 2001. Through its broadcast stations and cable carriers, Telemundo can reach over 84 percent of U.S. Hispanic households. Telemundo cooperates with the Cable News Network (CNN) to produce some Spanish-language news reports from CNN's Atlanta studios. It also has news bureaus in Mexico, New York, Washington, and Miami. However, most of Telemundo's programs come from its 50,000-square-foot facility in Hialeah, Florida.

In addition to its nightly news, *Noticiero Telemundo,* the network offers investigative reporting, issues programs, and entertainment. Among the most popular shows is Telemundo's talk show *Laura en America,* which, with more than a million viewers a day, is a rival to Univisión's *Cristina.* The network produces a very popular soap opera, *Betty La Fea* (Betty the Ugly). It also produces specials such as the popular *Esta Noche con Usted* (Tonight with You). This special program offers interviews with important Latin Americans.

Hispanic Internet

A Department of Commerce study in 2000 found that Hispanics were quite far behind other U.S. groups in the use of the Internet. Many believed that a reason for this was that only about 3 percent of Web sites were in the Spanish language, while more than 60 percent were in English. That same year several Spanish-language Web sites were launched, including Spanish versions of AOL and Yahoo!. The Spanish company Terra Networks also signed a deal with Lycos to target Hispanic Americans on the Web, while Yupi.com, another Spanish-language portal, made plans to offer stock to the public. To further boost the Hispanic presence on the Internet, Gateway invested $10 million in quepasa.com and Microsoft announced the creation of a new Spanish-language Web portal in Mexico.

A study done in 2002 revealed that Hispanic presence on the Internet had increased with 51 percent of Hispanics owning a personal computer in their home, and 44 percent of them accessing the Internet. The Hispanics on the Internet were spending more than half their time on Spanish-language Web sites.

14

Hispanic Americans in Sports

FACT FOCUS

- Hispanic Americans have influenced American sports, especially rodeo and baseball. They have also been successful in other sports such as boxing, football, and golf.
- The festival of Mexican cowboys is probably the grandfather of the American rodeo.
- Americans introduced baseball to Cuba in 1866. It quickly became popular there and spread to Mexico, Puerto Rico, and Venezuela.
- In the early 1900s, a color barrier kept blacks and darker-skinned Hispanics out of major league baseball. For this reason, many Hispanics played in the Negro leagues started for African Americans. Some Hispanics still made their way into the U.S. major leagues. Many of those who did had long and successful careers.
- The color barrier in baseball came down in 1947. In 2002, over 17 percent of major league players were Hispanic.

Sports have played a very important role in popular Hispanic culture. In the past, sports have offered recreation and entertainment to many, and have given some Hispanics a chance to change their lives, a chance at fame and fortune. Sports have also reflected the general Hispanic experience in American society.

Hispanic Americans have participated in a wide variety of sports in the United States.

On the field of play, Hispanics have mixed their Native American, Spanish, and African sports traditions with other sporting traditions. As a result some Hispanics have helped create the sports of the United States. Others have been very successful in mainstream American sports. Rodeo and baseball are the two American sports most influenced by Hispanics, and in the 2000s, Hispanic players are very visible in major league baseball.

WORDS TO KNOW

charro fiesta: a celebration and contest started by cowboys in northern Mexico. It was the first kind of rodeo.

color barrier: the rule that kept African Americans, Hispanic Americans, and other people of color from playing in American professional baseball. Jackie Robinson, an African American, broke through the color barrier on April 10, 1947.

horsemanship: the skill of riding and taking care of horses.

rodeo: a contest for cowboys in which they test their skill riding horses and cattle and using ropes.

segregation: separating people in schools and other public places because of their race or culture.

Early Spanish colonists introduced ranching and sports with horses and cattle to the New World. These Spanish sports soon mixed with traditional Native American sports. Later, these new sports were learned by Anglo Americans and other European immigrants. The American cowboy was born in this exchange. So was the rodeo. The influence of the *charrerías* (contests) of Mexican *vaqueros* (cowboys) can still be seen in today's rodeo.

Baseball was developed in the United States in the 1800s. It was introduced to Cuba and other Hispanic countries in the last part of that century. As the game became more serious, American players began to look for places to play during the winter. The weather and playing fields of Mexico and the Caribbean attracted many American players. These players, in turn, attracted more and more Hispanics to the sport.

Rodeo

When the Spaniards brought cattle ranching to the New World, they also brought their horse culture with them. They used their animals for work and also for play. These practices quickly blended with Native American customs for animal handling. As the number of haciendas (ranches) grew, so did the need for cowboys. The number of mestizo (those of mixed Spanish and Native American heritage) cowboys increased during the seventeenth, eighteenth, and nineteenth centuries. The *charros,* as the mestizo cowboys were called, developed their own culture. They had unique customs, clothing, music, and styles of horsemanship.

In the 1800s the charros' lifestyle captured the hearts of the Mexican people. Charro clothing and horsemanship became popular even in the cities of Mexico. It was so popular, in fact, that it became the national costume. Charros also served as models for American cowboys. Anglo cowboys worked alongside and learned from Mexican cowboys in Texas and California in the early 1800s.

The contests and games common to the charros also became the Mexican national sport. People came from hundreds of miles away to haciendas in order to see the skillful charros compete during their festivals. Dressed in their finest costumes, the charros

A vaquero, a Mexican cowboy. *Reproduced courtesy of the Bancroft Library, University of California.*

raced horses, rode wild horses and bulls, roped horses and steers, and threw bulls. They performed tricks while riding at top speed. This charro fiesta spread to become a standard celebration all along both sides of the U.S.-Mexican border. It was perhaps the grandfather of the American rodeo. Colonel W. F. "Buffalo Bill" Cody launched the American rodeo when he included many of the charro festival events in his Wild West Show. The five standard events in today's professional rodeo all have roots in these early events. They are bareback bronc rid-

ing, saddle bronc riding, bull riding, steer wrestling, and calf roping.

Between 1883 and 1916, Cody's show toured the major cities of the United States and Europe. Along with him came many Hispanic cowboys from the San Antonio, Texas, area. Among these were rodeo superstar Antonio Esquivel and roper Señor Francisco. But the most famous charro of all was Vicente Oropeza. Oropeza was the greatest trick roper of all time. He was a star of Cody's show for more than sixteen years.

He even influenced Will Rogers, one of America's greatest rodeo stars.

Baseball

Baseball has been a part of Hispanic popular culture since 1866. The story is told that in that year a group of sailors from an American ship anchored in a Cuban harbor came to shore. There, they invited local Cubans to join them in an American game. Together the Americans and Cubans built a diamond at Palmar del Junco. They played while the ship remained in the harbor. From this beginning Hispanic baseball has been closely linked to American baseball.

Latin American Baseball

By 1874 Cuban teams were playing each other regularly. A professional league formed in 1878, the Liga de Béisbol Profesional Cubana (the Cuban Baseball League). This was just seven years after the National Baseball Association was founded in the United States. By 1891 there were seventy-five teams playing on the island. From that time Cuban baseball has contributed to baseball in the United States. Cuban teams served as a training ground for players on their way to the American major leagues. At one time there was even a Triple A minor league team, the Cuban Sugar Kings. Major league teams practiced during the winter months and held their spring training on the island. Mexican, Puerto Rican, and Venezuelan baseball leagues started soon after the Cuban leagues. They offered similar services to the major leagues. All of these leagues helped make Hispanic players and teams an important part of their cultures.

Latin American baseball gave a lot to American baseball. Even so, Hispanic players did not always receive the benefits of this relationship. Until 1947 people of color could not play on mainstream American baseball teams. This was due to social attitudes about race and because of segregation. Segregation forced blacks and whites to keep separate in society. This color barrier also kept darker-skinned Hispanics off American teams. Instead, they competed with African American players in the many Negro leagues in the United States. Lighter-skinned and white Hispanics were allowed to play in the majors, however. Between 1871 and 1947, about fifty of them played for major league teams. Some eventually made it to the Hall of Fame. One even served as manager of a major league team.

Cuban, Mexican, Puerto Rican, and Venezuelan baseball leagues did not have a color barrier. For this reason they gave players of all colors a chance to play together. Darker-skinned Hispanic and African American baseball players could compete with white and lighter-skinned players. They could also compete with major league players who played in Latin America during the winter. This was long before baseball legend Jackie Robinson broke the color barrier on April 10, 1947.

Mexican baseball began to grow dramatically in the 1940s. In 1946 the wealthy Pasquel family in Mexico founded a professional league there. The family used its money to try to attract star players from the major leagues and the Negro leagues. Newspapers in the United States cried out that Mexico planned to rob the nation of its pastime. The U.S. State Department even filed a formal complaint with the Mexican government. Twenty-three players accepted Pasquel's offer. Seven years later financial problems forced the league to shut down. The northern teams joined with the Arizona-Texas and Arizona-Mexico leagues from 1953 to 1957.

The Mexican League started up again in 1955 and is still alive. Castro's Cuban Revolution raised a political barrier between the Cuban leagues and American baseball. This barrier has helped Mexican baseball grow. Several leagues started during the 1960s. They now supply young ballplayers to the American major leagues. They also give older major league players a chance to play after they have passed their prime.

Hispanics in the Negro Leagues

The color barrier in major league baseball in the United States blocked many Hispanics from playing in those leagues. The Negro leagues offered these Hispanics a chance to play. By the 1920s there were many Hispanics playing in the U.S. Negro leagues. Among the Hispanic greats to play in the Negro leagues were Cristóbal Torriente, Martín Dihigo, José Méndez, Orestes "Minnie" Miñoso, Alejandro Oms, and Luis Tiant, Sr.

As early as 1900, Cubans were a part of the U.S. Negro leagues. At that time two of the five black professional teams showed their Hispanic character in their names. The Cuban Giants played their home games in New York and later in Hoboken, New Jersey, and Johnstown, Pennsylvania. The Cuban X Giants played their home games in New York. In the 1920s there were teams named the Cuban Stars in both the Eastern

A newspaper montage for the Negro League Museum featuring Oscar Charleston, Pablo Mesa, and Alejandro Oms of the 1927 Cuban Stars. *Reproduced by permission of the Martin Agency.*

Colored League and the Negro National League. Cuban teams continued to be an important part of the Negro leagues from the 1920s through the 1940s.

There were also individual Hispanics playing on several other teams in the Negro leagues. The Indianapolis Clowns filled their roster with Hispanics. At one point this team was even managed by a Hispanic, Ramiro Ramírez. Over the course of his long career from 1916 to 1948, Ramírez had played with most of the Cuban teams, plus

JOSÉ MÉNDEZ

José Méndez was a Cuban baseball player from the turn of the twentieth century. He was a very talented pitcher, but because he was black he could not play in the U.S. major leagues. In 1909, Méndez and his team, the Cuban Stars, toured the United States to play the best teams in the Negro leagues. During the tour, he was the winning pitcher 44 times. He lost only two games. In Cuba, Méndez and the Cuban Stars played against the Philadelphia Phillies and the New York Giants. He beat the Phillies. In two games against the Giants, he pitched against two future Hall of Famers, Christy Mathewson and John McGraw. Méndez won one game and lost one.

this early major league. Later, teams in Washington, Cincinnati, Chicago, Cleveland, and Detroit regularly gave Hispanics the chance to play. By the turn of the twentieth century, however, no black Cubans were allowed to play in the major leagues.

Cubans and other Hispanics soon returned to major league baseball, but only lighter-skinned and white players. Some Americans still complained that these players contaminated the racial purity of the national pastime. For this reason some teams had to show proof that their players had pure Spanish ancestry. In 1911 the Cincinnati Reds had to show such proof when the team recruited Armando Marsans and Rafael Almeida from the Cuban Stars of the Negro league.

In 1912 Cuban Miguel González began playing for Boston as a catcher. He played for various teams during his seventeen-year career. He also served for fourteen years as a St. Louis Cardinals coach, the first Hispanic to do so. Adolfo Luque had perhaps the longest career among the early Hispanics in major league baseball. A dark-skinned Cuban pitcher, Luque played from 1914 to 1935. During those many years, he played for the Atlanta Braves, Cincinnati Reds, Brooklyn Dodgers, and New York Giants. He pitched in two World Series and won the final game of one. During his best season, 1923 with Cincinnati, he led the league with 27 wins, a 1.93 earned run average, and six shutouts. Despite his talent Luque faced many problems because of his color. Fans jeered at him and used racial slurs against him.

The Washington Senators was the major league team most open to Hispanic players.

the Baltimore Black Sox, the Bacharach Giants, and the Clowns. Hispanics also played regularly on teams such as the Cleveland Buckeyes, Memphis Red Sox, and New York Black Yankees.

Hispanics in the Major Leagues

The first Hispanic to play on a major league team in the United States was Esteban Bellán, a black Cuban. The Troy Haymakers recruited Bellán from Fordham College in New York. The team joined the National Baseball Association when it was founded in 1871. Bellán spent three years in

Roberto Clemente, four times the National League batting champion and voted the league's Most Valuable Player in 1966, is considered a national hero by Puerto Ricans for his generosity, outstanding athletic achievements, and heroism. *Reproduced by permission of AP/Wide World Photos.*

The team signed its first Hispanic player in 1911. From 1939 to 1947, it employed nineteen Hispanic players. Even though they could play for Washington and other teams, Hispanic players were not completely accepted. They suffered racial attacks from fans and sportswriters. They had separate housing, uniforms, equipment, and travel accommodations. In the 1940s the new Mexican league started to attract Hispanic players in the United States. This competition forced some American teams to improve conditions for their Hispanic players or face losing them.

After Jackie Robinson broke through the color barrier in 1947, things became much easier for Hispanic ballplayers of all colors and nationalities. Their numbers soon increased. By the 1970s, 9 percent of major league players were Hispanic. At about this same time, political and social changes in Cuba raised barriers to Cuban players. Their numbers dropped in the major leagues.

Dominican slugger and philanthropist Sammy Sosa. *Reproduced by permission of Archive Photos, Inc.*

Players from the Dominican Republic and Puerto Rico now were the largest groups represented. Venezuela and Mexico also made a strong showing.

Major league baseball in the United States will continue to attract Hispanic ballplayers. The large salaries offered by American teams attract talented young Hispanics as a way to a better life. American baseball also attracts talented Hispanic players because of the quality of play. In turn, these Hispanic players help to make American baseball even more competitive.

In the early 2000s, Hispanics are a very major presence in major league baseball. In 2001 they made up 17 percent of opening day rosters, more than doubling their pres-

ence in a decade. There are many Hispanic superstars making millions of dollars at the sport. Baseball scouts scour the Latin American baseball leagues for new players, and the Dominican Republic is often the first place they look. With summer weather all year and a long history of baseball it is a perfect place for talented players to get started.

Of Latin American countries, the Dominican Republic, in fact, provided the most Hispanic players to the major leagues in 2001. That year there were fifty-seven Dominican players, twenty-eight Puerto Ricans, twenty Venezuelans, and eight Mexicans.

In baseball's management positions, the representation of Hispanics has been very low in the past. In early 2002, Omar Minaya (notably the scout who discovered Sammy Sosa) became the first Hispanic to be general manager of a major league team. Other teams are bringing in more Hispanic officials, but there is a long way to go to achieve balance.

Other Sports

Rodeo and baseball are the two American sports most influenced by Hispanic athletes. Yet, Hispanics have made their mark in other sports. Boxing has a long history of Hispanic champions. In the lighter-weight classifications, many Cuban, Mexican, and Puerto Rican boxers have used their size and speed to great advantage. From the early days of Sixto Escobar and Kid Chocolate to the present, many young Hispanics have seen boxing as a way out of poverty. In the 2000s, there are many Hispanic superstars in boxing, among them Erik Morales, Oscar de la Hoya, Marco Antonio Barrera, Fernando Vargas, and John Ruiz. In 2002 Showtime

Jennifer Rodriguez races during the women's 1,500-meter speedskating competition at the Winter Olympic Games in Salt Lake City, Utah, 2002. Rodriguez finished the race at 1:55.32 to capture the bronze medal, her second at the games. *Reproduced by permission of AP/Wide World Photos.*

aired the "Latin Fury" matches from Las Vegas, featuring Antonio Diaz versus Antonio Margarito and Yory Boy Campas versus Daniel Santos. Many boxing promoters have commented that Hispanics seem to hold the keys to the future of boxing.

Now, more and more Hispanic athletes are playing other mainstream American sports. At American universities Hispanics have the chance to play football and basketball. Manny Fernández, Tom Flores, Anthony Muñoz, and Jim Plunkett have already shown their skills in the National Football League. Golfers such as Juan "Chi Chi" Rodríguez and Lee Treviño have become world-class competitors. The Winter Olympics of 2002 witnessed two Hispanics winning medals in speed skating. Derek Parra became the first Mexican American to win a medal at the Winter Olympics: a gold and a silver in speedskating. Cuban American speedskater Jennifer Rodriguez won two bronzes. In every field of U.S. sports, Hispanics are out there competing in greater numbers that are sure to increase over the next decades.

FURTHER READING

Acosta-Belén, Edna, ed. *The Puerto Rican Woman: Perspectives on Culture, History, and Society,* 2nd ed. New York: Praeger, 1986.

Acosta-Belén, Edna, and Barbara R. Sjostrom, eds. *The Hispanic Experience in the United States: Contemporary Issues and Perspectives.* New York: Praeger, 1988.

Acuña, Rodolfo. *Occupied America: A History of Chicanos.* New York: Harper & Row, 1981.

Bean, Frank D., and Marta Tienda. *The Hispanic Population of the United States.* New York: Russell Sage Foundation, 1987.

Boswell, Thomas D., and James R. Curtis. *The Cuban American Experience: Culture, Images, and Perspectives.* Totawa, NJ: Rowan and Allenheld, 1984.

Elías Olivares, Lucia, ed. *Spanish in the U.S. Setting: Beyond the Southwest.* Rosalyn, VA: National Clearinghouse for Bilingual Education, 1983.

Fitzpatrick, Joseph P. *Puerto Rican Americans: The Meaning of Migration to the Mainland,* 2nd ed. Englewood Cliffs, NJ: Prentice Hall, 1987.

García, Mario T. *Mexican Americans: Leadership, Ideology, and Identity, 1930–1960.* New Haven, CT: Yale University Press, 1989.

Gonzalez, Juan. *Harvest of Empire: A History of Latinos in America.* New York: Viking, 2000.

Kanellos, Nicolás, ed. *Hispanic Theater in the United States.* Houston: Arte Público Press, 1984.

Kanellos, Nicolás. *Thirty Million Strong: Reclaiming the Hispanic Image in American Culture.* Golden, CO: Fulcrum, 1998.

McKenna, Teresa Flora, and Ida Ortiz, eds. *The Broken Web: The Education Experience of Hispanic American Women.* Berkeley, CA: Floricante Press and the Tomás Rivera Center, 1988.

Meier, Kenneth J., and Joseph Stewart. *The Politics of Hispanic Education / un paso pálante y dos pátras.* Albany: State University of New York Press, 1991.

Molina, Carlos W., and Marilyn Aguirre-Molina, eds. *Latino Health in the United States: A Growing Challenge.* Washington, DC: American Public Health Association, 1994.

Morales, Ed. *The Latin Beat: The Rhythms and Roots of Latin Music from Bosa Nova to Salsa and Beyond.* Cambridge, MA: Da Capo, 2002.

Morales, Julio. *Puerto Rican Poverty and Migration: We Just Had to Try Elsewhere.* New York: Praeger, 1986.

Portes, Alejandro, and Robert L. Bach. *Latin Journey: Cuban and Mexican Immigrants in the United States.* Berkeley: University of California Press, 1985.

Rosales, Francisco A. *Chicano!: The History of the Mexican American Civil Rights Movement.* Houston: Arte Público Press, 1996.

Sandoval, Moisés. *On the Move: A History of the Hispanic Church in the United States.* Maryknoll, NY: Orbis Books, 1990.

Stavans, Ilan. *The Hispanic Condition: The Power of a People,* 2nd ed. New York: Rayo, 2001.

Suro, Roberto. *Strangers among Us: How Latino Immigration Is Transforming America.* New York: Knopf, 1998.

Weber, David. *The Mexican Frontier, 1821–1846: The American Southwest under Mexico.* Albuquerque: University of New Mexico Press, 1982.

INDEX

References to photos are marked by (ill.).